Pocket
PARIS

TOP SIGHTS • LOCAL LIFE • MADE EASY

Catherine Le Nevez

In This Book

QuickStart Guide

Your keys to understanding the city – we help you decide what to do and how to do it

Need to Know
Tips for a hassle-free trip

Neighbourhoods
What's where

Explore Paris

The best things to see and do, neighbourhood by neighbourhood

Top Sights
Make the most of your visit

Local Life
The insider's city

The Best of Paris

The city's highlights in handy lists to help you plan

Best Walks
See the city on foot

Paris' Best...
The best experiences

Survival Guide

Tips and tricks for a seamless, hassle-free city experience

Getting Around
Travel like a local

Essential Information
Including where to stay

Our selection of the city's best places to eat, drink and experience:

◉ **Sights**

✖ **Eating**

🚌 **Drinking**

★ **Entertainment**

🔒 **Shopping**

These symbols give you the vital information for each listing:

☏ Telephone Numbers	🍴 Family-Friendly
⊙ Opening Hours	🐾 Pet-Friendly
P Parking	🚌 Bus
Nonsmoking	⛴ Ferry
@ Internet Access	Ⓜ Metro
🛜 Wi-Fi Access	Ⓢ Subway
Vegetarian Selection	🚋 Tram
🗎 English-Language Menu	🚃 Train

Find each listing quickly on maps for each neighbourhood:

Bar Hemingway

16 🚌 Map p233, B2

Legend has it that Hemi self, wielding a machine erate this timber-pan ered bar during showpiece is a en by Papa ar town. Dress .com; Hôtel Rit ⊙6.30pm-2a

6 ◉ Plac Vc

Lonely Planet's Paris

Lonely Planet Pocket Guides are designed to get you straight to the heart of the city.

Inside you'll find all the must-see sights, plus tips to make your visit to each one really memorable. We've split the city into easy-to-navigate neighbourhoods and provided clear maps so you'll find your way around with ease. Our expert authors have searched out the best of the city: walks, food, nightlife and shopping, to name a few. Because you want to explore, our 'Local Life' pages will take you to some of the most exciting areas to experience the real Paris.

And of course you'll find all the practical tips you need for a smooth trip: itineraries for short visits, how to get around, and how much to tip the guy who serves you a drink at the end of a long day's exploration.

It's your guarantee of a really great experience.

Our Promise

You can trust our travel infor-mation because Lonely Planet authors visit the places we write about, each and every edition. We never accept freebies for positive coverage, so you can rely on us to tell it like it is.

QuickStart Guide   7

Top Sights 8
Local Life 12
Day Planner 14
Need to Know 16
Neighbourhoods 18

Explore Paris   21

22	Eiffel Tower & Les Invalides
34	Arc de Triomphe & Champs-Élysées
46	Louvre, Tuileries & Opéra
70	Sacré-Cœur & Montmartre
88	Centre Pompidou & the Marais
110	Notre Dame & the Islands
126	Latin Quarter
140	Musée d'Orsay & St-Germain des Prés

Worth a Trip:

Canal St-Martin & Around 84
Southeastern Paris 86
Père Lachaise 160
Versailles 162

The Best of Paris   167

Paris' **Best Walks**

Left Bank Literary Loop **168**

Seine-Side Romantic Meander **170**

Right Bank
Time Passages **172**

Paris' **Best...**

Architecture **174**

Cooking & Wine-Tasting
Courses **176**

Markets **177**

Museums **178**

History **180**

Eating **182**

Drinking **184**

Literary Paris **185**

Nights Out **186**

Gay & Lesbian Paris **188**

Parks & Gardens **189**

Fashion **190**

Churches **192**

Multicultural Paris **193**

Panoramas **194**

For Free **195**

Tours **196**

Gourmet Shops **197**

For Kids **198**

Survival Guide   199

Before You Go **200**

Arriving in Paris 202

Getting Around 203

Essential Information 205

Language **210**

QuickStart Guide

Top Sights 8

Local Life 12

Day Planner 14

Need to Know 16

Neighbourhoods 18

Welcome to Paris

Composer Cole Porter was spot on: whether you're here in the springtime, the autumn, the winter (when it drizzles) or the summer (when it sizzles!), the world's most romanticised city – with its tree-shaded boulevards, iconic monuments, lamplit bridges, wicker chair–lined cafe terraces, chic fashion sense and exquisite cuisine – has a way of seducing you every moment of the year.

Eiffel Tower (p24) and the Seine
IZZET KERIBAR/LONELY PLANET IMAGES ©

Paris
Top Sights

Eiffel Tower (p24)

No other monument is as synonymous with a city as this graceful wrought-iron spire is with Paris. Head to the top for panoramic views over the city, day and night.

Notre Dame (p112)

A vision of stained-glass rose windows, gothic gargoyles and flying buttresses, Paris' glorious cathedral lies at the heart of the city. Climbing its 422 spiralling steps takes you up into its towers.

Louvre (p48)

The *Mona Lisa* and the *Venus de Milo* are just two of the priceless treasures in the world's biggest museum, housed inside a resplendent former palace.

Arc de Triomphe (p36)

Standing sentinel at the top of the Champs-Élysées, this intricately carved triumphal arch epitomises Paris' pomp and ceremony, especially during festivals and celebrations. And yes, you can climb to the top of it, too.

Sacré-Cœur (p72)

In the fabled artists' neighbourhood of Montmartre, climb staircased, ivy-clad streets or catch the funicular that glides up to reach the dove-white domes of Paris' crowning basilica.

Centre Pompidou (p90)

Richard Rogers and Renzo Piano's 'inside-out' building is so striking you could spend hours looking at it without going inside. But do, for its exceptional collection of modern, postmodern and contemporary art.

Musée d'Orsay (p142)

Works by some of the most famous artists to have painted in Paris – including Van Gogh, Renoir and Monet –are spectacularly showcased in this turn-of-the-20th-century former railway station.

Jardin du Luxembourg (p144)

Do as Parisians do and corral one of the iconic 1923-designed sage-green metal chairs and find your own favourite part of the city's loveliest park.

Musée National du Moyen Âge (p128)

Gallo-Roman baths (c AD 200) and the 15th-century Hôtel de Cluny, Paris' finest civil medieval building, house France's fascinating National Museum of the Middle Ages.

Musée Rodin (p26)

Rodin's seminal sculptures, including *The Thinker*, are dotted through the rose-clambered gardens, while the 18th-century mansion's interior collection proves that Rodin's talents weren't limited to sculpture.

Père Lachaise (p160)

Paris is a collection of villages, and this 48-hectare cemetery of cobbled lanes and elaborate tombs qualifies as one in its own right. Famous 'residents' include Oscar Wilde, Jim Morrison and Édith Piaf.

Versailles (p162)

It's worth venturing outside central Paris to marvel at the sheer opulence of this colossal château, which was the seat of the royal court until the start of the French Revolution.

Paris
Local Life

Insider tips to help you find the real city

Paris' star attractions certainly justify the hype. But the real magic of Paris lies in the unexpected: hidden parks, small, specialised museums and galleries, and tucked-away bistros, boutiques and bars. Start exploring and see what you find.

The Spirit of Les Halles (p54)

▶ Cookware shops
▶ Late-night bistros

In the streets where Paris' wholesale markets were formerly located, their spirit lives on, with grocers' stalls, virtually unchanged bakeries, late-opening and 24-hour bistros, as well as cookware shops where Parisian chefs still buy the tools of their trade.

A Heads-Up on the Haut Marais (p94)

▶ Emerging designers
▶ Covered markets

The southern Marais used to attract all the hype but the *haut* (upper, ie northern) part of Paris'

hippest *quartier* (quarter) is rapidly becoming an art and fashion hub with edgy boutiques and galleries setting up amid long-standing neighbourhood haunts that are enjoying a revival.

Canal St-Martin & Around (p84)

▶ Funky boutiques
▶ Cool cafes

The banks of this picturesque canal and its surrounds are the epicentre of the city's *bobo* (bourgeois bohemian) culture, where artists, musicians and other creatives catch cutting-edge music and shop at offbeat new and secondhand boutiques.

Art in Montmartre (p74)

▶ Windmills
▶ Village squares

Picasso, Renoir and Van Gogh were just some of the seminal artists who once lived and worked in Montmartre, and although this quaint, village-like neighbourhood of higgledy-piggledy streets now teems with visitors, there are tangible reminders of the masters' artistic legacy, which endures to this day.

A Stroll Along Rue Mouffetard (p130)

▶ Market stalls
▶ Lively bars

This old Roman road in the Latin Quarter is

Stall at Marché aux Puces d'Aligre (p109) Puces d'Aligre

lined with colourful food market stalls, cheap eateries, quirky shops and student-filled bars. You can easily spend several hours here, but give it a miss on Monday when the markets are closed.

Southeastern Paris
(p86)

▸ National library
▸ Floating bars

Off the tourist radar, there are lots of reasons to explore this up-and-coming area, including exhibitions at the book-shaped national library, the national cinema institute and the national fashion institute, as well as floating bars or night-

clubs and even a floating swimming pool.

St-Germain des Prés' Storied Shops
(p146)

▸ Antique dealers
▸ Historic shops

St-Germain des Prés is dripping with designer boutiques but in between browsing through them you'll find a trove of storied shops in this soulful Left Bank neighbourhood, as well as the city's first-ever department store and its magnificent food hall that draws Parisians from across the city.

Other great places to experience the city like a local:

Place des Vosges (p98)

Rue Cler (p33)

Rue des Martyrs (p81)

Golden Triangle (p44)

Rue de Seine & Rue de Buci (p154)

Rue des Lombards (p65)

Café de la Nouvelle Mairie (p139)

Rue St-Martin (p105)

Rue de Lappe (p108)

Pletzl (p100)

Paris
Day Planner

Day One

One day in Paris? This itinerary covers the very top sights of the city. Start your visit at the iconic **Eiffel Tower** (p24) for superb views across the city. Back on solid ground, make your way to the **Louvre** (p48), which holds some of the world's greatest art treasures, including the *Mona Lisa* and *Venus de Milo*.

You'll want to spend at least a couple of hours at the Louvre; once you're finished, head to **Angelina** (p63) for outrageously decadent hot chocolates. Walk it off with a stroll along the Seine, finishing at the Île de la Cité to explore the island's beautiful churches, **Notre Dame** (p112) and **Ste-Chapelle** (p120). Spend the rest of the afternoon wandering the laneways and poking through the quirky shops of the Île St-Louis, stopping to sample a **Berthillon** (p122) ice cream.

Splash out on a gastronomic extravaganza and mesmerising Seine views at **La Tour d'Argent** (p136) – just make sure you book ahead. After dinner, visit the Ritz' **Bar Hemingway** (p63) for flawless martinis.

Day Two

Two days? Start your second day on the steps of **Sacré-Cœur** (p72), taking in the vistas from the steps out front and up inside its dome. Spend some time strolling Montmartre's backstreets, checking out bustling **place du Tertre** (p75) and works by the surrealist master at the **Dalí Espace Montmartre** (p78). Next, head to the **Centre Pompidou** (p90) to gaze at its eye-popping exterior, and to dine at its panoramic restaurant, **Georges** (p91).

After lunch, explore the Centre Pompidou's fabulous modern art museum. Spend the rest of the afternoon absorbing the atmosphere of the Marais, checking out the boutiques and galleries in the **haut Marais** (p94) and getting lost in the maze of medieval streets. Learn about Parisian history at the **Musée Carnavalet** (p98) and take a walk along the four-storey-high **Promenade Plantée** (p100).

The Marais is the centre of Paris' nightlife. Start off with a glass of wine at **Le Baron Rouge** (p106), before moving on to dinner at the beautiful art nouveau **Brasserie Bofinger** (p105). After dinner, hit the bars and clubs on **rue de Lappe** (p108).

Short on time?

We've arranged Paris' must-sees into these day-by-day itineraries to make sure you see the very best of the city in the time you have available.

Day Three

☀ Today will be spent on Paris' Left Bank. Start your day at the vast **Les Invalides complex** (p30), which incorporates a military museum, an exhibition on de Gaulle and Napoleon's tomb, before moving on to the **Musée Rodin** (p26), where the artist's sculptures are displayed in a beautiful mansion and its rose-filled garden. Continue the artistic theme at **Musée d'Orsay** (p142), which holds the nation's incredible impressionist and postimpressionist collections.

☀ Wander east through chic St-Germain des Prés, stopping for lunch at **Bouillon Racine** (p152) and checking out the area's **storied shops** (p146). Stop for a coffee at legendary literary hangout **Le Deux Magots** (p155), then mingle with **Sorbonne** (p136) students in the Latin Quarter's **rue Mouffetard** (p130), and visit the **Panthéon** (p134) mausoleum, the resting place of many of France's greatest thinkers.

☾ After dinner at the impossibly romantic townhouse restaurant **Le Coupe-Chou** (p136), head to the charming local wine bar **Café de la Nouvelle Mairie** (p139), before checking out the student nightlife or catching jazz in the medieval cellars of **Le Caveau de la Huchette** (p138).

Day Four

☀ Start your day with panoramic city views from the top of Paris' iconic **Arc de Triomphe** (p36), then take a walk down the grand avenue the **Champs-Élysées** (p40). Detour for high-end window shopping in the *haute couture* (high fashion) heartland of the **Golden Triangle** (p44), then meander through the World Heritage–listed **Jardin des Tuileries** (p58), and visit the wonderful **Musée de l'Orangerie** (p58) to view Monet's stunning *Water Lilies*.

☀ Spend the afternoon exploring the bohemian **Canal St-Martin** (p84) neighbourhood, starting with lunch on the canalside terrace at **Chez Prune** (p84), before checking out the area's funky boutiques. Then make your way to the world's most visited cemetery, **Père Lachaise** (p160), to visit famous graves including those of Édith Piaf, Oscar Wilde and Jim Morrison.

☾ Return to Canal St-Martin for dinner at the historic **Hôtel du Nord** (p84). Afterwards, check out the area's hip bars, catch the cancan dancers at the famous **Moulin Rouge** (p82) cabaret or take in a performance at the lavish **Palais Garnier** (p64) opera house.

Need to Know

For more information, see Survival
Guide (p199).

Currency
Euro (€)

Language
French

Visas
No restrictions for EU citizens. Generally
not required for most other nationalities
for stays of up to 90 days.

Money
ATMs widely available. Visa and
MasterCard accepted in most hotels, shops
and restaurants; fewer establishments
accept American Express.

Mobile Phones
Check with your provider before you
leave about roaming and French SIM card
options.

Plugs & Adaptors
Plugs in France have two round pins. Voltage
is 220V AC, 50Hz. Appliances rated US 110V
need a transformer to work safely.

Time
Central European Time (GMT/UTC plus one
hour)

Tipping
Already included in prices under French
law, though if service is particularly good,
you might tip an extra five to 10 per cent in
restaurants. Round taxi fares up to the nearest
euro.

① Before You Go

Your Daily Budget

Budget less than €80
▶ Dorm beds €25–€35
▶ Self-catering supermarkets and markets
▶ Inexpensive public transport, stand-by theatre tickets

Midrange €80–€180
▶ Double room €80–€180
▶ Two-course dinner with glass of wine €20–€40
▶ Affordable museums

Top End over €180
▶ Historic luxury hotels
▶ Gastronomic restaurants
▶ Designer boutiques

Useful Websites

Lonely Planet (www.lonelyplanet.com/paris) Destination information, bookings, traveller forum and more.

Paris Info (www.parisinfo.com) Comprehensive tourist-authority website.

Secrets of Paris (www.secretsofparis.com) Loads of resources and reviews.

Advance Planning

Two months before Organise opera, ballet or cabaret tickets and make reservations for high-end or popular restaurants.

Two weeks before Sign up for a free, local-led tour, book a sightseeing balloon 'flight' and start narrowing down your choice of museums.

Two days before Pack your most comfortable shoes!

2 Arriving in Paris

Paris' two main airports are its largest, Charles de Gaulle, and the smaller, Orly; the quickest and easiest transport options are listed below. Some budget carriers including Ryanair use Beauvais airport, linked by shuttle bus (see p203). Gare du Nord train station is also a major entry point for UK travellers (see p203)

✈ From Charles de Gaulle Airport

Destination	Best Transport
Champs-Élysées, Arc de Triomphe	Air France bus 2
St-Germain des Prés (Gare Montparnasse)	Air France bus 4
Bastille (Gare de Lyon)	Air France bus 4
Châtelet–Les Halles, Notre Dame	RER train B
St-Germain des Prés, Latin Quarter (Denfert Rochereau)	RER train B
Opéra	Roissybus

✈ From Orly Airport

Destination	Best Transport
Les Invalides	Air France bus 1
Champs-Élysées, Arc de Triomphe	Air France bus 1
St-Germain des Prés (Gare Montparnasse)	Air France bus 1
St-Germain des Prés, Latin Quarter (Denfert Rochereau)	Orlybus
Châtelet–Les Halles, Notre Dame	Orlyval, then RER train B
Latin Quarter	Orlyval, then RER train B

3 Getting Around

Walking is a pleasure in Paris, but it also has one of the most efficient and inexpensive public transport systems in the world, making getting around the city a breeze.

Ⓜ Metro & RER

Paris' underground rail network has two separate but linked systems: the metro, with 16 lines and some 300 stations, spaced around 500m apart; and the RER (Réseau Express Régional), a network of five suburban services (designated A to E) that pass through the city centre and are good for quick cross-city journeys. Each metro line is marked by a number, colour and final destination. You'll save money by purchasing a *carnet* (book) of 10 tickets.

🚌 Bus

The extensive bus network is a slower but scenic alternative to the metro and easier for those with limited mobility.

🚲 Cycling

The Vélib' pick-up, drop-off bike system has revolutionised travel in Paris, with over 20,000 bikes and 1800 bike stations around 300m apart throughout the city. Subscriptions are super-cheap and the first 30 minutes of use are free.

⛴ Boat

The city's most beautiful 'boulevard', the Seine, runs right through the centre of the city. Boat cruises are plentiful; the hop-on, hop-off Batobus has eight stops serving some of Paris' top sights.

🚕 Taxi

You'll find ranks around major intersections or you can hail taxis in the street.

Paris
Neighbourhoods

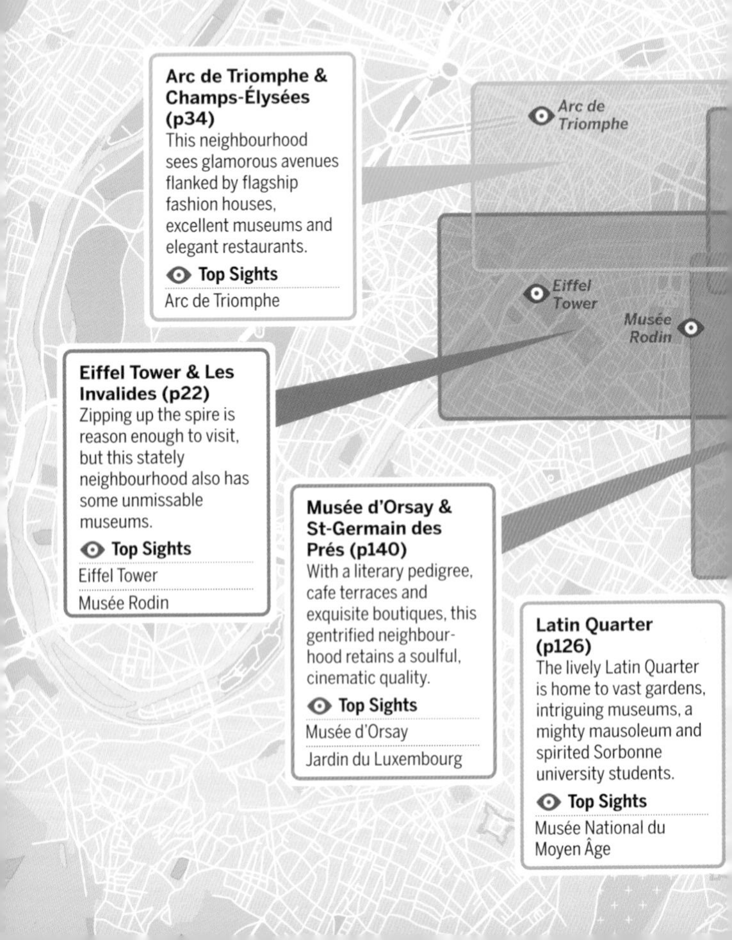

Arc de Triomphe & Champs-Élysées (p34)

This neighbourhood sees glamorous avenues flanked by flagship fashion houses, excellent museums and elegant restaurants.

⊙ **Top Sights**

Arc de Triomphe

Eiffel Tower & Les Invalides (p22)

Zipping up the spire is reason enough to visit, but this stately neighbourhood also has some unmissable museums.

⊙ **Top Sights**

Eiffel Tower

Musée Rodin

Musée d'Orsay & St-Germain des Prés (p140)

With a literary pedigree, cafe terraces and exquisite boutiques, this gentrified neighbourhood retains a soulful, cinematic quality.

⊙ **Top Sights**

Musée d'Orsay

Jardin du Luxembourg

Latin Quarter (p126)

The lively Latin Quarter is home to vast gardens, intriguing museums, a mighty mausoleum and spirited Sorbonne university students.

⊙ **Top Sights**

Musée National du Moyen Âge

⊙ Arc de Triomphe

⊙ Eiffel Tower

Musée Rodin ⊙

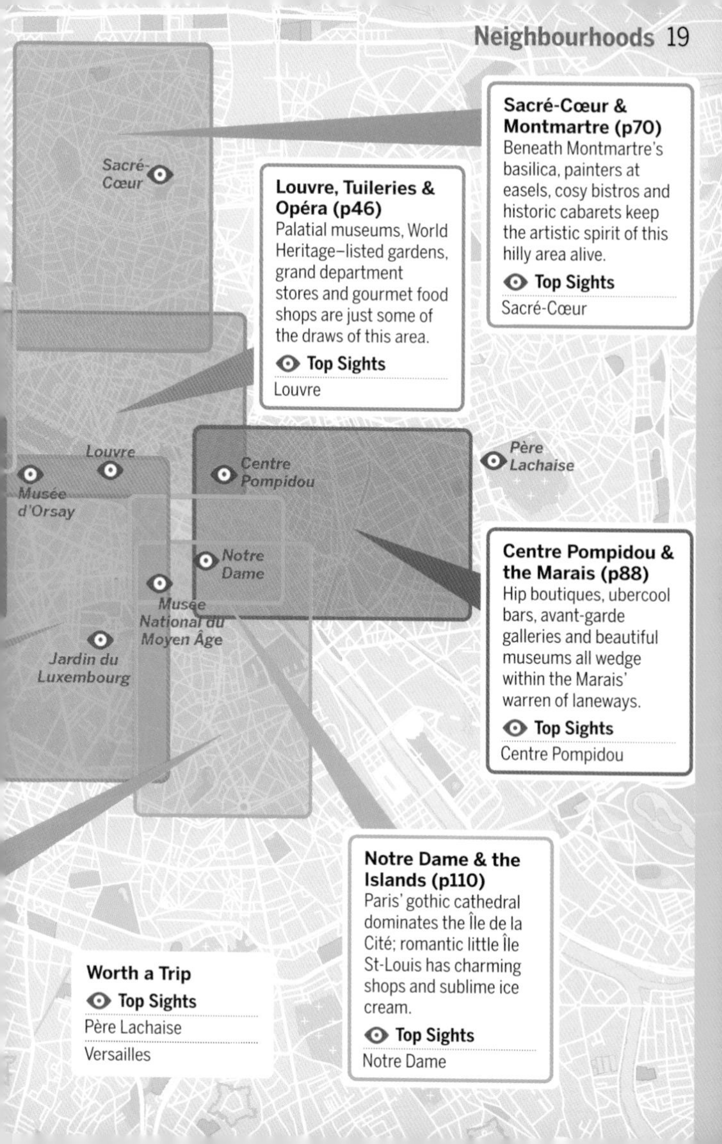

Sacré-Cœur & Montmartre (p70)
Beneath Montmartre's basilica, painters at easels, cosy bistros and historic cabarets keep the artistic spirit of this hilly area alive.

⊙ Top Sights
Sacré-Cœur

Sacré-Cœur ⊙

Louvre, Tuileries & Opéra (p46)
Palatial museums, World Heritage–listed gardens, grand department stores and gourmet food shops are just some of the draws of this area.

⊙ Top Sights
Louvre

Louvre ⊙

⊙
Musée d'Orsay

⊙ Centre Pompidou

Père ⊙ Lachaise

⊙ Notre Dame

Musée National du Moyen Âge

⊙
Jardin du Luxembourg

Centre Pompidou & the Marais (p88)
Hip boutiques, ubercool bars, avant-garde galleries and beautiful museums all wedge within the Marais' warren of laneways.

⊙ Top Sights
Centre Pompidou

Notre Dame & the Islands (p110)
Paris' gothic cathedral dominates the Île de la Cité; romantic little Île St-Louis has charming shops and sublime ice cream.

⊙ Top Sights
Notre Dame

Worth a Trip
⊙ Top Sights
Père Lachaise
Versailles

Explore
Paris

Eiffel Tower & Les Invalides — 22

Arc de Triomphe
& Champs-Élysées — 34

Louvre, Tuileries & Opéra — 46

Sacré-Cœur & Montmartre — 70

Centre Pompidou
& the Marais — 88

Notre Dame & the Islands — 110

Latin Quarter — 126

Musée d'Orsay
& St-Germain des Prés — 140

Worth a Trip
Canal St-Martin & Around 84
Southeastern Paris 86
Père Lachaise......................160
Versailles 162

Pont Neuf (p120) and the Seine
RICHARD L'ANSON/LONELY PLANET IMAGES ©

Explore

Eiffel Tower & Les Invalides

Stretching west along the Seine's southern bank, the broad boulevards and imposing architecture of the Eiffel Tower and Les Invalides area are Paris at its most bombastic. In this *grande dame* of a neighbourhood you can get up close and personal with the city's symbolic tower and discover its evolving history.

The Sights in a Day

A river cruise is the ideal way to start (and/or end) a day in this iconic area, with several companies stopping near the Eiffel Tower. Spend the morning exploring the **Musée Rodin** (p26), allowing time to soak up the serenity of its sculpture garden, then head to **Les Invalides** (p30) to learn about French military history through the ages and pay homage at Napoleon's tomb.

After lunch at **Café Branly** (p33) or a picnic in the **Parc du Champ de Mars** (p30) beneath the Eiffel Tower, check out the indigenous art as well as the striking architecture of the **Musée du Quai Branly** (p30). If you and your olfactory senses are game, you could take a walk below ground in the Paris sewers at the **Musée des Egouts** (p30).

Sunset is the best time to ascend the **Eiffel Tower** (p24), to experience both the dizzying views during daylight and then the glittering *la ville lumière* (the city of light) by night. There are restaurants in the tower itself, or for stunning views of it head to **Les Ombres** (p31).

Top Sights

Eiffel Tower (p24)

Musée Rodin (p26)

Best of Paris

Architecture
Eiffel Tower (p24)

Musée du Quai Branly (p30)

Eating
Le Jules Verne (p31)

L'Arpège (p31)

Drinking
Bar à Champagne (p25)

Multicultural Paris
Musée du Quai Branly (p30)

Panoramas
Eiffel Tower (p24)

Getting There

M Metro Bir Hakeim (line 6) or Champ de Mars–Tour Eiffel (RER C) are the most convenient stations for reaching the tower.

M Metro From the Right Bank's Alma Marceau (line 9), it's an easy stroll over the Pont de l'Alma bridge.

⚓ Boat In addition to river cruises, the hop-on, hop-off Batobus (p204) starts and ends its run at the Eiffel Tower.

Top Sights
Eiffel Tower

No one could imagine Paris today without its signature spire. But Gustave Eiffel constructed this graceful tower – the world's tallest, at 320m, until it was eclipsed by Manhattan's Chrysler Building some four decades later – only as a temporary exhibit for the 1889 Exposition Universelle (World Fair). Luckily, the tower's popularity assured its survival beyond the fair and its elegant art nouveau webbed-metal design has become the defining fixture of the city's skyline.

👁 Map p28, C2

www.tour-eiffel.fr

Champ de Mars, 7e

lift to 2nd fl €8.20/6.60, 3rd fl €13.40/11.80

🕙9am–midnight mid-Jun–Aug, 9.30am–11pm Sep–mid-Jun

Ⓜ Bir Hakeim

Don't Miss

The Trip Up

Lifts (elevators) yo-yo up and down the north, west and east pillars to the tower's three platforms (57m, 115m and 276m); change lifts on the 2nd level for the final ascent to the top. (There's wheelchair access to the 1st and 2nd levels.) If you're feeling athletic, you can take the south pillar's 1665 **stairs** (€4.70/3.70; ☺9am-midnight mid-Jun–Aug, 9.30am-6pm Sep–mid-Jun) as far as the 2nd level.

The Views

Views from the top extend up to 60km. Visibility is hampered by cloud cover and rain, so try to time your visit for a clear day if you can (access is restricted in severe weather). Telescopes and panoramic maps placed around the tower pinpoint locations in Paris and beyond.

The Lighting

Each night, the tower's twin searchlight beacons beam an 80km radius around the city (look up from the top platform to see the 6000-watt lamps). And every hour, for 10 minutes on the hour, the entire tower sparkles with 20,000 gold-toned lights. It took 25 mountain climbers five months to install the bulbs.

Gustave Eiffel's Office

Historic exhibits throughout the tower include Gustave Eiffel's restored top-level office, where wax models of Eiffel and his daughter Claire greet Thomas Edison, who visited the tower in 1889.

Story Windows

The 2nd level's story windows give a nuts-and-bolts overview of the lifts' mechanics.

Vision Well

Gaze down (and down, and d-o-w-n) through glass panels on the 2nd level to the ground.

☑ Top Tips

▶ Save time by buying tickets ahead online. You'll need to print out online tickets or use a smart-phone that can be read by the scanner at the entrance.

▶ The top can be breezy, especially at night – bring a jacket.

▶ Inexpensive buffets and snack bars are located in and around the tower, or you can feast on the views from the 1st-level restaurant 58 Tour Eiffel (p32), or sublime 2nd-level Le Jules Verne (p31).

▶ Did you know... the tower's size varies by up to 15cm; its 7000 tons of iron and 2.5 million rivets expand in warm weather and contract when it's cold.

✕ Take a Break

Toast being at the top at the sparkling new **Bar à Champagne** (champagne per glass €10-20; ☺noon-10pm).

Top Sights
Musée Rodin

Auguste Rodin was more than just a sculptor: he painted, sketched, engraved and collected. And his former workshop and showroom, the beautiful 1730-built Hôtel Biron, is more than just a museum. Rodin donated his entire collection to the French state in 1908 on the proviso they dedicate the Hôtel Biron to displaying his works. They're now installed not only in the mansion itself but also in its rose-clambered garden, which is one of the most peaceful places in central Paris.

Map p28, G3

www.musee-rodin.fr

79 rue de Varenne, 7e

permanent exhibition €6/5, garden €1

⊙ 10am-5.45pm Tue-Sun

Ⓜ Varenne

Auguste Rodin's *The Thinker (Le Penseur)*, Musée Rodin

Don't Miss

The Thinker

Rodin's famous sculpture *The Thinker* (*Le Penseur*) universally symbolises philosophy. The first large-scale cast, made from bronze and marble and completed in 1902, resides in the museum's garden – the perfect place to contemplate this heroic naked figure that was conceived by Rodin to represent intellect and poetry (it was originally titled *The Poet*).

The Gates of Hell

The Gates of Hell (*La Porte de l'Enfer*) was commissioned as the entrance for a Decorative Arts Museum in 1880. Although the museum was never built, Rodin worked on his sculptural masterpiece until his death in 1917. Standing 6m high by 4m wide, its 180 figures comprise an intricate scene from Dante's *Inferno*.

The Kiss

Originally part of *The Gates of Hell,* the marble monument to love, *The Kiss* (*Le Baiser*), was first titled *Francesca da Rimini* (after the 13th-century Italian noblewoman in Dante's *Inferno*). The sculpture's entwined lovers caused controversy on its completion due to Rodin's then-radical approach of depicting women as equal partners in ardour.

Camille Claudel Sculptures

Rodin's muse and protégé, sculptor Camille Claudel (sister of writer Paul Claudel), also became his mistress. Both teacher and student had a major influence on each other's creations. Fifteen of Claudel's sculptures are displayed in the museum.

Collections

In addition to Rodin's own paintings and sketches, don't miss his prized collection of works by artists including Van Gogh and Renoir.

☑ Top Tips

▶ Save money by purchasing a combined ticket (€12 if you visit both on the same day) with the nearby Musée d'Orsay (p142).

▶ Admission to the museum and garden is free on the first Sunday of the month.

▶ Save time queuing by buying tickets ahead online. Preprint tickets or use a smart-phone that can be read by the scanner at the entrance.

▶ Check out more of Rodin's work in the Varenne metro station.

✗ Take a Break

▶ Award-winning baked goodies, include baguettes made right in front of you, at *boulangerie* and *patisserie* **Besnier** (Map p28, H3; 40 rue de Bourgogne, 7e; ⏱7am-8pm Mon-Fri).

▶ For rich flavours from Burgundy try **Tante Marguerite** (Map p28, H2; ☎01 45 51 79 42; www.bernard-loiseau. com; 5 rue de Bourgogne, 7e; lunch/dinner menus €35/49; ⏱lunch & dinner Mon-Fri).

A | B | C | D

Av d'Eylau

Av Kléber

Av du Président Wilson

Pl d'Iéna

Ⓜ Iéna

Alma Marce

1

Ⓔ Av Georges Mandel

Trocadéro

Ⓜ

Pl du Trocadéro et du 11 Novembre

Av d'Iéna

R Fresnel

R Albert de Mun

Passerelle Debilly

Pont d l'Alma

Cimetière de Passy

Av de New York

Av Paul Doumer

R Scheffer

R Vineuse

16e

Jardins du Trocadéro

Pl de Varsovie

Av des Nations Unies

Port de la Bourdonnais

Musée du Quai Branly ⓞ 4

2

R de la Tour

Bd Delessert

Pont d'Iéna

R de l'Université ⓧ 9

Allée Paul Deschanel

Q Branly

Eiffel Tower ⓞ

Av de la Bourdonnais

R de Monttessuy

Av Rapp

R de Passy

Place de Costa Rica

Allée Léon Bourgeois

Av Elisée Reclus

R Raynouard

Passy Ⓜ

Champ de Mars-Tour Eiffel ⓞ

Allée Adrienne Lecouvre

Av Desch

3

R de Lamballe

Av du Président Kennedy

Pont de Bir Hakeim

Stade Émile Anthoine

Av Gustave Eiffel

Av de Suffren

Pl Jacques Rueff

Av Joseph Bouvard

Parc du Champ de Mars ⓞ 5

Av Anatole Fra

R Jean Rey

Pl des Martyrs Juifs du Vélodrome d'Hiver

Allée Thomy Thier

Av Pierre L

4

Av de Lamballe

Allée des Cygnes

Q de Grenelle

R Nélaton

Bir Hakeim Ⓜ

R St-Saëns

R de la Fédération

R Desaix

R Edgar Faure

Av Charles Floquet

15e

R du Docteur Finlay

Pl A Sauvy

R de Presles

R Dupleix

R Émeriau

R St-Charles

Pl Dupleix

5

Place de Brazzaville

R Viala

R Juge

Dupleix Ⓜ

Av de Champaubert

Bd de Grenelle

La Motte Picquet Grenelle Ⓜ

Place St-Charles

R Ruelle

R de Lourmel

R Fondary

R Violet

R Tiphaine

R Letellier

Place Cambronne

R du Commerce

R Frémicour

For reviews see

ⓞ Top Sights	p24
ⓞ Sights	p30
ⓧ Eating	p31
Ⓓ Drinking	p33
ⓕ Entertainment	p33

Ⓝ 0 ____ 400 m
0 ____ 0.2 miles

E
F
G
H

Pl de
la Reine
Astrid
de l'Alma

Cours la Reine

Cours Albert 1er

Pl de la
Concorde

Port de la Conférence

1

Pont de
l'Alma

Seine

Pont des
Invalides

Pont
Alexandre III

Pont de la
Concorde

Musée des
Égouts de Paris

Q de Solférino

Q d'Orsay

Pl de
Finlande

Invalides

Q Anatole
France

de la
sistance

Assemblée Nationale

Bd St-Germain

2

R Malar

Esplanade
des Invalides

R de l'Université

Pl du
Palais
Bourbon

R Ste-Dominique

R Fabert

R St-Dominique

R Amélie

Square
S Rousseau

Av de Bosquet

R de Grenelle

R Clerc

R Duvivier

Pl des
Invalides

R de Constantine

R de Bourgogne

R Las Cases

Pl Santiago
du Chili

R de Grenelle

**La Tour
Maubourg**

Square
Santiago
du Chili

Square
d'Ajaccio

R du Champ de Mars

*Musée
de l'Armée*

**FAUBOURG
ST-GERMAIN**

R de Bellechasse

7e

R Chevert

Hôtel des
Invalides

Varenne

R de Varenne

3

École
Militaire

Jardin du
l'Intendant

*Église
du Dôme*

Musée
Rodin

Av de Tourville

R Barbet de Jouy

la Motte-Picquet

Pl Vauban

**LEFT
BANK**

Square des
Missions
Étrangères

4

École
Supérieure
de Guerre

Av Duquesne

R Bixio

Av de Villars

Bd des Invalides

R de Babylone

École
Militaire

Av de Lowendal

R d'Estrées

Av de Breteuil

Pl du
Prést
Mithouard

St-François
Xavier

R Vaneau

Jardin
Catherine
Labouré

Place de
Fontenoy

Square
de l'Abbé
Esquerré

Laennec

UNESCO

Av de Saxe

Esplanade
du Souvenir
Français

R Éblé

R Oudinot

R Rousselet

Av de Suffren

Av de Ségur

R Éblé

Bd des Invalides

Vaneau

5

bronne

R Pérignon

Pl de
Breteuil

R Duroc

R de Sèvres

6e

Cambronne

Sights

Hôtel des Invalides   HISTORIC SITE

1 Map p28, G3

Built in the 1670s to provide housing for thousands of *invalides* (infirm veterans), this immense complex is fronted by the 500m Esplanade des Invalides lawns. (www.invalides.org; 129 rue de Grenelle, 7e; admission €9/7; ⏰10am-6pm Mon & Wed-Sat, 10am-9pm Tue, 10am-6.30pm Sun Apr-Sep, to 5pm Oct-Mar, closed 1st Mon of month; Ⓜ Invalides or Varenne)

Musée de l'Armée   MUSEUM

2 Map p28, G3

Sobering wartime footage screens at the Hôtel des Invalides' military museum, which also has weaponry, flag and medal displays. In the Cour de Valeur wing, a multimedia area is dedicated to Charles de Gaulle (p32). Hôtel des Invalides entry includes admission here; hours are the same.

Église du Dôme   CHURCH, TOMB

3 Map p28, G3

Within the Hôtel des Invalides complex is the grand Église du Dôme, which receives its name from its gilded dome that is visible throughout the city. Beneath it, Napoleon's remains lie in the **Tombeau de Napoléon 1er** (Napoleon I's Tomb). Entry is included with admission to Hôtel des Invalides. (⏰10am-6pm Apr-Sep, to 5pm Oct-Mar, closed 1st Mon of month)

Musée du Quai Branly   MUSEUM

4 Map p28, D2

Raked ramps lead through this urban-industrial building to darkened, mesh-encased rooms, which form a sharp contrast to the ancient art and arte-facts from Africa, Oceania, Asia and the Americas that are displayed here, along with fascinating temporary ex-hibitions. (www.quaibranly.fr; 37 quai Branly, 7e; admission €8.50/6; ⏰11am-7pm Tue, Wed & Sun, to 9pm Thu-Sat; Ⓜ Bir Hakeim or RER Pont de l'Alma)

Parc du Champ de Mars   PARK

5 Map p28, D3

Sprawled at the base of the Eiffel Tower, the expansive Parc du Champ de Mars lawns are as scenic a picnic spot as you'll find in Paris. (Champ de Mars, 7e; ⏰24hr; Ⓜ Bir Hakeim or RER Champ de Mars-Tour Eiffel)

Musée des Égouts de Paris   MUSEUM

6 Map p28, E1

Raw sewage runs beneath your feet along 480m of subterranean tunnels at this working-sewer museum. Exhib-its demonstrate the development of Paris' waste-water disposal system, as well as its resident rats (an estimated one in the sewers for every Parisian above ground). (www.egouts.tenebres.eu, in French; opposite 93 quai d'Orsay, 7e; admission €4.20/3.40; ⏰11am-5pm Sat-Wed May-Sep, to 4pm Sat-Wed Oct-Apr, closed 2 weeks mid-Jan & when rainfall threatens flood-ing; Ⓜ Alma-Marceau or RER Pont de l'Alma)

Eating

Le Jules Verne GASTRONOMIC €€€

The renowned Alain Ducasse and chef Pascal Féraud have elevated the cuisine on the 2nd level of the Eiffel Tower (see  Map p28, C2), accessed by private lift, to be on a par with its incomparable setting. Reserve well ahead. (☎01 45 55 61 44; www.lejulesverne-paris.com; Champ de Mars, 7e; lunch/dinner menus from €85/100; ☺lunch & dinner by reservation; Ⓜ Bir Hakeim or RER Champ de Mars-Tour Eiffel)

L'Arpège GASTRONOMIC €€€

7 ✖ Map p28, H3

Triple Michelin-starred chef Alain Passard specialises in vegetables and inspired desserts, like his signature tomatoes stuffed with a veritable orchard of a dozen dried and fresh fruits and served with aniseed ice cream. Book at least two weeks ahead. (☎01 47 05 09 06; www.alain-passard.com, in French; 84 rue de Varenne, 7e; menus from €120; ☺lunch & dinner Mon-Fri; Ⓜ Varenne)

Les Ombres GASTRONOMIC €€€

Paris not only gained the new Musée du Quai Branly (see 4 ◎ Map p28, D2), it also gained this 5th-floor restaurant.

Hôtel des Invalides and Pont Alexandre III

Named 'the shadows' for the patterns cast by the Eiffel Tower's ironwork and its own roof webbing, the dramatic views are complemented by dishes like prawns with peppered fennel foam, and cardamom crème brûlée. (📞01 47 53 68 00; www.lesombres -restaurant.com; 27 quai Branly, 7e; lunch/ dinner menus from €38/65; ⊙lunch & dinner, tearoom service 3-5.30pm; Ⓜ Alma-Marceau or Bir Hakeim)

58 Tour Eiffel   BRASSERIE €€

If Le Jules Verne is beyond your booking window and/or budget, this 1st-level restaurant in the Eiffel Tower (see ◉ Map p28, C2) serves inexpensive 'chic picnic' lunches (*menus* from €18; no booking necessary) and contemporary evening meals (*menus* from €67; reserve ahead), along with

stunning Seine views. (📞01 45 55 20 04; www.restaurantstoureiffel.com; Champ de Mars, 7e; ⊙lunch & dinner; Ⓜ Bir Hakeim or RER Champ de Mars-Tour Eiffel)

Café de l'Alma   CAFE €€

8 ✗ Map p28, E2

At this table-fronted cafe, the bistro-style fare is as stylish as the contemporary charcoal-, rose- and violet-hued decor. (www.cafe-de-l-alma.com; 5 av Rapp, 7e; mains €7-40; ⊙breakfast, lunch & dinner; Ⓜ Alma-Marceau or RER Pont de l'Alma)

Les Deux Abeilles   SALON DE THÉ €€

9 ✗ Map p28, D2

The faded floral wallpaper and even the somewhat stuffy service make this tearoom a charmingly old-fashioned stop for authentic baked treats such

Understand
Charles de Gaulle & WWII

The WWII battle for France began in earnest in May 1940 and by 14 June France had capitulated. Paris was occupied, and almost half the population evacuated. General Charles de Gaulle, France's undersecretary of war, fled to London. In a radio broadcast on 18 June 1940, he appealed to French patriots to continue resisting the Germans. He set up a French government-in-exile and established the Forces Françaises Libres (Free French Forces), fighting the Germans alongside the Allies. Paris was liberated on 25 August 1944 by an Allied force spearheaded by Free French units.

De Gaulle returned to Paris and set up a provisional government, but in January 1946 he resigned, wrongly believing that the move would provoke a popular outcry for his return. De Gaulle formed his own party (Rassemblement du Peuple Français) and remained in opposition until 1958, when he was brought back to power to prevent a military coup in 1958 over the uprising in Algeria. He resigned as president in 1969, succeeded by the Gaullist leader Georges Pompidou.

Pastry shop on rue Cler

Q Local Life
Rue Cler

Pick up fresh bread, sandwich fill-ings, pastries and wine for a picnic along the 7e's **rue Cler** (Map p28, E3; ⏱7am or 8am-7pm or 7.30pm Tue-Sat, 8am-noon Sun), which buzzes with local shoppers, especially on weekends.

Quai Branly (see 4 ◎ Map p28, D2) sits amid reflecting pools and gardens, making it an idyllic coffee break. It also serves light meals like *tartines* (open sandwiches). (www.quaibranly.fr; 27 quai Branly; ⏱9.30am-6pm Tue, Wed & Sun, to 8pm Thu, Fri & Sat; Ⓜ Alma-Marceau, Bir Hakeim or RER Pont de l'Alma)

as fluffy quiche, Madeleine cakes and *clafoutis aux cerises* (cherry flan). (☎01 45 55 64 04; 189 rue de l'Université, 7e; mains €12-18; ⏱9am-7pm Mon-Sat; Ⓜ Alma-Marceau, Bir Hakeim or RER Pont de l'Alma)

Drinking

Café Branly   CAFÉ, SALON DE THÉ

With ringside views of the Eiffel Tower, the cafe at the Musée du

Entertainment

La Pagode   CINEMA

10 ☆   Map p28, G4

This 19th-century Japanese pagoda was converted into a cinema in the 1930s and remains the most atmos-pheric spot in Paris to catch arthouse and classic films. (☎01 45 55 48 48; www. etoile-cinema.com; 57bis rue de Babylone; ⏱vary; Ⓜ St-François Xavier)

Explore

Arc de Triomphe & Champs-Élysées

Pomp and grandeur reign: Baron Haussmann famously reshaped the Parisian cityscape around the Arc de Triomphe, from which 12 avenues radiate like the spokes of a wheel. The most celebrated (and the scene of major celebrations) is the Champs-Élysées. The neighbourhood's splendour extends to its *haute cuisine* restaurants and *haute couture* fashion houses.

The Sights in a Day

☀️ Climb above the **Champs-Élysées** (p40) to the top of the **Arc de Triomphe** (p36), then stroll – and shop – along this famous avenue.

☀️ After lunch at the beautiful tea-room of the **Musée Jacquemart-André** (p40), wander among the flagship fashion houses of the **Golden Triangle** (p44) and be dazzled by the glittering crystal at the **Galerie Musée Baccarat** (p41) and ornate Asian arte-facts at the **Musée Guimet des Arts Asiatiques** (p40). Visit the resident fish at the **Cinéaqua** (p41) aquarium, snap a postcard-perfect photo of the Eiffel Tower from the terrace of the **Palais de Chaillot** (p41), and admire modern art at the **Musée d'Art Mod-erne de la Ville de Paris** (p40).

🌙 Options for dinner in the area extend from smart neighbour-hood bistros like **Le Hide** (p43) to gastronomic heavyweights such as **Alain Ducasse au Plaza Athénée** (p43). Then catch cabarets like **Le Lido** (p44) or head out to a nightclub such as **Le Showcase** (p44).

 Top Sights

Arc de Triomphe (p36)

💜 **Best of Paris**

Architecture
Cité de l'Architecture et du Patri-moine (p42)

Museums
Musée d'Art Moderne de la Ville de Paris (p40)

Galerie Musée Baccarat (p41)

Eating
Le Hide (p43)

Muticultural Paris
Musée Guimet des Arts Asiatiques (p40)

Panoramas
Arc de Triomphe (p36)

Getting There

Ⓜ **Metro** Charles de Gaulle–Étoile (lines 1, 2, 6 and RER A) is adja-cent to the Arc de Triomphe.

Ⓜ **Metro** The Champs-Élysées' other stops are George V (line 1), Franklin D Roosevelt (lines 1 and 9) and Champs-Élysées–Clemenceau (1 and 13).

🚣 **Boat** The hop-on, hop-off Batobus (p204) stops near the Champs-Élysées by Pont Alex-andre III.

Top Sights
Arc de Triomphe

If anything rivals the Eiffel Tower as the symbol of Paris, it's this magnificent 1836-built monument to Napoleon's 1805 victory at Austerlitz, which he commissioned the following year. The intricately sculpted triumphal arch stands sentinel in the centre of the Étoile (star), the world's largest roundabout, with some of the best views in Paris from the top.

◉ Map p38, C1

www.
monumentsnationaux.fr

place Charles de Gaulle, 8e

viewing platform €9.50/6

🕑10am-11pm Apr-Sep, to 10.30pm Oct-Mar

Ⓜ Charles de Gaulle–Étoile

Don't Miss

The Architecture
Inspired by the Roman Arch of Titus, architect Jean-François Chalgrin gave the Arc de Triomphe its imposing stature through its outsized dimensions: a proud 50m high, 45m long and 22m wide.

The Sculptures
The most famous of the four high-relief panels at the base is to the right, when facing the arch from the av des Champs-Élysées side. It's entitled Départ des Volontaires de 1792 (also known as La Marseillaise). Higher up, a frieze running around the whole monument depicts hundreds of figures.

The Climb to the Top
Scaling 284 steps brings you to the top of the arch to its panoramic terrace. Tickets are sold in the underground passage that surfaces on the northeastern side of the Champs-Élysées.

The Axe Historique
The Arc de Triomphe is the highest point of Paris' line of monuments known as the *axe historique* (historic axis; also called the grand axis). Views swoop east down the Champs-Élysées to the Louvre's glass pyramid, and west along the *axe historique* to the modern, box-like Grande Arche in the business district of La Défense (p177).

The Tomb of the Unknown Soldier
Honouring the 1.3 million French soldiers who lost their lives in WWI, the Unknown Soldier was laid to rest under the arch in 1921, beneath an eternal flame (rekindled daily at 6.30pm).

Bastille Day Celebrations
The military parade commemorating France's national Bastille Day (14 July) kicks off from the arch (adorned by a billowing tricolour).

☑ Top Tips

▶ Don't try to cross the traffic-choked roundabout above ground. Stairs on the northern side of the Champs-Élysées lead beneath the Étoile to pedestrian tunnels (not linked to metro tunnels) that bring you out safely beneath the arch.

▶ Admission to the terrace at the top is free on the first Sunday of the month from November to March.

▶ Visitors frequently pause while crossing the road to photograph the arch from the middle of the Champs-Élysées and risk getting skittled by traffic – take care.

▶ There *is* a lift (elevator) at the arch, but it's only for visitors with limited mobility or those travelling young children, and there are still some unavoidable steps.

✗ Take a Break

Footsteps from the arch, Publicis Drugstore (p45) is great for a brasserie meal, drink or snack.

A

Place du
Gal Patton

R des
Acacias

17e

B

Av Carnot

R Troyon

13

R de Tilsitt

C

Av Hoche

R Beaujon

Pl G Guillaumi

D

R du Faubou
St-Honoré

Argentine

Av de la Grande Armée

Charles de
Gaulle–Étoile

Av de Friedland
Charles de Gaulle–Étoile

1

R Duret

Arc de Triomphe

R Lord Byron

R Washington

Av Foch

Pl Charles
de Gaulle

Av des Champs-Élysées

25   28

R Vernet

22

R de Presbourg

15

Kléber

19

George V

23

2

R Paul Valéry

R de Bassano

Av d'Iéna

R R Galilée

R de Bassano

TRIANGLE
D'OR

Av Victor Hugo

R Copernic

R La Pérouse

Av Kléber

R Jean Giraudoux

Av Marceau

R Quentin Bauchart

R Pierre Charr

16

R Lauriston

R de Belloy

Pl des
États-Unis

Galerie
Musée
Baccarat

6

Pl Amiral
de Grasse

Lycée
Assomption

R de Chaillot

Av Pierre 1er de Serbie

R C Marot

R de
Trém

18

R du Boccador

3

Boissière

R Galilée

R Boissière

16e

R de Lübeck

Musée Galliera
de la Mode de la
Ville de Paris

Av George V

R de

Av Raymond Poincaré

Musée Guimet des
Arts Asiatiques
R de Longchamp

4

Iéna

Pl d'Iéna

12

Square
Brignole
Galliéra

24

Alma
Marceau

Pl de
la Reine
Astrid

4

Av d'Iéna

11

Palais
de Tokyo

Musée d'Art
2 Moderne de la
Ville de Paris

Pl de
l'Alma

Pont de
l'Alma

Trocadéro

Av du Président Wilson

Av d'Iéna

R Fresnel

Av de New York

Passerelle
Debilly

Pont de
l'Alma

Pl de la
Résistance

5

Cimetière
de Passy

Palais de
Chaillot

7

Cinéaqua

5

Pl de
Varsovie

8

Jardins du
Trocadéro

Av des
Nations Unies

Av Albert de Mun

Q Branly

Port de la
Bourdonnais

Av Rapp

Av Bosquet

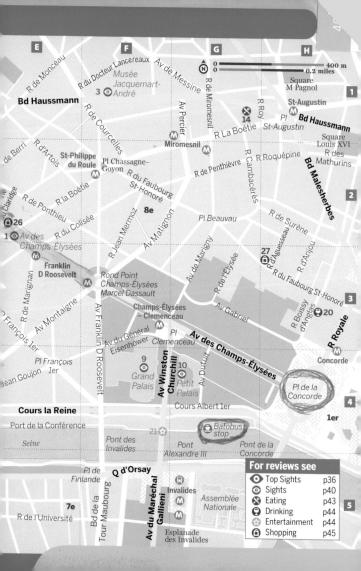

E   F   G   H

0   400 m
0   0.2 miles

R de Monceau

R du Docteur Lancereaux

Av de Messine

Square
M Pagnol

Musée
Jacquemart-
André   3

Bd Haussmann

R de Miromesnil

St-Augustin

14

R Roy

Pl
St-Augustin

Bd Haussmann

R de Courcelles

Av Percier

Miromesnil

R La Boétie

Square
Louis XVI

R des
Mathurins

de Berri

R d'Artois

St-Philippe
du Roule

Pl Chassagne-
Goyon

R de Penthièvre

R Roquépine

R de Cambacérès

Bd Malesherbes

R la Boétie

R du Faubourg
St-Honoré

8e

R de Surène

Claridge   26

R de Ponthieu

R du Colisée

Pl Beauvau

R du Faubourg St-Honoré

R d'Anjou

1   Av des
Champs-Élysées

R Jean Mermoz

Av Matignon

27

R d'Aguesseau

Franklin
D Roosevelt

Av de Marigny

R de l'Élysée

R Boissy
d'Anglas

20

R de Marignan

Rond Point
Champs-Élysées
Marcel Dassault

Av Gabriel

R Royale

Av Montaigne

Champs-Élysées
– Clemenceau

Pl
Clemenceau

Av des Champs-Élysées

Concorde

François 1er

Av Franklin D Roosevelt

Av du Général
Eisenhower

Av Winston Churchill

9
Grand
Palais

Av Dutuit

10
Petit
Palais

Pl de la
Concorde

Pl François
1er

Jean Goujon

Cours la Reine

Cours Albert 1er

1er

Port de la Conférence

Seine

Pont des
Invalides

21

Pont
Alexandre III

Batobus
stop

Pont de la
Concorde

Pl de
Finlande

Q d'Orsay

Invalides

7e

R de l'Université

Bd de la
Tour Maubourg

Av du Maréchal Gallieni

Assemblée
Nationale

Esplanade
des Invalides

For reviews see	
⊙ Top Sights	p36
◉ Sights	p40
✕ Eating	p43
☻ Drinking	p44
☆ Entertainment	p44
⌂ Shopping	p45

Sights

Av des Champs-Élysées STREET

1 Map p38, E2

No trip to Paris is complete without strolling this broad, tree-shaded avenue lined with luxury shops (including car showrooms). Named for the Elysian Fields ('heaven' in Greek mythology), the Champs-Élysées is the final stretch of the Tour de France, and is where Paris turns out for organised and impromptu celebrations. (MCharles de Gaulle-Étoile, George V, Franklin D Roosevelt or Champs-Élysées–Clemenceau)

Musée d'Art Moderne de la Ville de Paris MUSEUM

2 Map p38, C4

Housed in the Electricity Pavilion from the 1937 Exposition Universelle (World Fair), Paris' Modern Art Museum spans virtually every major

---

☑ Top Tip

La Colline des Musées Pass

The Cité de l'Architecture et du Patrimoine, Palais de Tokyo, Musée Quai Branly and Musée d'Art Moderne de la Ville de Paris offer reduced admission to the second and third museums and free admission to the fourth, including temporary exhibitions, no matter what order you visit them within five days. Download the pass at www.lacollinedesmusees.com.

---

artistic movement of the 20th and nascent 21st centuries – Fauvism, cubism, dadaism, surrealism, the School of Paris, expressionism, abstractionism and so on – by artists including Matisse, Picasso and Chagall. (www.mam.paris.fr; 11 av du Président Wilson, 16e; admission free; ⊗10am-6pm Tue, Wed & Fri-Sun, to 10pm Thu; Mléna)

Musée Jacquemart-André MUSEUM

3 Map p38, F1

Works by Rembrandt, Van Dyck, Bernini, Botticelli and Donatello, among other masterpieces collected by Édouard André and his portraitist wife Nélie Jacquemart, are intimately displayed in this exquisite mid-19th-century residence. A double-helix marble staircase dominates its tropical plant-filled winter garden. Be sure to at least peek at the frescoed tearoom. (www.musee-jacquemart-andre.com; 158 bd Haussmann, 8e; admission €10/8.50; ⊗museum 10am-6pm, until 9.30pm Mon & Sat during exhibitions, tearoom 11.45am-5.45pm; MMiromesnil)

Musée Guimet des Arts Asiatiques MUSEUM

4 Map p38, B4

France's leading museum of Asian art incorporates sculptures, paintings and *objets d'art* from Afghanistan, India, Nepal, Pakistan, Tibet, Cambodia, China, Japan and Korea. Buddhist art is displayed at the nearby annexe **Galeries du Panthéon Bouddhique du**

BRUCE BI/LONELY PLANET IMAGES ©

Wall at Palais de Tokyo (p42)

Japon et de la Chine (Buddhist Pantheon Galleries of Japan & China; 19 av Iéna; admission free; 9.45am-5.45pm Wed-Mon); afterwards, zen out in the Galeries' Japanese gardens. (www.museeguimet. fr; 6 place d'Iéna, 16e; admission €7.50/5.50; 10am-6pm Wed-Mon; M Iéna)

Cinéaqua
AQUARIUM

5 Map p38, B5

'Ciné' refers to the cinema screens and animation studio at this state-of-the-art, kid-friendly attraction, but the main draw is the 'aqua'. Over 500 aquatic species, including sharks, glide through this aquarium. One of its huge tanks forms the backdrop to the onsite Japanese café–restaurant, Ozu. (www.cineaqua.com; 2 av des Nations

Unies, 16e; admission €19.50/15.50; 10am-7pm; M Trocadéro)

Galerie Musée Baccarat
MUSEUM

6 Map p38, B3

Showcasing services designed for illustrious dining tables over the centuries, this crystal museum occupies striking rococo-style premises in the ritzy 16e, and has a glittering gastronomic restaurant onsite. (www.baccarat. com; 11 place des États-Unis, 16e; admission €5/3.50; 10am-6.30pm Mon & Wed-Sat; M Boissière or Iéna)

Palais de Chaillot
MUSEUM

7 Map p38, A5

The Palais' western wing incorporates the **Musée de l'Homme** (Museum of

Mankind; ⏱closed for renovations until 2015) and the **Musée de la Marine** (Maritime Museum; www.musee-marine.fr, in French; admission €7/5; ⏱11am-6pm Mon & Wed-Fri, to 7pm Sat & Sun), with an amazing collection of model ships. Architecture and history intertwine at the **Cité de l'Architecture et du Patrimoine** (www.citechaillot.fr, in French; admission €8/5; ⏱11am-7pm Mon, Wed & Fri-Sun, to 9pm Thu) in the eastern wing. (place du Trocadéro et du 11 November, 16e; Ⓜ Trocadéro)

Jardins du Trocadéro GARDENS

 8 ◎ Map p38, A5

For knockout views of the Eiffel Tower head to these fountained gardens, adjacent to the Palais de Chaillot, which are dramatically floodlit at night. (Ⓜ Trocadéro)

Grand Palais EXHIBITIONS

9 ◎ Map p38, F4

Erected for the 1900 Exposition Universelle, the Grand Palais now houses the Galeries Nationales beneath its huge 8.5-ton art nouveau glass roof. Some of Paris' biggest exhibitions are held here, lasting three to four months. In the same building, the Nave also stages special events, which require a separate ticket. Booking in advance for either is recommended. (www.grandpalais.fr; 3 av du Général Eisenhower, 8e; admission varies; ⏱vary; Ⓜ Champs-Élysées–Clemenceau)

Petit Palais MUSEUM

10 ◎ Map p38, G4

Like the Grand Palais, this architectural stunner was also built for the 1900 Exposition Universelle, and is home to the Paris municipality's Museum of Fine Arts. It specialises in medieval and Renaissance *objets d'art* such as porcelain and clocks, tapestries, drawings and 19th-century French painting and sculpture, plus standout works by artists including Rembrandt. (www.petitpalais.paris.fr; av Winston Churchill, 8e; admission free; ⏱10am-6pm Tue-Sun; Ⓜ Champs-Élysées–Clemenceau)

Palais de Tokyo MUSEUM

11 ◎ Map p38, C4

Created for the 1937 Exposition Universelle (and undergoing renovations at the time of research) the Tokyo Palace has no permanent collection – instead its shell-like interior of polished concrete and steel is the stark backdrop for rotating, often interactive art installations. There's an excellent international restaurant and cafe on the premises. (www.palaisdetokyo.com; 13 av du Président Wilson, 16e; admission €3/1; ⏱noon-9pm Tue-Sun; Ⓜ Iéna)

Musée Galliera de la Mode de la Ville de Paris MUSEUM

12 ◎ Map p38, C4

This Italianate villa and its luxuriant gardens are a fitting backdrop for Paris' Fashion Museum. (www.galliera.paris.fr; 10 av Pierre 1er de Serbie, 16e; ⏱closed for renovations until spring 2013; Ⓜ Iéna)

Eating

Le Hide

FRENCH €€

13 Map p38, B1

This tiny 33-seater neighbourhood bistro fills up faster than you can scurry down the steps at the nearby Arc de Triomphe. Scrumptious traditional French fare spans snails to baked shoulder of lamb and monkfish in lemon butter, followed by lush desserts like strawberry soup. (☑01 45 74 15 81; www.lehide.fr; 10 rue du Général Lanrezac, 17e; 2-/3-course menus €22/29; ⏱lunch Mon-Fri, dinner Mon-Sat; ⓂCharles de Gaulle-Étoile)

Le Bistrot du Sommelier

GASTRONOMIC €€€

14 Map p38, G1

If you like *haute cuisine* with your wine (rather than the other way around), this brainchild of star sommelier Philippe Faure-Brac offers superb degustation *menus* (fixed-price meals) with pre-paired wines. On Fridays, wine tastings are followed by a three-course lunch (€50) and five-course dinner (€75). (☑01 42 65 24 85; www.bistrotdusommelier.com; menus without/with wine from €33/43; 97 bd Haussmann, 8e; ⏱lunch & dinner Mon-Fri; ⓂSt-Augustin)

Maison Prunier

GASTRONOMIC €€€

15 Map p38, B2

The highlight of this erstwhile restaurant, a 1925 art deco treasure, is Prunier's own brand of caviar, along with seafood and vodkas. (☑01 44 17 35 85; www.prunier.com, in French; 16 av Victor Hugo, 16e; lunch/dinner menus from €45/65; ⏱lunch & dinner Mon-Sat; ⓂCharles de Gaulle-Étoile)

Charbon Rouge

STEAK €€€

16 Map p38, D3

Japanese wagyu beef tops the price list at this sophisticated steakhouse, where meat is treated like fine wine; there are also more affordable French, American and Argentinian cuts. (☑01 40 70 09 99; www.charbonrouge.com; 25 rue Marbeuf, 8e; mains €27-180; ⏱noon-11.30pm; ⓂGeorge V)

Alain Ducasse au Plaza Athénée

GASTRONOMIC €€€

17 Map p38, D4

Seated beneath 10,000 crystal shards glittering from the ceiling's chandeliers, dine on triple Michelin-starred fare like Iranian caviar with langoustines while sipping vintages from the 1001-strong wine list. (☑01 53 67 65 00; www.alain-ducasse.com; Hôtel Plaza Athénée, 25 av Montaigne, 8e; menus €95-360; ⏱lunch Thu & Fri, dinner Mon-Fri; ⓂAlma Marceau)

El Mansour

MOROCCAN €€

18 Map p38, D3

Couscous and *tajines* are elevated to fine-dining status at this elegant restaurant. (☑01 47 23 88 18; www.elmansour.fr, in French; 7 rue de la Trémoille, 8e; menus from €38; ⏱lunch Tue-Fri, dinner Mon-Sat; ⓂAlma Marceau)

Drinking

Sir Winston
BAR

19 Map p38, B2

A baroque interior, deep armchairs and nightly DJs make this British-style bar an urbane spot to lounge. (www.sirwinston.fr, in French; 5 Rue de Presbourg, 16e; ⊘9am-4pm; M Charles de Gaulle-Étoile)

Buddha Bar
BAR

20 Map p38, H3

An iridescent two-storey-high golden Buddha and multitude of flickering candles provide a spectacular backdrop for sipping cocktails. (www.buddhabar. com; 8-12 rue Boissy d'Anglas, 8e; ⊘noon-late Mon-Fri, 4pm-late Sat & Sun; M Concorde)

Entertainment

Le Showcase
NIGHTCLUB

21 Map p38, F4

In a former boatshed beneath the Alexandre III bridge, this huge club hosts live music, kickin' DJs and parties. (www.showcase.fr, in French; beneath Pont Alexandre III, 8e; ⊘11.30pm-dawn Fri & Sat; M Champs-Élysées–Clemenceau)

Le Lido
CABARET

22 Map p38, D2

In 1946, postwar Paris embraced the opening of this sparkling cabaret venue, and the lavish sets, towering feather headdresses, sequinned gowns and synchronised dancing still dazzle the crowds today. (☎01 40 76 56 10; www. lido.fr; 116bis av des Champs-Élysées, 8e; M George V)

Le Queen
GAY & LESBIAN

23 Map p38, D2

These days this doyen of a club is as popular with a straight crowd as it is with its namesake clientele but Monday's disco nights are still prime dancing queen territory. Events and parties are posted on the website. (www.queen. fr, in French; 102 av des Champs-Élysées, 8e; ⊘vary; M George V)

Le Baron
NIGHTCLUB

24 Map p38, D4

Ensconced in a former brothel, this hipper-than-thou club, frequented by an endless list of celebs, is renowned for its formidable door policy. Try to look as famous as possible. (www. clublebaron.com; 6 av Marceau, 8e; ⊘11pm-dawn; M Alma Marceau)

 Local Life

Golden Triangle

The designer-heeled **Triangle d'Or** (Golden Triangle; Map p38, D2; M George V, Franklin D Roosevelt or Alma Marceau) is home to historic *haute couture* flagships including Chanel, Christian Dior, Christian Lacroix, Commes des Garçons, Givenchy, Hermès, Jean-Paul Gaultier, Lanvin, Louis Vuitton and Yves Saint Laurent.

Shopping

Publicis Drugstore
CONCEPT SHOP

25 🔒 Map p38, C2

An institution since 1958, Publicis incorporates cinemas plus a glassed-in brasserie and bar, *épicerie* (specialist grocer), pharmacy and newsagent (all open from 8am to 2am weekdays and from 10am weekends); and a wine *cave* (cellar), cigar bar and beauty salon (all open from 11am to 11.30pm). (www.publicisdrugstore.com; 133 av des Champs-Élysées; M Charles de Gaulle-Étoile)

Guerlain
PERFUME, SPA

26 🔒 Map p38, E2

At this 1912 *parfumerie* you can shop for scents including the namesake of the shop's address, the gold-and-pink-packaged Champs-Élysées, or take a decadent beauty treatment at the glistening toffee-tiled spa. (📞 spa bookings 01 45 62 11 21; www.guerlain.fr; 68 av des Champs-Élysées, 8e; ⏰9am-7pm Mon-Wed & Sat, to 9pm Thu, to 8pm Fri; M Franklin D Roosevelt)

Chloé
FASHION

27 🔒 Map p38, H3

Bold prints, bohemian layers and uneven hemlines have given street cred to this 1950s-established Parisian

Louis Vuitton shop, Champs-Élysées

label. (www.chloe.com, in French; 54 rue du Faubourg St-Honoré, 8e; ⏰10.30am-7pm Mon-Sat; M Champs-Élysées–Clemenceau)

Lancel
ACCESSORIES

28 🔒 Map p38, C2

Open racks of luscious totes fill this handbag designer's gleaming premises. (www.lancel.com; 127 av des Champs-Élysées; ⏰10.30am-10pm Mon-Sat, to 8pm Sun; M Charles de Gaulle-Étoile) Re qui optur at. Dunt quo im venesequam simolorest occumque rendae

Explore

Louvre, Tuileries & Opéra

Carving its way through the city, Paris' *axe historique* passes through the Tuileries gardens before reaching IM Pei's glass pyramid at the entrance to world's largest museum, the Louvre. Gourmet shops garland the Église de la Madeleine, while further north are the splendid Palais Garnier opera house and art nouveau department stores of the Grands Boulevards.

The Sights in a Day

☀️ Navigating the labyrinthine **Louvre** (p48) takes a while, so it's an ideal place to start your day. Other nearby museums well worth a visit include the **Musée de l'Orangerie** (p58), showcasing Monet's enormous *Water Lilies,* and photography at the **Jeu de Paume** (p59), both in the elegantly laid-out gardens of the **Jardin des Tuileries** (p58).

☀️ After visiting the **Église de la Madeleine** (p58), whet your appetite browsing place de la Madeleine's gourmet shops such as **Hédiard** (p66), then stay for lunch. Go behind the scenes of the opulent **Palais Garnier** (p64) opera house and shop at the beautiful **Galeries Lafayette** (p66) and **Le Printemps** (p66) department stores, taking time to admire the panoramic views from their rooftops.

🌙 Book ahead for dinner at any number of excellent restaurants in the area, such as **Frenchie** (p61). Then relax at the art deco cinema **Le Grand Rex** (p65), hit the dance floor of its legendary nightclub, **Rex Club** (p66), or catch a jazz session on **rue des Lombards** (p65).

For a local's day in the Les Halles area, see p54.

 Top Sights
Louvre (p48)

🔍 **Local Life**
The Spirit of Les Halles (p54)

💜 **Best of Paris**

Architecture
Galeries Lafayette (p66)
Louvre Pyramid (p48)

Museums
Musée de l'Orangerie (p58)
Jeu de Paume (p59)

History
Louvre (p48)
Place de la Concorde (p60)
Forum des Images (p65)

Getting There

Ⓜ **Metro** The Louvre has two metro stations: Palais Royal–Musée du Louvre (lines 1 and 7), and Louvre–Rivoli (line 1).

Ⓜ **Metro** Châtelet–Les Halles is Paris' main hub, with numerous metro and RER lines converging here.

⚓ **Boat** The hop-on, hop-off Batobus (p204) stops outside the Louvre.

Top Sights
Louvre

Stretching 700m along the Seine, it's estimated it would take nine months just to *glance* at every artwork in the world's largest museum. Constructed as a fortress by Philippe-Auguste in the early 13th century, the Palais du Louvre was rebuilt in the mid-16th century as a royal residence; and in 1793 the Revolutionary Convention turned it into France's first national museum. The late President Mitterrand doubled its exhibition space, and new and renovated galleries now see some 35,000 works displayed.

◉ Map p56, E5

www.louvre.fr

place du Louvre, 1er

permanent collections €11/free

⊙ 9am–6pm Mon, Thu, Sat & Sun, to 9.45pm Wed & Fri

Ⓜ Palais Royal–Musée du Louvre

Sully Wing and IM Pei's pyramid, Louvre

Don't Miss

Collections

The rambling palace houses priceless treasures from antiquity to the 19th century, within eight curatorial departments: Near Eastern Antiquities, Egyptian Antiquities, Greek, Etruscan and Roman Antiquities, Islamic Art, Sculptures, Decorative Arts, Paintings (split into three main categories: the French school, the Italian and Spanish schools, and the Northern European schools – German, Flemish and Dutch), and Prints and Drawings.

Louvre Pyramid

A new entrance was necessary to accommodate the crowds but when it was unveiled in 1989, few people thought IM Pei's futurist glass pyramid, standing 20.6m high with a base of four 35m sides (plus three smaller pyramids), was in keeping with the centuries-old palace. But the bold juxtaposition works and today no one could imagine the Louvre without it.

Hall Napoléon

The split-level public area under the glass pyramid is known as the **Hall Napoléon** (⏱9am-10pm Wed-Mon). In addition to a helpful information desk, there's a temporary exhibition hall (p52) and a bookshop and souvenir store selling extensive guides (up to 475 pages long!) for dedicated Louvre-goers, plus a cafe and auditoriums for lectures and films.

Mona Lisa
ROOM 6, 1ST FLOOR, DENON WING

The Louvre's star attraction, Leonardo Da Vinci's early 16th-century painting *La Joconde (Mona Lisa)*, resides in a climate-controlled enclosure behind a wooden railing and bulletproof glass in

☑ Top Tips

▶ Save time by pre-purchasing your ticket from machines at the shopping centre Carrousel du Louvre (p69).

▶ Avoid queues at the pyramid by entering via the Carrousel du Louvre or the Musée du Louvre exit from the Palais Royal–Musée du Louvre metro station.

▶ Rough out an itinerary before setting off. Free English-language maps are available online and from information desks.

▶ Multimedia guides (€6/2) help you get the most out of your visit.

▶ Tickets are valid all day, so you can take a break any time.

▶ The Louvre is closed on Tuesdays and some sections are shut on other days. Check for closures online or at the information desk.

✕ Take a Break

The Louvre's nine cafes and restaurants include Café Marly (p61).

the glass-roofed Salle des Etats. For background on the painting, see p50.

Venus de Milo
ROOM 16, GROUND FLOOR, SULLY WING

Standing 203cm high, the c 100–130 BC Greek marble sculpture Aphrodite of Milos, better known as the Venus de Milo, is slightly larger than life size. The graceful statue (discovered in 1820 without its arms) depicts Aphrodite, the Greek goddess of beauty and love.

Winged Victory of Samothrace
OPPOSITE ROOM 1, 1ST FLOOR, DENON WING

This c 190 BC marble sculpture of the Greek goddess Nike (Victory), the Winged Victory of Samothrace (also known as the Nike of Samothrace), was discovered in 1863 (minus her head and arms) and has been displayed at the Louvre since 1884.

The Raft of the Medusa
ROOM 77, 1ST FLOOR, DENON WING

Théodore Géricault's large-scale *The Raft of the Medusa* was inspired by the French Royal Navy frigate, the *Medusa*, shipwrecked in 1816 en route to colonise Senegal. The shortage of lifeboats meant a raft had to be built for 150 people, which drifted for 13 days and ultimately saved only 10 lives.

Nineteenth-Century French Works
2ND FLOOR, SULLY WING

Works by Delacroix, along with artists such as Corot and Fragonard, are housed on the 2nd floor of the Sully Wing. Look out for Ingres' *Turkish*

Understand
Behind the World-Famous Smile

Leonardo Da Vinci's *Mona Lisa* is widely regarded as the world's most famous painting, but for centuries the identity of the subject was as enigmatic as her ghost of a smile. Canadian scientists recently used infrared technology to peer through the *Mona Lisa's* paint layers, confirming her identity as mother-of-five Lisa Gherardini, wife of Florentine merchant Francesco de Giocondo, hence the painting's alternative title *La Joconde*, meaning 'de Giocondo'. The name *Mona Lisa* comes from the Italian *ma donna* (my lady), which contracts to *madonna* and is shortened to *mona*. The same scientists also discovered that her dress was covered in a transparent gauze veil typically worn in early 16th-century Italy by pregnant or new mothers; it's surmised that the work was painted to commemorate the birth of her second son around 1503, when she was aged about 24. In another discovery, French engineer Pascal Cotte concluded from ultrahigh-resolution scans that eyebrows and lashes were originally painted but have disappeared gradually, possibly from over-cleaning.

LOUVRE

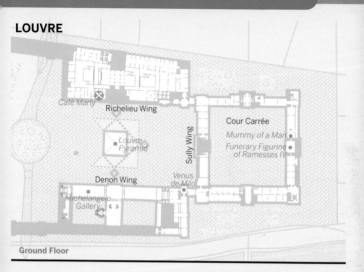

Café Marly

Richelieu Wing

Louvre Pyramid

Denon Wing

Michelangelo Gallery

Cour Carrée

Mummy of a Man

Funerary Figurine of Ramesses IV

Sully Wing

Venus de Milo

Ground Floor

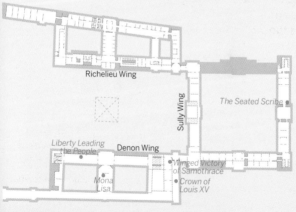

Richelieu Wing

Sully Wing

The Seated Scribe

Liberty Leading the People

Denon Wing

Mona Lisa

Winged Victory of Samothrace

Crown of Louis XV

First Floor

Bath (off Room 60, 2nd Floor, Sully Wing).

Pharaonic Egypt Collections
SULLY WING

The eastern side of the Sully Wing's ground and first floors houses the Louvre's astonishing cache of Pharaonic Egyptian art, artefacts and treasures. Don't miss the Mummy of a Man (Room 15, Ground Floor, Sully Wing; closed Friday) and the funerary figurine of pharaoh Ramesses IV (Room 13, Ground Floor, Sully Wing; closed Friday).

The Seated Scribe
ROOM 22, 1ST FLOOR, SULLY WING

Sitting cross-legged, The Seated Scribe, the painted limestone statue with rock-crystal inlaid eyes, dates *way* back to c 2620–2500 BC. Measuring 53.7cm high by 44cm wide, the unknown figure is depicted holding a papyrus scroll in his left hand; he's thought to have been holding a brush in his right hand that has since disappeared.

Michelangelo Gallery
ROOM 4, GROUND FLOOR, DENON WING

Created between 1513 and 1516, Michelangelo's marble masterpiece *The Dying Slave* is one of many magnificent 16th- to 19th-century Italian sculptures in the Michelangelo Gallery. Other artists represented in the majestic marble-floored gallery include Canova.

Italian Paintings
1ST FLOOR, DENON WING

In addition to Da Vinci's crowd-pleaser, the *Mona Lisa,* Renaissance works by Raphael, Botticelli and Titian are among the Louvre's collection of Italian paintings along the southern side of the Denon Wing's 1st floor.

Flemish & Netherlands Paintings
2ND FLOOR, RICHELIEU WING

Works by Peter Paul Rubens and Pieter Bruegel the Elder are among the standouts housed in the Louvre's collection of Flemish and Netherlands paintings.

Crown of Louis XV
ROOM 66, 1ST FLOOR, DENON WING

French kings traditionally had crowns made for their coronations, which was the only time Louis XV wore this 1722 embroidered satin cap. Topped by openwork arches and a fleur-de-lis, the crown was originally adorned with pearls, sapphires, rubies, topazes, emeralds and diamonds; in 1729 the stones were replaced with the paste imitations you see today.

Temporary Exhibitions

The Hall Napoléon mounts excellent **temporary exhibitions** (€12; 9am-6pm Mon, Thu & Sun, 9am-10pm Wed, 9am-8pm Sat). Combination tickets for permanent collections and temporary exhibitions cost €15. Note that year-round free admission to the Louvre on the first Sunday of the month doesn't include temporary exhibitions.

Crowds at Da Vinci's *Mona Lisa* (p49), Louvre

Thematic Trails

The Louvre has an array of innovative, entertaining self-guided thematic trails, from 'masterpieces of the Louvre' to 'the art of eating,' as well as a *Da Vinci Code* tour and many trails that kids will enjoy, including 'hunting for lions' (ie lion sculptures). Trails can be downloaded from the website; alternatively brochures (in French) are available from information desks.

Guided Tours

If you'd like expert guidance, introductory **guided tours** (90-min tours €9/6 plus museum admission; ⏰11am & 2pm Wed-Mon except 1st Sun of month) in English depart from the Hall Napoléon, in the area marked Acceuil des Groupes (Groups

Reception). Groups are limited to 30 people – sign up at least 30 minutes before departure times.

Other Palais du Louvre Museums
ROHAN WING

The Louvre shelters three **additional museums** (www.lesartsdecoratifs.fr; 107 rue de Rivoli, 1er; admission for all 3 museums €9/7.50; ⏰11am-6pm Tue, Wed & Fri-Sun, to 9pm Thu; Ⓜ Palais Royal-Musée du Louvre): the **Musée des Arts Décoratifs**, featuring furniture, ceramics and glassware; the **Musée de la Publicité**, displaying advertising, including posters dating from the 13th century; and the **Musée de la Mode et du Textile**, showcasing couture and fabrics.

Local Life
The Spirit of Les Halles

In 1137 Louis VI created *halles* (markets) – for merchants who converged on the city centre to sell their wares – and for over 800 years they were, in the words of Émile Zola, the 'belly of Paris'. Although the wholesalers moved out to the suburb of Rungis in 1971, the markets' spirit lives on here.

....

❶ Pigs' Trotters for Brunch

...or breakfast, or any time, in fact. Enduring brasserie **Au Pied de Cochon** (www.pieddecochon.com; 6 rue Coquillière, 1er; 2-/3-course menu €17.90/23.90; ⏱24hr; Ⓜ Les Halles), specialising in grilled pigs' trotters and traditional cheese-topped onion soup, opens around the clock – just as it did when marketeers started and ended their day in its lamplit interior.

2 Cookware Shopping

Paris' professional chefs still come to this neighbourhood to stock up on knives, whisks, sieves, slicers, ladles, grinders, pastry moulds, pots, pans, chopping blocks, champagne buckets, duck presses and more at venerable cookware shops, including the 1820-established **E Dehillerin** (📞01 42 36 53 13; www.e-dehillerin.fr; 18 rue Coquillière, 1er; ⏱9am-6pm Mon-Sat; Ⓜ Les Halles).

3 Cookbook Shopping

There are more esteemed cookware shops on rue Montmartre, as well as Paris' leading food bookshop **Librairie Gourmande** (www.librairie-gourmande.fr, in French; 92 rue Montmartre, 2e; ⏱11am-7pm Mon-Sat; Ⓜ Sentier or Étienne Marcel) – the ultimate place to pick up inspiration. All the classic texts are here, along with cutting-edge collections and cocktail recipe books.

4 A Stroll Along Rue Montorgueil

A splinter of the historic *halles,* rue Montorgueil was its oyster market. At the northern end (rue des Petite Carreaux), look for horse-meat butcher J Davin at No 9. On rue Montorgueil proper, 1846-founded oyster restaurant **Au Rocher de Cancale** (📞01 42 33 50 29; www.aurocherdecancale.fr, in French; 78 rue Montorgueil, 2e; lunch mains €8-14.90, dinner mains €17-19; ⏱8am-2am; Ⓜ Les Halles or Étienne Marcel) is virtually unchanged since the markets' days; its salads are great value, as are its oysters from Cancale, Brittany's foremost oyster port. Grocery and speciality street stalls set up daily, except Monday.

5 Gourmet Goods Shopping

If the foie gras, truffles, caviar and other delicacies at the 1894 *épicerie* (specialist grocer) **Comptoir de la Gastronomie** (www.comptoir.gastronomie. com; 34 rue Montmartre, 1er; mains €17-35; ⏱épicerie 6am-11pm Mon-Sat, to 7pm Sun, restaurant 11am-11pm Mon-Sat, to 7pm Sun; Ⓜ Les Halles) tantalise, you can enjoy them at its adjacent restaurant.

6 Apéro at Christ Inn's Bistrot

A Parisian jewel, the heritage-listed hole-in-the-wall **Christ Inn's Bistrot** (15 rue Montmartre, 1er; ⏱10am-11pm Mon-Sat; Ⓜ Les Halles), until recently known as Le Conchon à l'Oreille, serves bistro fare and retains 1890-laid tiles depicting vivid market scenes of the old *halles* and a handful of railway-carriage-style slatted wooden seats. Hours can vary.

7 Late-Night Dinner at Le Tambour

Salvaged street furniture and old metro maps make the good-natured bistro and bar **Le Tambour** (41 rue Montmartre, 2e; mains €14-21; ⏱noon-6am Tue-Sat, 6pm-6am Sun & Mon; Ⓜ Étienne Marcel), in the words of its proprietor (a former *halles* butcher), a 'temple to know the soul of Paris'. Don't miss the legendary *tarte tatin* (upside-down caramelised-apple tart).

A

B

Square
Louis
XVI

Bd Haussmann

R des Mathurins

Bd Malesherbes

8e

R de Surène

R de l'Arcade

R d'Anjou

R Tronchet

R Vignon

17

40

35

34

39

3

36

42

Église de la Madeleine

Pl de la
Madeleine

Madeleine

43

R du Faubourg St-Honoré

R Royale

R Duphot

Av Gabriel

Av des
Champs-Élysées

Place
de la
Concorde

10

Concorde

7

Jeu de
Paume

14

R St-Honoré

R du Mont Thabor

24

46

Musée de
l'Orangerie

2

Pont de la
Concorde

1

Jardin des
Tuileries

Q des Tuileries

Assemblée
Nationale

Musée
d'Orsay

Q Anatole France

7e

Musée
d'Orsay

R du Bac

Q Voltaire

C

Havre
Caumartin

38

Pl Diaghilev

R Auber

Auber

37

R Gluck

R Scribe

Roissybus

Musée du
Parfum

9

Pl Ch
Garnier

33

R Scribe

Bd des Capucines

R de Sèze

R Cambon

R des Capucines

R Daunou

R de la Paix

23

8

Place
Vendôme

R Danielle
Casanova

Av de l'Opéra

48

R d'Alger

47

R St-Roch

Tuileries

R de Rivoli

R St-Honoré

Jardin du
Carrousel

6

Arc de
Triomphe
du Carrousel

Seine

Q des Tuileries

Pont
Royal

Pont du
Carrousel

D

R de Provence

R de la Chaussée d'Antin

R de Mogador

9e

R La Fayett

Chaussée
d'Antin

R du Helder

Pl J
Rouché

Pl Ch

R Halévy

27

Opéra

Pl de
l'Opéra

Bd des Italien

R du Quatre
Septembre

Quatre
Septembre

R Gaillon

22

Pyramides

Paris Convention &
Visitors Bureau

R Thérè

44

R St-Honoré

R de Richel

49

Palais Royal
Musée du Louv

16

Cour
Napoléc

Musée
du Louvre

For reviews see

◉	Top Sights	p48
◎	Sights	p58
✕	Eating	p60
▣	Drinking	p63
★	Entertainment	p64
⌂	Shopping	p66

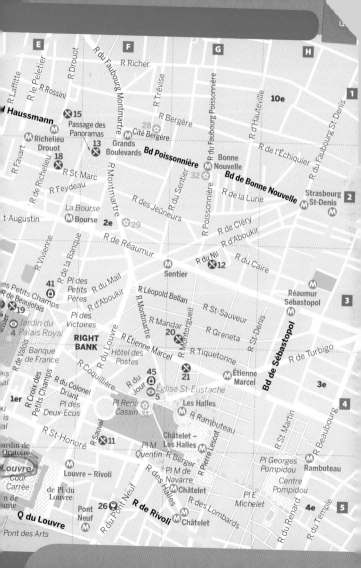

E

F

G

H

R Laffitte

R le Peletier

R Rossini

R Drouot

R du Faubourg Montmartre

R Richer

R Trévise

R du Faubourg Poissonnière

R d'Hauteville

10e

R de l'Échiquier

R du Faubourg St-Denis

1

◀ Haussmann

❌ 15

Passage des Panoramas

Richelieu Drouot

18

R de Richelieu

R Favart

R St-Marc

R Feydeau

R Montmartre

28

Cité Bergère

13

Grands Boulevards

R Bergère

R du Sentier

Bd Poissonnière

32

R Poissonnière

Bonne Nouvelle

Bd de Bonne Nouvelle

R de la Lune

Strasbourg St-Denis

2

R Vivienne

La Bourse

Bourse

2e

29

R des Jeûneurs

R de Cléry

R d'Aboukir

t-Augustin

R de la Banque

41

PI des Petits Pères

R du Mail

R d'Aboukir

R de Réaumur

R du Nil

12

R du Caire

Réaumur Sébastopol

3

es Petits Champs R de Beaujolais

19

Jardin du Palais Royal

PI des Victoires

RIGHT BANK

Sentier

R Léopold Bellan

R St-Sauveur

R Montmartre

R Mandar

20

R Montorgueil

R Greneta

R St-Sauveur

R St-Denis

R de Turbigo

R Valois

Banque de France

R du Louvre

R Étienne Marcel

Hôtel des Postes

R Tiquetonne

21

Étienne Marcel

Bd de Sébastopol

3e

1er

R Croix des Petits Champs

R du Colonel Driant

R Coquillière

R du Jour

45

Église St-Eustache

Les Halles

R St-Martin

R Beaubourg

4

is al

u is al

jardin de l'Oratoire

PI des Deux-Écus

PI René Cassin

R St-Honoré

R Sauval

11

Louvre

Cour Carrée

n de ante

Louvre – Rivoli

Châtelet – Les Halles

PI M Quentin

R Rambuteau

R Berger

PI M de Navarre

R des Halles

Châtelet

R Pierre Lescot

PI Georges Pompidou

Centre Pompidou

PI E Michelet

Rambuteau

4e

5

de PI du Louvre

26

Pont Neuf

R du Pont Neuf

R de Rivoli

Châtelet

R des Lombards

R du Renard

R du Temple

Q du Louvre

Pont des Arts

Sights

Jardin des Tuileries GARDENS

1 ⊚ Map p56, B4

Bisected by the *axe historique,* these 28-hectare formal gardens are where Parisians paraded their finery in the 17th century. Now a Unesco World Heritage Site, the paths, ponds and merry-go-round make it as enchanting as ever for a stroll. A funfair sets up here in midsummer. (⏲7am-11pm Jun-Aug, 7am-9pm Apr, May & Sep, 7.30am-7.30pm Oct-Mar; Ⓜ Tuileries or Concorde)

Musée de l'Orangerie MUSEUM

2 ⊚ Map p56, A4

Monet's prized cycle of eight enormous *Water Lilies,* which he conceived specifically for this former palace greenhouse, wrap around two skylit oval rooms. The lower level houses an astonishing collection of additional works by Monet and many by Sisley, Renoir, Cézanne, Gauguin, Picasso, Matisse and Modigliani, as well as Derain's *Arlequin & Pierrot.* (www.musee-orangerie.fr; Jardin des Tuileries, 1er; admission €7.50/5.50 or €13 with combined admission to Musée d'Orsay within 4 days; ⏲9am-6pm Mon-Wed; Ⓜ Concorde)

Église de la Madeleine CHURCH

3 ⊚ Map p56, B2

Styled like an austere Greek temple, with 52 Corinthian columns, the interior of the Church of St Mary Magdalene is much more ornate, decorated with gilt, marble and frescoes. The colossal organ above the main entrance on the southern side is played during Sunday Mass. (www.eglise-lamadeleine.com, in French; place de la Madeleine, 8e; ⏲9.30am-7pm; Ⓜ Madeleine)

Jardin du Palais Royal GARDENS

4 ⊚ Map p56, E3

Flanked by colonnaded shopping arcades selling everything from silverware and music boxes to Marc Jacobs' designerwear, this park is just north of the Palais Royal, where a young Louis XIV once resided (and which now houses government buildings). The black-and-white-striped columns at its southern end created by sculptor Daniel Buren in 1986 prompted a public outcry that interrupted construction; installation wasn't completed until 1995. (place du Palais Royal, 1er; ⏲7.30am-10pm Apr & May, 7am-11pm Jun-Aug, 7am-9.30pm Sep, 7.30am-8.30pm Oct-Mar; Ⓜ Palais Royal-Musée du Louvre)

Église St-Eustache CHURCH

5 ⊚ Map p56, F4

Constructed between 1532 and 1637, this magnificent church is primarily Gothic, with a neoclassical façade added on the western side in the mid-18th century. Inside, some exceptional Flamboyant Gothic arches support the chancel ceiling; most of the ornamentation is Renaissance and classical. The gargantuan organ is played during Sunday Mass. (www.saint-eustache.org, in French; place du Jour, 1er; ⏲9.30am-7pm Mon-Fri, 10am-7pm Sat, 9am-7pm Sun; Ⓜ Les Halles)

Arc de Triomphe du Carrousel
MONUMENT

6 ⊙ Map p56, D4

Although smaller than the famous Arc de Triomphe, this 1805 triumphal arch, located in the Jardin du Carrousel at the eastern end of the Tuileries, is more ornate. Its eight pink marble pillars are each topped with a statue of a soldier in Napoleon's army. (place du Carrousel, 1er; M Palais Royal-Musée du Louvre)

Jeu de Paume
MUSEUM

7 ⊙ Map p56, B3

In the northwestern corner of the Jardin des Tuileries, this former royal tennis court is now France's national photography centre, featuring rotating exhibitions of photography, cinema, video and installations that span the 19th to 21st centuries. (www.jeudepaume. org; 1 place de la Concorde, 8e; admission €7/5; ⊙ noon-9pm Tue, to 7pm Wed-Fri, 10am-7pm Sat & Sun; M Concorde)

Place Vendôme
SQUARE

8 ⊙ Map p56, C3

In 1796 Napoleon married Josephine in building No 3 of this octagonal 'square'. Its colonnades now shelter boutiques and the posh Hôtel Ritz. The square's 43.5m bronze-and-stone column commemorates Napoleon's

JOHN SONES/LONELY PLANET IMAGES ©

Ferris wheel between Arc de Triomphe du Carrousel and place de la Concorde (p60)

battle at Austerlitz, with bas-reliefs illustrating his subsequent victories and a crowning statue depicting the leader as a Roman emperor. (Tuileries or Opéra)

Musée du Parfum
MUSEUM

 9 ◉ Map p56, C2

In a beautiful 1860 townhouse, the secrets of perfume-making are revealed by Grasse-based *parfumerie* Fragonard. Its essences are sold mainly to factories, so you're unlikely to recognise the scents, but you can, of course, buy them here cheaply. Its 1900-built annexe, the **Théâtre-Musée des Capucines** (39 bd des Capucines, 2e; admission free; ☉9am-6pm Mon-Sat), concentrates on the bottling process and bottles, including Bohemian crystal. (www.fragonard.com; 9 rue Scribe, 2e; admission free; ☉9am-6pm Mon-Sat, to 5pm Sun; Ⓜ Opéra)

Place de la Concorde
SQUARE

10 ◉ Map p56, A3

Paris spreads around you, with views of the Eiffel Tower, the Seine and along the Champs-Élysées, when you stand in the city's largest square, laid out in 1775. Its 3300-year-old pink granite obelisk was a gift from Egypt in 1831. (Ⓜ Concorde)

Eating

Yam'Tcha
FUSION €€€

 11 Map p56, F4

Adeline Grattard's ingeniously fused French and Chinese flavours recently earned her a Michelin star. Dishes on the frequently changing menu can be paired with exotic teas (as well as wines, of course). Book well ahead. (☎01 40 26 08 07; 4 Rue Sauval, 1er; lunch/dinner menus from €50/85; ☉lunch Wed-Sat, dinner Wed-Sun; Ⓜ Louvre-Rivoli)

Local Life
Forum des Halles

Ever since Paris' old markets were forsaken for the banal shopping mall the **Forum des Halles** (Map p56, F4; www.forum-des-halles.com; 1 rue Pierre Lescot, 1er; ☉shops 10am-8pm Mon-Sat; Ⓜ Les Halles), Parisians have been up in arms. Four decades later, the dodgy park and dated arbours that topped the underground shopping mall have been demolished, to be replaced by architects Patrick Berger and Jacques Anziutti's giant, rainforest-inspired glass canopy and landscape designer David Mangin's opened-up gardens (completion is due by the end of 2016). The mall itself will receive a relatively light renovation in stages; hence business should continue more or less as usual, with minimal disruption to city's largest metro and RER hub. Keep tabs on developments at www.parisleshalles.fr.

Frenchie

FRENCH €€

12 Map p56, G3

There are just two choices for each course at this little alleyway bistro, but the food is so good even that can cause dilemmas. Bookings are notoriously hard to nail down but persistence pays off. (📞 01 40 39 96 19; www.frenchie-restaurant.com; 5 rue du Nil, 2e; menus €34-45; ⊙dinner Mon-Fri; Ⓜ Sentier)

Passage 53

GASTRONOMIC €€€

13 Map p56, F2

Easily missed inside the city's oldest covered arcade (see p172), Passage 53 is setting Paris' food scene alight with its intricate combinations of flavours, such as haddock with oyster foam. Prices are a steal, particularly at lunch, considering it recently gained a second Michelin star. (📞 01 42 33 04 35; www.passage53.com; 53 Passage des Panoramas, 2e; lunch/dinner menus from €60/110; ⊙lunch & dinner Tue-Sat; Ⓜ Grands Boulevards)

Le Soufflé

SOUFFLÉS €€

14 Map p56, B3

Savoury soufflés in flavours including snail and foie gras, and sweet soufflés ranging from pear and chocolate to Grand Marnier are the specialties of this family-friendly spot. (📞 01 42 60 27 19; www.lesouffle.fr, in French; 36 rue du Mont Thabor, 1er; soufflés €11-18; ⊙lunch & dinner; Ⓜ Concorde)

Le J'Go

SOUTHWESTERN FRANCE €€

15 Map p56, E1

Fronted by a tomato-red façade, the rugby-player-founded Le J'Go serves enormous dishes to share, such as roast leg of lamb or a whole side of pork, plus Basque tapas in its bar. (📞 01 40 22 09 09; www.lejgo.com; 4 rue Drouot, 9e; 2-/3-course menus from €15/20; ⊙lunch Mon-Fri, dinner Mon-Sat; Ⓜ Richelieu Drouot)

Café Marly

INTERNATIONAL €€

16 Map p56, D4

The glittering views of IM Pei's glass pyramid and of the French movers, shakers and stars who frequent this cafe, do their best to distract from Marly's classy fare, including its sumptuous pastas. (📞 01 46 26 06 60; rue de Rivoli, 1er; mains €12-40; ⊙8am-2am; Ⓜ Palais Royal-Musée du Louvre)

Le Roi du Pot au Feu

FRENCH €€

17 Map p56, B1

True to its name (King of Hotpots), this homey 1930s bistro dishes up wonderful hotpots, with the herb-infused stock served as an entrée and the beef and root vegetables as the main, as well as classic desserts like crème caramel. There are no bookings; just turn up. (34 rue Vignon, 9e; 2-/3-course menus from €18/30; ⊙lunch & dinner Mon-Sat; Ⓜ Havre Caumartin)

Aux Lyonnais
LYONNAIS €€

18 Map p56, E2

Beneath Alain Ducasse's ever-expanding umbrella, this beautiful art nouveau venue turns out classical Lyonnais cuisine focusing on frogs' legs, free-range poultry and pork. (☎01 42 96 65 04; www.auxlyonnais.com; 32 rue St-Marc, 2e; mains €20-32; ☺lunch Tue-Fri, dinner Tue-Sat; MRichelieu Drouot)

Le Grand Véfour
GASTRONOMIC €€€

19 Map p56, E3

Chef Guy Martin preserves the reputation of this 1784-established splendour, replete with gilt-edged mirrors and chandeliers, whose past guests include Napoleon. A sommelier pairs Martin's opuses – such as chicken and foie gras with ginger-infused tofu – with France's finest wines. (☎01 42 96 56 27; www.grand-vefour.com, in French; 17 rue de Beaujolais, 1er; lunch menu €96, mains €80-100; ☺lunch & dinner Mon-Fri; MPyramides)

Stohrer
PATISSERIE, DELICATESSEN

20 Map p56, G3

Opened in 1730, this beautiful patisserie's pastel murals were added in 1864 by Paul Baudry, who also decorated the Garnier Opèra's Grand Foyer. All of the cakes, pastries, ice cream

WILL SALTER/LONELY PLANET IMAGES ©

Café Marly (p61)

and savoury delicacies are made on the premises, including specialities invented here such as *baba rhum* (rum-drenched brioche) and *puit d'amour* (cream-filled, caramel-topped puff pastry). (www.stohrer.fr, in French; 51 rue Montorgueil, 2e; dishes €11.50-14.90; ⏱7.30am-8.30pm; Ⓜ Étienne Marcel or Sentier)

L'Escargot
FRENCH €€€

21 Map p56, G4

A giant gold snail adorns the forest-green façade of this heritage-listed monument. Snails also feature on the menu, along with frogs' legs, Chateaubriand steak with Béarnaise sauce, veal sweetbreads and whisky-flambéed Breton lobster. Past guests range from Proust to Bogie and Bacall. (☎01 42 36 33 51; 38 rue Montorgueil, 1er; menus €80-150; ⏱lunch Sun-Fri, dinner daily; Ⓜ Les Halles)

Drinking

Harry's New York Bar
BAR

22 Map p56, C2

This mahogany-panelled beauty of a bar's great gift to the world was, allegedly, the Bloody Mary, which was invented here in 1921 following the advent of canned tomato juice. (Harry's also invented the Blue Lagoon in 1960 but we'll forgive it for that.) The basement piano bar knocks out jazz tunes. (www.harrys-bar.fr; 5 rue Daunou, 2e; ⏱noon-2am Sun-Thu, to 3am Fri & Sat; piano bar 10pm-2am Tue-Thu, to 3am Fri & Sat; Ⓜ Opéra)

Bar Hemingway
BAR

23 Map p56, C2

Legend has it that Hemingway himself, wielding a machine gun, helped liberate this timber-panelled, leather-upholstered bar during WWII. Today the Ritz's showpiece is awash with photos taken by Papa and has the best martinis in town. Dress to impress. (www.ritzparis.com; Hôtel Ritz Paris, 15 place Vendôme, 1er; ⏱6.30pm-2am; Ⓜ Concorde or Madeleine)

Angelina
SALON DE THÉ

24 Map p56, C3

Beneath the rue de Rivoli's cloisters, this 1903 belle époque tearoom is so renowned for its decadent African hot chocolate (served with a pot of whipped cream) that queues regularly stretch out the door. (www.angelina-paris.fr, in French; 226 rue de Rivoli, 1er; ⏱7.30am-7pm Mon-Fri, from 8.30am Sat & Sun; Ⓜ Tuileries)

Verjus
WINE BAR

25 Map p56, E3

The switched-on foodie duo behind this newly opened wine bar cooks smart bar fare and is set to have opened an adjacent restaurant by the time you're reading this. One to watch. (www.verjusparis.com; 47 rue de Montpensier, 1er; ⏱6-11pm Mon-Sat; Ⓜ Tuileries)

Kong BAR

26 ⊖ Map p56, F5

Late nights at this Philippe Starck–designed riot of iridescent champagne-coloured vinyl booths, Japanese cartoon cutouts and garden gnome stools see Paris' glam young set guzzling Dom Pérignon and shaking their designer-clad booty on the tables. But the best time to visit this bar–restaurant–club is at sunset, when you have incredible views of the river. (www.kong.fr; 1 rue du Pont Neuf, 1er; ⊙bar noon-2am Sun-Thu, to 3am Fri & Sat; ⓂPont Neuf)

Entertainment

Palais Garnier OPERA HOUSE

27 ⭐ Map p56, C1

The fabled 'phantom of the opera' lurked in this opulent Charles Garnier–designed opera house. Some seats have limited or no visibility, though this is being improved. You can also take a 90-minute guided tour or visit the attached museum, with three centuries' worth of costumes, backdrops, scores and other memorabilia, which includes a self-guided behind-the-scenes peek (except during matinees and rehearsals). (☎08 92 89 90 90, tours 08 25 05 44 05; www.operadeparis.fr; place de l'Opéra, 9e; tours €13.50/9.50, museum €9/6; ⊙English-language tours 11.30am & 2.30pm daily during school holidays, museum 10am-5pm; ⓂOpéra)

Top Tip

Booking Agencies

Booking agency **Agence Perrossier & SOS Théâtres** (Map p56, B2; ☎01 42 60 58 31, 01 44 77 88 55; www.agencedetheatresdeparis.fr; 6 place de la Madeleine, 8e; ⊙10am-7pm Mon-Sat; ⓂMadeleine) sells theatre tickets, while **Kiosque Théâtre Madeleine** (Map p56, B2; www.kiosquetheatre.com, in French; opposite 15 place de la Madeleine, 8e; ⊙12.30-8pm Tue-Sat, 12.30-4pm Sun; ⓂMadeleine) sells discounted theatre tickets – see p56.

Au Limonaire CHANSONS

28 ⭐ Map p56, F1

Traditional *chansons* enthral audiences at this perfect little Parisian wine bar. (http://limonaire.free.fr, in French; 18 cité Bergère; admission free; ⊙7pm-midnight Mon, 6pm-midnight Tue-Sun; ⓂGrands Boulevards)

Social Club NIGHTCLUB

29 ⭐ Map p56, F2

These subterranean rooms, showcasing electro, hip-hop and funk, and live acts, are a magnet for clubbers who take their music seriously. (www.parissocialclub.com; 142 rue Montmartre, 2e; ⊙11pm-3am Tue & Wed, to 6am Thu-Sat; ⓂBourse)

Comédie Française

THEATRE

30 Map p56, D4

Founded in 1680, France's oldest theatre stages works by playwrights such as Molière, Racine and Beaumarchais. The 'French Comedy' encompasses the main **Comédie Française Salle Richelieu** (place Colette, 1er), just west of the Palais Royal, as well as the **Comédie Française Studio Théâtre** (99 rue de Rivoli, 1er) and the **Théâtre du Vieux Colombier** (p157). (www.comedie-francaise.fr; place Colette, 1er; ⊙box office 11am-6pm; ⓜPalais Royal-Musée du Louvre)

Forum des Images

CINEMA

31 Map p56, F4

This archive centre, devoted to Paris on film, has cinemas showing films set in Paris and various art-house screenings and festivals. It also has a new library and research centre with newsreels, documentaries and advertising. (www.forumdesimages.net, in French; 1 Grande Galerie, Porte St-Eustache, Forum des Halles, 1er; ⊙12.30-11.30pm Tue-Fri, from 2pm Sat & Sun; ⓜLes Halles)

Le Grand Rex

CINEMA

32 Map p56, G2

In addition to screenings, this 1932 art deco icon runs hugely entertaining 45-minute behind-the-scenes tours (English soundtracks available). Tracked by a sensor slung around your neck, you're directed up in the lift behind the giant screen, and put on a soundstage and in a recording studio,

with whizz-bang special effects along the way. A winner with kids (and adults too). (www.legrandrex.com, in French; 1 bd Poissonnière, 2e; tour €9.80/8; ⊙tours 10am-7pm Wed-Sun; ⓜBonne Nouvelle)

L'Olympia

LIVE MUSIC

33 Map p56, C2

Opened in 1888 by the founder of the Moulin Rouge, this hallowed concert hall's past performers include Johnny Hallyday, Hendrix and Piaf, as well as

---

Local Life
Rue des Lombards

Parisian jazz buffs flock to the city's greatest concentration of clubs on rue des Lombards. **Le Baiser Salé** (Map p56, G5; ☎01 42 33 37 71; www.lebaisersale.com, in French; 58 rue des Lombards, 1er; ⊙5pm-6am; ⓜChâtelet) unearths trad, Afro- and fusion-jazz talent, and hosts pop-rock and *chansons*. Revamped venue **Le Duc des Lombards** (Map p56, G5; ☎01 42 33 22 88; www.ducdeslombards.com, in French; 42 rue des Lombards, 1er; ⊙9pm-4am; ⓜChâtelet) has an inexpensive restaurant on-site. Or head to **Sunset & Sunside** (Map p56, G5; ☎01 40 26 46 60; www.sunset-sunside.com, in French; 60 rue des Lombards, 1er; ⊙8pm-4am; ⓜChâtelet): world music–oriented electric and fusion is found downstairs at Sunset, acoustic upstairs at Sunside.

Jeff Buckley, who considered 'Live at the Olympia' his best-ever gig. Today you might see anything from kids' musicals to bands like The Kills. (www.olympiahall.com; 28 bd des Capucines, 9e; Ⓜ Opéra)

Rex Club
NIGHTCLUB

Attached to Le Grand Rex (see **32** ⭐ Map p56, G2), Paris' premier house and techno venue's 70-speaker, multidiffusion sound system is tested to the limits by some of the world's hottest DJs. (www.rexclub.com, in French; 5 bd Poissonnière, 2e; ⏱ 11.30pm-6am Wed-Sat; Ⓜ Bonne Nouvelle)

Shopping

Hédiard
FOOD & DRINK

34 🔒 Map p56, B2

Since 1880 this gourmet emporium has sold exotic teas and luxury gourmet goods. The upstairs tearoom and restaurant serves sumptuous brunches. (www.hediard.com; 21 place de la Madeleine, 8e; ⏱ tearoom 3-6pm Mon-Sat, restaurant breakfast, lunch & dinner Mon-Sat; Ⓜ Madeleine)

Eres
FASHION

35 🔒 Map p56, B2

Before you and your suntan oil hit Paris Plages (the city's summertime beaches, which set up along the Seine from mid-July to mid-August), shimmy into a swimsuit from this sleek beachwear boutique. In addition to shapely one-pieces and bikinis (with tops and bottoms sold separately), Eres also does its own line of lingerie. (www.eres.fr; 2 rue Tronchet, 8e; ⏱ 10am-7pm Mon-Sat; Ⓜ Madeleine)

Fauchon
FOOD & DRINK

36 🔒 Map p56, B2

Many a lavish Parisian dinner party has been catered for with goods from this famous pair of glossy black-and-fuchsia-pink shops. Beautifully wrapped delicacies include pâté de foie gras and jams. (www.fauchon.fr; 24-26 place de la Madeleine, 8e; ⏱ 8am-9pm Mon-Sat; Ⓜ Madeleine)

Galeries Lafayette
DEPARTMENT STORE

37 🔒 Map p56, D1

Beneath a stained-glass dome, this opulent department store stocks designer labels and stages free **fashion shows** (bookings 📞 01 42 82 30 25; ⏱ 3pm Fri Mar-Jul & Sep-Dec). Don't miss the fabulous rooftop panorama over Paris. Its homewares store, Lafayette Maison, is at 35 bd Haussmann. (www.galerieslafayette.com, in French; 40 bd Haussmann, 9e; ⏱ 9.30am-8pm Mon-Wed, Fri & Sat, to 9pm Thu; Ⓜ Auber or Chaussée d'Antin)

Le Printemps
DEPARTMENT STORE

38 🔒 Map p56, C1

One of Paris' most resplendent *grands magasins* (department stores), Le Printemps' fashion, accessories and homewares span three neighbouring buildings, including its original

Jardin des Tuileries (p58)

building topped by a stained-glass, 7th-floor art nouveau cupola, with great views from the rooftop. Multilingual personal shoppers are on hand for free advice. (www.printemps.com; 64 bd Haussmann, 9e; ⊘9.35am-8pm Mon-Wed, Fri & Sat, to 10pm Thu; MHavre Caumartin)

La Maison de la Truffe
FOOD & DRINK

39 Map p56, B2

Buy pricey 'black diamond' truffles (which can be cooked) and even pricier elusive white truffles (always eaten raw) here; taste them in pastas, eggs and other dishes at the onsite restaurant, or take away truffle-laced sandwiches. (www.maison-de-la-truffe.com; 19 place de la Madeleine, 8e; ⊘shop 10am-10pm Mon-Sat, restaurant noon-10.30pm Mon-Sat; MMadeleine)

La Maison du Miel
FOOD & DRINK

40 Map p56, B1

More than 50 varieties of honey produced throughout France and the world gleam on the shelves of this 1898-established, family-run 'honey house'. (www.maisondumiel.com; 24 rue Vignon, 9e; ⊘9.30am-7pm Mon-Sat; MMadeleine)

Legrand Filles & Fils
WINE

41 Map p56, E3

Opening onto Galerie Vivienne (p172), this wondrous wine and wine accoutrement emporium is Paris' oldest. (www.caves-legrand.com, in French; 1 rue de la

Banque, 2e; 11am-7pm Mon, 10am-7.30pm Tue-Fri, 10am-7pm Sat; Ⓜ Pyramides)

Marché aux Fleurs Madeleine

MARKET

42 Map p56, B2

This colourful flower market has been trading since 1832. (place de la Madeleine, 8e; 8am-7.30pm Mon-Sat; Ⓜ Madeleine)

Boutique Maille

FOOD

43 Map p56, B2

You can buy Maille's specialty mustard premade or have it prepared to complement different cuisines. Maille also sells high-quality vinegars, mayonnaises and oils. (www.maille.com, in French; 6 place de la Madeleine, 8e; 10am-7pm Mon-Sat; Ⓜ Madeleine)

Antoine

ACCESSORIES

44 Map p56, D3

Founded in 1785 under Louis XV's royal decree, M and Mme Antoine rented out the first-ever 'public umbrellas'. The shop now sells dozens of umbrellas and parasols as well as new and antique walking canes. (www.antoine1745.com, in French; 10 av de l'Opéra, 2e; 10.30am-6.30pm Mon-Sat; Ⓜ Palais Royal-Musée du Louvre or Pyramides)

Understand

Flâneurie

The single best way to acquaint yourself with any city is walking or, in Paris' case, flâneurie. Writer Charles Baudelaire (1821–67) came up with the whimsical term flâneur to describe a 'gentleman stroller of city streets' or a 'detached pedestrian observer of a metropolis' (the metropolis being Baudelaire's native Paris).

Paris' ornate arcades were closely tied to the concept of flâneurie in philosopher Walter Benjamin's Arcades Project – an unfinished collection of writings from 1927 to 1940, which was published posthumously. Known as passages couverts (covered passages), these marble-floored, iron-and-glass-roofed shopping arcades, streaming with natural light, were the elegant forerunners to department stores and malls. For a walk linking some of the best-preserved passages, see p172.

The term flâneurie is now widely used, especially in the context of architecture and town planning. But Paris – with its village-like backstreets, its riverbank paths (particularly down the steps at the water's edge), its parks and gardens and its passages – remains the ultimate place for a flâneur to meander without any particular destination in mind.

agnès b
FASHION

45 Map p56, F4

Parisian-label-turned-global-empire agnès b is synonymous with durable basics in muted colours, such as well-cut jackets, body-hugging shirts and snap-fastened cardigans, plus quirky items such as artist-designed humanitarian T-shirts. As well as the women's shop, there's also a men's shop and a children's shop on the same street. (www.agnesb.com; 6 rue du Jour, 1er; 10am-7pm Mon-Fri, to 7.30pm Sat; Les Halles)

Galignani
BOOKS

46 Map p56, C3

Beneath rue de Rivoli's cloisters is France's first-ever English-language bookstore, which also stocks French literature. (http://galignani.com; 224 rue de Rivoli, 1er; 10am-7pm Mon-Sat; Tuileries)

Colette
FASHION, ACCESSORIES

47 Map p56, C3

The thumping music reverberating from this uberhip concept shop means you'll probably hear it before you spot its discreet signage. Streetwear, music and hi-tech gadgets that change with the zeitgeist fill the ground floor. Upstairs are serious party frocks and menswear, cosmetics and collectors' items. The basement 'water bar' serves dozens of varieties of water, as well as champagne. (www.colette.fr; 213 rue St-Honoré,1er; 11am-7pm Mon-Sat; Tuileries)

Maroquinerie Saint-Honoré
ACCESSORIES

48 Map p56, C3

Behind this boutique's black-enamelled antique façade (which bears the name B Biberon & Fils in gold letters), you'll find affordable handbags including coveted Frederic T designs. (334 rue St-Honoré, 1er; 10.30am-6.30pm Mon-Sat; Tuileries)

Carrousel du Louvre
SHOPPING CENTRE

49 Map p56, D4

IM Pei's inverted glass pyramid is the focal point of this underground shopping centre's upmarket shops selling fashion, jewellery and electronics, as well as beauty boutiques and international restaurants and cafes. (www.carrouseldulouvre.com, in French; 99 rue de Rivoli, 1er; 8am-11pm; Palais Royal-Musée du Louvre)

Explore

Sacré-Cœur & Montmartre

Montmartre's slinking streets, lined with crooked ivy-clad buildings, retain a fairy tale charm, despite the area's popularity. Crowned by the Sacré-Cœur basilica, Montmartre is the city's steepest quarter (*mont* means hill; the martyr was St Denis, beheaded here in about AD 250); the lofty views, wine-producing vines and hidden village squares have lured painters since the 19th century.

The Sights in a Day

Montmartre makes for an enchanting stroll, especially in the early morning or midweek when tourists are few. Start at the top of the Butte de Montmartre at the striking **Sacré-Cœur** (p72) basilica for exceptional views (especially from inside its dome), then check out the **Dalí Espace Montmartre** (p78).

After lunch at **Le Relais Gascon** (p79), wander through the peaceful **Cimetière de Montmartre** (p78), before visiting one of Paris' loveliest small museums, the **Musée de la vie Romantique** (p78), dedicated to author George Sand. For a romantic museum of an altogether different kind, you might want to check out the **Musée de l'Érotisme** (p78) in Montmartre's southern neighbour, the red-light district (albeit a safe, tame one) Pigalle, before an *apéro* (predinner drink) at **La Fourmi** (p81).

Continue down **rue des Martyrs** (p81) to neighbourhood bistro **Le Miroir** (p81) for dinner, then catch a cabaret at the **Moulin Rouge** (p82) or a concert at **La Cigale** (p82).

For local insight into Montmartre's artistic legacies, see p74.

 Top Sights

Sacré-Cœur (p72)

Local Life

Art in Montmartre (p74)

Best of Paris

Museums
Dalí Espace Montmartre (p78)

Eating
Le Miroir (p81)

Drinking
Les Deux Moulins (p78)

Nights Out
Moulin Rouge (p82)
Au Lapin Agile (p75)

Churches
Sacré-Cœur (p72)

Getting There

M Metro Anvers (line 2) is the most convenient for Sacré-Cœur and its funicular.

M Metro Abbesses and Lamarck–Caulaincourt (line 12) are in the heart of Montmartre.

M Metro Blanche and Pigalle (line 2) are your best bet for the clubs and cabarets around Pigalle.

Top Sights
Sacré-Cœur

Visible from across the city, the striking white domes of the Basilique du Sacré-Cœur (Sacred Heart Basilica) crown the 130m-high Butte de Montmartre (Montmartre Hill). The basilica's travertine stone exudes calcite, ensuring that it remains white despite weathering and pollution, while its lofty vantage point offers dizzying Parisian vistas from its steep surrounding streets, steps, and above all, its main dome.

◉ Map p76, D4

www.sacre-coeur
-montmartre.com

Parvis du Sacré-Cœur,
18e

admission free

⊙6am-10.30pm, dome
9am-7pm Apr-Sep, to
5.30pm Oct-Mar

Ⓜ Anvers, or funicular

Don't Miss

The History

Designed by architect Paul Abadie and begun in 1873 as a means for France to atone for the Franco-Prussian War (1870–71), the Roman-Byzantine basilica was funded largely by private, often small, donations. It was completed in 1914 but wasn't consecrated until after WWI in 1919.

The Blessed Sacrament

In a sense, atonement here has never stopped: a prayer 'cycle' that began in 1835 (before the basilica's consecration) continues around the clock, with perpetual adoration of the Blessed Sacrament that's on display above the high altar.

The Dome

The sublime views from Sacré-Cœur get even better when you climb the 234 steps spiralling inside its 83m-high main **dome** (admission €5, cash only; ⏲9am-7pm Apr-Sep, to 5.30pm Oct-Mar). From here, you can see up to 30km on a clear day.

The Crypt

Admission to the dome also includes entry to Sacré-Cœur's huge, chapel-lined crypt.

France's Largest Bell

'La Savoyarde' in the basilica's huge square bell tower is the largest in France. Donated by the four dioceses of the Savoy in 1895, it can be heard ringing out across the neighbourhood and beyond.

The Christ in Majesty Mosaic

The magnificent apse mosaic *Christ in Majesty,* designed by Luc-Olivier Merson in 1922, is one of the largest of its kind in the world. Its golden hues lighten Sacré-Cœur's otherwise dark interior.

☑ Top Tips

▶ To save you some of the climb up to the basilica, a **funicular** (⏲6am-midnight) railway shuttles up and down a 36m-long hillside track, offering some stunning views of its own during the 90-second ride. Metro tickets and travel passes are valid on the funicular; there are also ticket booths at the funicular's upper and lower stations.

▶ Photography and filming are forbidden inside the basilica; for etiquette tips see p192.

▶ Keep one eye on the mesmerising views and the other on your belongings, as the base of the basilica attracts pickpockets and touts.

✗ Take a Break

The area has more than its fair share of tourist traps, but for great-value French dishes in atmospheric surrounds head to neighbourhood bistro Chez Marie (p79).

Local Life
Art in Montmartre

For centuries Montmartre was a bucolic country village filled with *moulins* (mills) that supplied Paris with flour. But after it was incorporated into the capital in 1860, its picturesque charm and low rents attracted painters including Manet, Degas, Renoir, Van Gogh, Toulouse-Lautrec, Dufy, Picasso, Utrillo, Modigliani and Dalí in its late 19th- and early 20th-century heyday.

1 The Ninth Art
Bandes dessinées (comics) are known as *le neuvième art* (the ninth art), and the colourful little shop **Temps Libre** (28 rue Lepic, 18e; ⊙ 3.30-7.30pm Mon, 11am-7.30pm Tue-Sat, 11am-1pm Sun; M Blanche) is perfect for whiling away time poring over its huge selection of comics and graphic novels, from *Tintin* and *Asterix* to Marvel and manga editions.

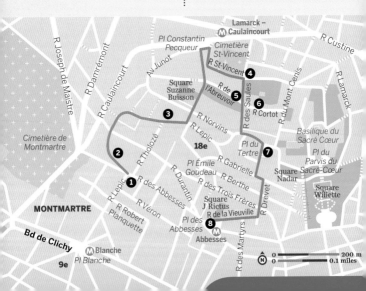

❷ Van Gogh's House

Théo Van Gogh owned the house at 54 rue Lepic; his brother, the artist Vincent, stayed with him on the 3rd floor for two years from 1886.

❸ Renoir's Dance Hall

Montmartre's two surviving windmills are the Moulin Blute-Fin and, 100m east, the Moulin Radet (now a restaurant). In the 19th century, the windmills were turned into the open-air dance hall Le Moulin de la Galette, immortalised by Renoir in his 1876 tableau *Le Bal du Moulin de la Galette* (now on display at the Musée d'Orsay).

❹ Gill's Mural

Look for caricaturist André Gill's mural *Le Lapin à Gill* of a rabbit jumping out of a cooking pot on the façade of legendary local cabaret **Au Lapin Agile** (☏01 46 06 85 87; www.au-lapin-agile.com; 22 rue des Saules, 18e; tickets €24/17, no concession Sat; ⏱9pm-2am Tue-Sun; Ⓜ Lamarck-Caulaincourt), and return later for a show.

❺ Lunch at La Maison Rose

Rendered in lithographs by Utrillo, the hillside-perched, rose-pink cottage **La Maison Rose** (☏01 42 57 66 75; 2 rue de l'Abreuvoir, 18e; menu €17; ⏱lunch daily, dinner Fri-Sun; Ⓜ Lamarck-Caulaincourt) serves well-priced, authentic bistro fare in its cosy rooms and tiny terrace. Hours vary; confirm ahead.

❻ Local History Lessons

Local history comes to life through paintings and documents at the **Musée de Montmartre** (www.museedemontmartre.fr, in French; 12 rue Cortot, 18e; admission €8/6; ⏱10am-6pm; Ⓜ Lamarck-Caulaincourt), housed in Montmartre's oldest building – a 17th-century garden-set manor where Renoir, Utrillo and Dufy once lived.

❼ Artists at Work

The main square of the original village before it was incorporated into Paris proper, **place du Tertre** (Ⓜ Abbesses) has drawn countless painters in its time. While it's awash with visitors, local, often very talented, artists paint, sketch and sell their creations at stalls here, and the portraitists, buskers and crowds create an unmissable carnival-like atmosphere.

❽ The Art of Travel

With its original glass canopy and twin wrought-iron lamp posts illuminating the dark-green-on-lemon-yellow *Metropolitain* sign still intact, Abbesses is the finest remaining example of art nouveau designer Hector Guimard's metro station entrances.

MONTMARTRE

Sacré-Cœur

18e

17e

Bd Ney

For reviews see	
◉ Top Sights	p72
◉ Sights	p78
⊗ Eating	p79
◎ Drinking	p81
◎ Entertainment	p82
◎ Shopping	p83

R Faubourg Poissonnière

24 ⓜ

Barbès Rochechouart

R du Delta

R de Dunkerque

R Pétrelle

R de Rochechouart

10e

Poissonnière ⓜ

R du Faubourg Poissonnière

R Talul

R d'Orsel

Anvers ⓜ
Anvers

R Gérando

R Turgot

R Rodier

R Condorcet

Av Trudaine

R de la Tour d'Auvergne

Square de
Montholon

R Lamartine

R Bleue

R Trévise

R Richer

R Ste-Cécile

R Bergère

R Dancourt

13 Bd de Rochechouart

17

R Lallier

R des Martyrs

R Choron

Cadet ⓜ
R Cadet

R du Faubourg Montmartre

Grands
Boulevards ⓜ

25 ⓜ

16

Abbesses ⓜ

15

R Victor Massé

R Navarin

Pl
Kossuth

Notre Dame
de Lorette ⓜ

Le Peletier ⓜ

R le Peletier

Richelieu
Drouot ⓜ

R Drouot

2e

Pigalle ⓜ

Pigalle

St-Georges ⓜ

Notre Dame
de Lorette

R de la Rochefoucauld

R d'Aumale

Pl St-Georges

9e

R St-Georges

R de la Victoire

R Laffitte

Bd Haussmann ⓜ

Musée
de la vie
Romantique

8

2

R Jean Baptiste Pigalle

R Chaptal

R la
Bruyère

R St-Lazare

R de Châteaudun

R Taitbout

R de Provence

Trinité ⓜ

R Blanche

Pl Blanche ⓜ

23 ⓜ

Bd de Clichy

Bruxelles Blanche

R de Douai

R Ballu

R Moncey

Square
d'Estienne
d'Orves

Pl d'Estienne
d'Orves

R de la Chaussée d'Antin

R de Mogador

Chaussée
d'Antin ⓜ

Pl Diaghilev

R Gluck

Pl J
Rouché

Pl Blanche

Pl de 9
Clichy ⓜ

Place de 9

R de Vintimille

R de Clichy

Havre
Caumartin ⓜ

Auber ⓚ

R Auber

5 13

Bd des
Batignolles

R de Turin

Pl de
Dublin

R Clapeyron

R d'Amsterdam

R de St-Pétersbourg

R de Liège

Liège ⓜ

Pl de
Budapest

R d'Athènes

Pl de Londres

8e

Gare
St-Lazare ⓜ

St-Lazare ⓜ

Pl G-Péri

R St-Lazare

R de Rome

Bd Haussmann

R Tronchet

R de l'Arcade

Pl de
l'Europe

Europe ⓜ

400 m

0.2 miles

Ⓝ

Sights

Dalí Espace Montmartre   MUSEUM

1 Map p76, D4

Catalan surrealist Dalí's illustrations, sculptures, engravings and furniture, such as his 'lips' sofa, are dramatically displayed against black-painted walls. (www.daliparis.com; 11 rue Poulbot, 18e; admission €10/7; ⊙10am-6pm, to 8pm Jul & Aug; MAbbesses)

Musée de la vie Romantique   MUSEUM

2 Map p76, B6

In the district once known as 'New Athens', the Museum of the Romantic Life is devoted to the life and work of Amandine Aurore Lucile Dupin, Baronne Dudevant (aka George Sand; 1804–76) and her intellectual circle. It's full of paintings, *objets d'art* and personal effects; don't miss the tiny but enchanting garden. (www.vie-romantique.paris.fr, in French; 16 rue Chaptal, 9e; admission free; ⊙10am-6pm Tue-Sun; MBlanche or St-Georges)

Clos Montmartre   VINEYARD

3 Map p76, D3

Planted in 1933 to thwart real estate development, the small Clos Montmartre is central Paris' only remaining vineyard. Its 2000 vines produce an average of 800 bottles each year, which are auctioned off for charity. You can view it from the street; alternatively contact the Montmartre Tourist Office (p208) about occasional tours. (18 Rue des Saules, 18e; MLamarck-Caulaincourt)

Cimetière de Montmartre   CEMETERY

4 Map p76, B4

Famous graves in this cobbled cemetery, established in 1798, include those of writers Emile Zola, Alexandre Dumas and Stendhal (Marie-Henri Beyle), composer Jacques Offenbach, artist Edgar Degas, film director François Truffaut and dancer Vaslav Nijinsky. Pick up a free map from the conservation office. Hours vary seasonally. (Conservation office 20 av Rachel, 18e; admission free; ⊙9am-5.30pm; MPlace de Clichy)

Musée de l'Érotisme   MUSEUM

5 Map p76, B5

Surprisingly artistic exhibits represent the history of erotica from around the world, incorporating 5000-plus stat-

Local Life

Les Deux Moulins

The arty cafe where the title character of the quirky film *Amélie* (itself a work of art) waitressed, **Les Deux Moulins** (Map p76, B4; Two Windmills; 15 rue Lepic, 18e; ⊙7am-2am Mon-Sat, 8am-2am Sun; MBlanche), remains a down-to-earth local where you can watch Montmartre go by.

ues, paintings by artists including Degas, black-and-white 1920s silent porn and mind-boggling toys. (If you're inspired, there's a sex supermarket, complete with shopping trolleys, next door.) (www.musee-erotisme.com; 72 bd de Clichy, 18e; admission €9/6; ⊙10am-2am; Ⓜ Blanche)

Cimetière St-Vincent   CEMETERY

6 Map p76, C3

Painter Maurice Utrillo (1883–1955) and film director Marcel Carné (1906–96) are among the celebrity 'residents' of this small cemetery. Hours vary seasonally. (6 rue Lucien-Gaulard, 18e; ⊙9am-5.30pm; Ⓜ Lamarck-Caulaincourt)

Eating

Le Relais Gascon   FRENCH €€

7 🍴 Map p76, C5

Climbing the wooden staircase to this narrow townhouse's 1st-floor dining room rewards with rooftop views of Montmartre. The menu includes steak with Roquefort sauce, but the reason people pack its communal tables is to tuck into one of Gascon's gargantuan salads, served in bowls with thin-sliced fried potatoes sautéed in garlic. (www.lerelaisgascon.fr, in French; 6 rue des Abbesses, 18e; menu €25.50; salads €10.50-15.50; ⊙10am-2am; Ⓜ Abbesses)

À la Cloche d'Or   FRENCH €€

8 🍴 Map p76, B5

Once owned by actress Jeanne Moreau's family, the 'Golden Bell' has vaudeville charm, with photos of stars, an open fire in winter, and a timeless steak tartare. (☎01 48 74 48 88; www.alaclochedor.com, in French; 3 rue Mansart, 9e; 2-/3-course menus €18.50/29.50; ⊙lunch & dinner to 4am Mon-Sat; Ⓜ Blanche or Pigalle)

Charlot, Roi des Coquillages   SEAFOOD €€€

9 🍴 Map p76, B5

Renowned for its good-value seafood platters, the art deco 'King of Shellfish' also does delicious grilled sardines and bouillabaisse to make any Marseillais homesick. (☎01 53 20 48 00; www.charlot-paris.com, in French; 12 place de Clichy, 9e; menus/platters from €22.10/33.15; ⊙lunch & dinner; Ⓜ Place de Clichy)

Chez Marie   FRENCH €

10 🍴 Map p76, D4

If you're after simple French standards such as onion soup followed by veal or perfectly cooked sole, with robust house wines, this little place, découpaged with old theatre and advertising posters, is a treat. (☎01 42 62 06 26; www.chezmarierestaurant.com; 27 rue Gabrielle, 18e; menus €12.50-19; ⊙lunch & dinner; Ⓜ Abbesses)

Understand
Village Life

- - - - - - - - - - - - - - - - - - - -

Within the Walls

Paris is defined by its walls (that is, the *Périphérique* or ring road), the interior of which spans 105 sq km. *Intra-muros* (Latin for 'within the walls'), the city has a population of just under 2.2 million, while the greater metropolitan area – the Île de France *région,* encircled by rivers – has over 12 million inhabitants, about 19% of France's total population. This makes Paris – the capital of both the *région* and the nation – in effect an 'island within an island' (or, as residents of other regions might say, a bubble). And in this highly centralised country, Paris is the principal place where the national identity is defined and embraced.

Communal Living

Paris isn't merely a commuter destination, however – its dense inner-city population defines city life. Paris' shops, street markets, parks and other facets of day-to-day living evoke a village atmosphere, and its almost total absence of high-rises gives it a human scale.

Single-occupant dwellings make up more than half of all households in central Paris. On top of this, space shortages mean residential apartments are often minuscule. As a result, communal spaces are the living and dining rooms and backyards of many Parisians, while neighbourhood shops are cornerstones of community life.

This high concentration of city dwellers is why most bars and cafes close around 2am, due to noise restrictions, and why nightclubs in the inner city are few.

Parisian Dogs

The city's dense residential makeup is also why some 200,000 domestic dogs live in Paris. Dogs are treated with adulation here: they're welcomed in shops and restaurants, ride the metro (with their own ticket), are coiffed, perfumed and psychoanalysed by top-dollar professionals, and sport the latest fashions from specialised boutiques. But the days when dog owners wouldn't deign to clean up are fading into the past, boosted by the introduction of hefty fines, and the pavements (which are washed every day) are the cleanest they've ever been. Still, watch your step.

Chez Toinette   FRENCH €€

`11` 🍴 Map p76, C5

Game features among the dishes chalked on the blackboard of this authentic bistro, along with the house speciality, duck fillet with thyme and honey. (📞01 42 54 44 36; http://chez toinette.com; 20 rue Germain Pilon, 18e; mains €16-23; ⏰dinner Mon-Sat; Ⓜ Abbesses)

Café de la Butte   BISTRO €€

`12` 🍴 Map p76, C3

The price-to-quality ratio is outstanding at this art-adorned bistro serving French classics. (71 rue Caulaincourt, 18e; 2-/3-course menus €19/27; ⏰lunch Tue-Sun, dinner Tue-Sat; Ⓜ Lamarck-Caulaincourt)

Marché des Batignolles   MARKET €

`13` 🍴 Map p76, A5

Saturday mornings see this *marché biologique* (organic market) busy with shoppers stocking up for the week. (bd des Batignolles btwn rue des Batignolles & rue Puteaux, 8e & 17e; ⏰7am-3pm Sat; Ⓜ Place de Clichy or Rome)

Drinking

Café Le Refuge   CAFE

`14` 🍷 Map p76, C3

Perfect for a sundowner on the terrace, this *café du quartier* (local cafe) has fantastic interior vintage tiling, a gleaming timber bar and *sympa* (cool)

🔍 Local Life
Rue des Martyrs

Sought out by Parisian foodies, gourmet shops along rue des Martyrs include award-winning baguettes at *boulangerie* **Arnaud Delmontel** (Map p76, D6; www.arnaud -delmontel.com, in French; 39 rue des Martyrs, 9e; ⏰7am-8.30pm Wed-Mon; Ⓜ St-Georges). For a sit-down meal, the delightful, unassuming bistro **Le Miroir** (Map p76, D5; 📞01 46 06 50 73; 94 rue des Martyrs, 18e; lunch/ dinner menus from €18/25; ⏰lunch & dinner Tue-Sat; Ⓜ Abbesses) serves scrumptious pâtés and rillettes like guinea hen with dates, duck with mushrooms, haddock and lemon, followed by well-prepared standards like stuffed veal shoulder, and has its own wine shop across the street.

staff. (72 rue Lamarck, 18e; ⏰7.30am-2am; Ⓜ Lamarck-Caulaincourt)

La Fourmi   BAR

`15` 🍷 Map p76, D5

Spread over two levels and wrapping around a zinc bar, this Pigalle stalwart has a dynamic energy both day and night, and is a great spot to pick up leaflets and flyers on club and DJ nights. (74 rue des Martyrs, 18e; ⏰8am-2am Mon-Thu, to 4am Fri & Sat, 10am-2am Sun; Ⓜ Pigalle)

Entertainment

Le Divan du Monde   NIGHTCLUB

16 ⭐ | Map p76, C5

Anything goes – from rock parties to big-name DJs to obscure acts – at this Pigalle party spot. (www.divandumonde.com, in French; 75 rue des Martyrs, 18e; Ⓜ Pigalle)

La Cigale   LIVE MUSIC

17 ⭐ | Map p76, D5

A heritage-listed monument, this 1887 music hall overhauled by Philippe Starck presents edgy rock, jazz and roots (Primal Scream, Ani Di Franco et al). (www.lacigale.fr; 120 bd de Rochechouart, 18e; Ⓜ Anvers or Pigalle)

Moulin Rouge   CABARET

18 ⭐ | Map p76, B5

Immortalised in the posters of Toulouse-Lautrec and later on screen by Baz Luhrmann, the Moulin Rouge twinkles beneath a 1925 replica of its original red windmill. Yes, it's rife with bus-tour crowds, but from the opening bars of music to the last high kick it's a whirl of fantastical costumes, sets, choreography and champagne. (☏ 01 53 09 82 82; www.moulinrouge.fr; 82 bd de Clichy, 18e; Ⓜ Blanche)

Folies-Bergère   CABARET

19 ⭐ | Map p76, D8

This is the legendary club where Charlie Chaplin, WC Fields and Stan Laurel appeared on stage together one night in 1911, and where Josephine Baker – accompanied by her diamond-collared pet cheetah and wearing only stilettos and a skirt made from bananas – bewitched audience members including Hemingway. Shows span solo acts to musicals. (www.foliesbergere.com, in French; 32 rue Richer, 9e; Ⓜ Cadet)

Cinéma des Cinéastes   CINEMA

20 ⭐ | Map p76, A5

Avant-garde flicks are shown at this cinema, whose founders include *Betty Blue* director Jean-Jacques Beineix. There are thematic screenings, documentaries and talks, and a wine bar.

MANFRED GOTTSCHALK/LONELY PLANET IMAGES ©

Moulin Rouge

(www.cinema-des -cineastes.fr, in French; 7 av de Clichy, 17e; **M** Place de Clichy)

Shopping

Tombées du Camion   BRIC-A-BRAC

21 Map p76, B4

Trumpets, stamps, antique locks and Smurf figurines are among the 'old and forgotten' treasures at this quaint curio shop. (www.tombeesducamion.com, in French; 17 rue Joseph de Maistre, 18e; ☺1-10pm Mon-Fri, from 11am Sat & Sun; **M** Blanche)

Zut!   ANTIQUES

22 Map p76, C4

If you're looking for a conversation piece to dominate your lounge room – a turn-of-the-20th-century railway clock or other oversized industrial objects – Zut's proprietor, Frédéric Daniel, can help you track it down. Even if you're not, it's worth visiting to see some resplendent relics of Paris' past. (☎01 42 59 69 68; www.antiquites -industrielles.com; 9 rue Ravignan, 18e; ☺11am-1pm & 4-7pm Wed-Sat, 11am-1pm Sun & by appointment; **M** Abbesses)

Transmondia   TOYS

23 Map p76, B5

Train enthusiasts will adore this trio of model railway shops selling locomotives (even gold-plated ones!), carriages, cabooses, tracks, gauges, scenery and much more. (www.transmondia-transeurop. com, in French; 48-50 rue de Douai, 18e; ☺10.30am-7pm Tue-Sat; **M** Blanche)

Understand
Daily Bread

Some 80% of Parisians eat bread with *every* meal, hence the aromas wafting from Paris' *boulangeries* (bakeries) throughout the day. The shape of a baguette (literally 'stick' or 'wand') evolved when Napoleon Bonaparte ordered army bakers to create loaves for soldiers to stuff down their trouser legs on the march. Common variations include a *baguette tradition* ('une tradi'), a shorter, pointier version with a coarse, handcrafted surface; a wide *bâtard;* thin, crunchy breadstick-like *ficelle;* thick *flûte;* and a *pain* (the generic word for bread, which also specifically refers to a wide, soft loaf with a chewy crust).

Tati   FASHION

24 Map p76, E5

This bargain-filled, rough-and-tumble, frill-free department store is every fashionable Parisian's guilty secret. (www.tati.fr, in French; 4 bd de Rochechouart, 18e; ☺10am-7pm Mon-Fri, 9.30am-7pm Sat; **M** Barbès Rochechouart)

Ets Lion   FOOD & DRINK

25 Map p76, C5

Gourmet goodies here include homemade jams, multicoloured Eiffel Tower pasta, sweets, wine and olive oils. (www.epicerie-lion.fr, in French; 7 rue des Abbesses, 18e; ☺10.30am-8pm Tue-Sat, 11am-7pm Sun; **M** Abbesses)

Local Life
Canal St-Martin & Around

Getting There

Canal St-Martin is about 4km north of Notre Dame.

M Metro République (lines 3, 5, 8, 9 and 11) is centrally located.

M Metro Château d'Eau, Jacques Bonsergent, Gare de l'Est and Parmentier are also useful stations.

Bordered by shaded towpaths and criss-crossed with iron footbridges, Canal St-Martin wends through the city's northern *quartiers* (quarters). You can float past these areas on a canal cruise (see p196), but strolling among this rejuvenated neighbourhood's cool cafes, offbeat boutiques and hip bars and clubs lets you see why it's beloved by Parisian *bobos* (bourgeois bohemians).

❶ Coffee with the Locals
Kick off at **Le Petit Château d'Eau** (34 rue du Château d'Eau, 10e; ◷9am-2am Mon-Fri, closed Aug; ⓂJacques Bonsergent or Château d'Eau), an unchanged-in-decades neighbourhood cafe (cracked lemon-and-lime tiles, oversized mirrors, time-worn maroon-leather booths), where locals chat with staff over the zinc bar.

❷ Retro Clothes Shopping
Flip through colour-coded racks of cast-offs at vintage boutique **Frivoli** (26 rue Beaurepaire, 10e; ◷11am-7pm Tue-Sun; ⓂJacques Bonsergent).

❸ Lunchtime
The **Hôtel du Nord** (☎01 40 40 78 78; www.hoteldunord.org; 102 quai de Jemmapes, 10e; mains €16-22; ◷cafe 9am-1.30am, restaurant lunch & dinner; ⓂJacques Bonsergent) is the setting for Marcel Carné's 1938 film of the same name; author Eugène Dabit, whose stories formed the film's basis, lived here. It's now a wonderful book-lined cafe–restaurant.

❹ Cultural Centre Cool
Within a converted warehouse, cultural centre and nightclub **Point Éphémère** (www.pointephemere.org, in French; 200 quai de Valmy, 10e; ◷bar-restaurant noon-2am Mon-Sat, 2pm-9pm Sun; ⓂJaurès) has resident artists and musicians, no-holds-barred art exhibitions and a chilled, inexpensive bar-restaurant. Pop back at night to catch live music, DJs and clubbing events.

❺ Canalside Cafes
Watch the passing boats from spirited **L'Atmosphere** (www.latmosphere.fr, in French; 49 rue Lucien-Sampaix, 10e; ◷9.30am-2am; ⓂJacques Bonsergent). Three blocks south is Paris' original *bobo* hangout **Chez Prune** (71 quai de Valmy, 10e; ◷8am-2am Mon-Sat, 10am-2am Sun; ⓂJacques Bonsergent).

❻ Hilltop Haven
A far cry from its former incarnation as a rubbish tip and quarry for Baron Haussmann's 19th-century reformation (p174), the hilly, forested 25-hectare **Parc des Buttes Chaumont** (rue Manin & rue Botzaris, 19e; ◷7.30am-11pm May-Sep, to 9pm Oct-Apr; ⓂButtes Chaumont or Botzaris) conceal grottoes, artificial waterfalls and a temple-topped island reached by footbridges.

❼ Dinnertime
Looking every bit the classic Parisian bistro, the gorgeously old-fashioned **L'Estaminet** (☎01 43 57 34 29; http://estaminet.comu.fr, in French; 116 rue Oberkampf, 11e; ◷lunch Tue-Fri, dinner Tue-Sat, mains €14.50-17; ⓂMénilmontant) serves street-smart fare like goats cheese and eggplant *mille feuilles* (layered stacks).

❽ Nightcap, Nightlife
Finish with a drink at the distressed belle époque **Café Charbon** (www.lecafecharbon.com; 109 rue Oberkampf, 11e; ◷9am-2am Sun-Wed, to 4am Thu-Sat; ⓂParmentier) or kick on at its annexed live music and DJ venue, **Le Nouveau Casino** (www.nouveaucasino.net).

Local Life
Southeastern Paris

Getting There

Southeast Paris is about 3km southeast of Notre Dame.

M **Metro** Gare de Lyon (lines 1 and 14) and Place d'Italie (lines 5, 6 and 7) are convenient start and end points.

Spanning both banks of the Seine, Paris' southeast is an eclectic mix of *quartiers* (quarters) that makes for a fascinating stroll if you've stood in one tourist queue too many. But while it's an authentic slice of local life, there are plenty of big-hitting attractions here too, including France's national cinema institute and national library.

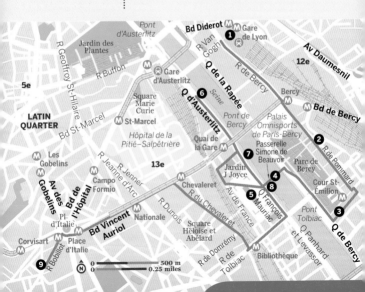

1 Railway Station Splendour

Start your journey in style with a drink or classical fare like beef tartare prepared at your table at belle époque showpiece **Le Train Bleu** (📞01 43 43 09 06; www.le-train-bleu.com; 26 pl Louis Armand, Gare de Lyon, 12e; menus €55-68; 🕐bar 7.30am-11pm Mon-Sat, 10am-11pm Sun, restaurant lunch & dinner; Ⓜ Gare de Lyon).

2 Cinematic History

Cinephiles shouldn't miss **Cinémathèque Française** (📞01 71 19 33 33; www.cinemathequefrancaise.com, in French; 51 rue de Bercy, 12e; museum €5/4, cinema €6.50/5; 🕐museum noon-7pm Mon-Sat, 10am-8pm Sun, cinema daily; Ⓜ Bercy), showcasing the history of French cinema at its museum and library, as well as screening classics and edgy new films.

3 Village Spirit

There are more cinemas at **Bercy Village** (📞01 40 02 90 80; www.bercyvillage.com, in French; 28 rue François Truffaut, 12e; 🕐shops 11am-9pm, restaurants to 2am; Ⓜ Cour St-Émilion), but the main draw is its cobblestone strip of designer shops, bars and restaurants.

4 Crossing the Bridge

The oak-and-steel foot- and cycle-bridge **Passerelle Simone de Beauvoir**, links the Right and Left banks.

5 Hitting the Books

Topped by four sunlit glass towers shaped like open books, a rainforest wraps around the subterranean reading rooms of the **Bibliothèque Nationale de France** (National Library; www.bnf.fr; 11 quai François Mauriac, 13e; exhibitions from €7/5, library €3.50; 🕐exhibitions 10am-7pm Tue-Sat, 1-7pm Sun, library 2-7pm Mon, 9am-7pm Tue-Sat, 1-7pm Sun; Ⓜ Bibliothèque), which mounts excellent exhibitions.

6 Dockside Fashion

Transformed warehouse **Docks en Seine** (www.paris-docks-en-seine.fr; 30 quai d'Austerlitz, 13e; Ⓜ Gare d'Austerlitz), aka the Cité de la Mode et du Design, is the French fashion institute HQ with exhibitions and events.

7 Swimming on the Seine

Splash on (not in!) the Seine at the floating swimming pool **Piscine Joséphine Baker** (📞01 56 61 96 50; www.paris.fr, in French; quai de la Gare; admission €3/1.70; 🕐2-9pm; Ⓜ Quai de la Gare).

8 Drinking, Dining and Dancing on the Seine

Board three-mast Chinese junk **La Dame de Canton** (http://damedecanton.com, in French; opposite 11 quai François Mauriac, 13e; 🕐restaurant & nightclub 8pm-late Tue-Sat; Ⓜ Quai de la Gare) or fire engine-red tugboat **Le Batofar** (www.batofar.org, in French; opposite 11 quai François Mauriac, 13e 🕐restaurant lunch & dinner Tue-Sat, nightclub varies; Ⓜ Quai de la Gare).

9 Neighbourhood Dinner

If you'd rather dine on terra firma, cosy bistro **L'Avant-Goût** (📞01 53 80 24 00; www.lavantgout.com; 26 rue Bobillot, 13e; lunch/dinner menus from €14/32; 🕐lunch & dinner Tue-Sat; Ⓜ Place d'Italie) is renowned for its pork hotpot.

Explore

Centre Pompidou & the Marais

Paris' *marais* (marsh) was cleared in the 12th century but Hauss-mann's reformations left its tangle of medieval laneways largely intact. Hip bars and restaurants, emerging clothing and homewares designers' boutiques and the city's thriving gay and Jewish com-munities all squeeze into this vibrant neighbourhood, which is a see-and-be-seen spot for a *soirée* (evening out) on the town.

The Sights in a Day

The twice-weekly **Marché Bastille** (p103) is one of the largest, liveliest street markets in Paris –catch it if you can before visiting Paris' fascinating history museum, the **Musée Carnavalet** (p98); and the **Musée Victor Hugo** (p98), the author's former home on scrumptious **place des Vosges** (p98).

Join the locals queuing at the takeaway window of **L'As du Felafel** (p104) or sit down for lunch at **Chez Marianne** (p101). Stroll along the **Promenade Plantée** (p100), or simply spend the afternoon browsing the Marais' trove of colourful and quirky shops, stopping for ice cream at **Pozzetto** (p103) or afternoon tea at **Le Loir dans la Théière** (p101).

The **Centre Pompidou** (p90) stays open late, so head here in the late afternoon to see its amazing collection of modern and contemporary art and the awesome views from its roof. After dinner at its rooftop restaurant, **Georges** (p91), kick off a bar crawl at **Andy Wahloo** (p106).

For a local's day in the hip haut Marais, see p94.

 Top Sights

Centre Pompidou (p90)

Local Life

A Heads-Up on the Haut Marais (p94)

Best of Paris

Architecture
Centre Pompidou (p90)

Opéra Bastille (p107)

Pavillon de l'Arsenal (p99)

Markets
Marché Bastille (p103)

Marché aux Enfants Rouges (p95)

Marché aux Puces d'Aligre (p109)

Getting There

M Metro Rambuteau (line 11) is the most convenient for the Centre Pompidou.

M Metro Other central metro stations include Hôtel de Ville (lines 1 and 11), St-Paul (line 1) and Bastille (lines 1, 5 and 8).

Boat The hop-on, hop-off Batobus (p204) stops outside the Hôtel de Ville.

Top Sights
Centre Pompidou

The building housing Paris' premier cultural centre is so iconic that you could spend hours looking at it without ever going inside. But you should! As well as containing France's national modern and contemporary art museum, the Musée National d'Art Moderne (MNAM), the centre's cutting-edge cultural offerings include temporary exhibition spaces, a public library, cinemas and entertainment venues.

👁 Map p96, A2

www.centrepompidou.fr

place Georges Pompidou, 4e

admission varies

⊙ Wed-Mon

Ⓜ Rambuteau

Don't Miss

The Architecture

Former French President Georges Pompidou wanted an ultra-contemporary artistic hub and he got it: competition-winning architects Renzo Piano and Richard Rogers effectively designed the building inside out, with utilitarian features such as plumbing, pipes, air vents and electrical cables forming part of the external façade, freeing up the interior space for exhibitions and events.

The Views of the Building

When the 1977-completed building is viewed from a distance, such as from Sacré-Cœur, its primary-coloured, boxlike form amid a sea of muted-grey Parisian rooftops makes it look like a child's Meccano set abandoned on someone's elegant living room rug.

The Views from the Building

Although the Centre Pompidou is just six storeys high, Paris' low-rise cityscape means stupendous views extend from its roof (reached by external escalators enclosed in tubes). Rooftop admission is included in museum and exhibition admission. Otherwise, for admission to the roof only, you'll need a **panorama ticket** (€3; ⊘11am-11pm Wed-Mon).

Forum du Centre Pompidou

The vast open space on the Centre Pompidou's ground floor, the **Forum du Centre Pompidou** (⊘11am-10pm Wed-Mon), has temporary exhibits and information desks to help you get your bearings.

Musée National d'Art Moderne (MNAM)

The **Musée National d'Art Moderne** (National Museum of Modern Art; admission €12/9; ⊘11am-9pm

☑ Top Tips

▶ The Centre Pompidou opens late every night (except Tuesday, when the entire centre's closed), so head here around 5pm to avoid the daytime crowds.

▶ Skip the queues by purchasing tickets to the museum, exhibitions, shows and other events ahead of time online. In most cases you need to preprint your tickets and bring them with you.

✗ Take a Break

Encased in aluminium sheeting with modular white seats, the Centre Pompidou's hyperindustrial 6th-floor restaurant, **Georges** (☎01 44 78 47 99; mains €18-45; ⊘11am-9pm Wed-Mon), has a chic menu and stunning views over Paris. It's accessed by a free lift (elevator) – look for the red door to the left of the main entrance.

Inexpensive Café Mezzanine is on the 1st floor, or you could try nearby Café La Fusée (p105).

Wed-Mon) picks up more or less where the Musée d'Orsay leaves off, showcasing France's national collection of art from 1905 on (some 60,000 pieces) including works by the surrealists and cubists (Pablo Picasso among them), pop art and contemporary creations.

Museum Collections: Matisse
A highlight of the Musée National d'Art Moderne is its fabulous 245-piece collection of drawings, sculptures, prints and paintings by form-breaking French artist Henri Matisse. Don't miss his cut-outs *Deux danseurs* (Two Dancers; 1937–38) and *Nu bleu II* (Blue Nude II; 1952), and oil painting *Liseuse sur fond noir* (Woman Reading, Black Background; 1939).

Museum Collections: Surrealism
Max Ernst, Man Ray, Joan Miró, René Magritte and Salvador Dalí are just some of the surrealist artists whose works are on show at the museum.

Museum Collections: Pop Art
Mid-20th-century pop art drew its inspiration from popular culture. Major artists from the movement whose works are displayed here include Roy Lichtenstein, James Rosenquist and Andy Warhol.

Museum Collections: Kandinsky
The Musée National d'Art Moderne is one of the major holders of Moscow-born artist Vassily Kandinsky's work, with around 700 pieces. The museum's collection charts his journey from impressionist-style works to abstract paintings, such as *Auf Weiss II* (On White II; 1923), for which he's best known. The Kandinsky Society is also headquartered here.

Museum Collections: Klein
Yves Klein's monochromes, including a 1960 marine-blue monochrome that gave rise to the term 'Klein blue' are held in the museum's collection, as well as one of the famous 'sponge' sculptures (1962) that Klein created as a metaphor for the transmission of artistic sensibility.

Bibliothèque Publique d'Information
The **Bibliothèque Publique d'Information** (BPI, public library; www.bpi.fr; enter via rue du Renard; admission free; ☉noon-10pm Mon & Wed-Fri, 11am-10pm Sat & Sun) has a great range of resources including free internet terminals and wi-fi (time limits apply). Check the website for off-peak times to visit during the busy academic year (summer is fine).

Place Georges Pompidou
Outside the main entrance to the Centre Pompidou, the sloping concourse of place Georges Pompidou (and its surrounding streets) is a hub for busking musicians, mime artists, jugglers and street artists, and can be a lot of fun.

Place Igor Stravinsky
Adjacent to place Georges Pompidou is the much-photographed place Igor

Le Rhinocéros, Xavier Veilhan, Centre Pompidou

Stravinsky. Its mechanical fountains are a riot of skeletons, dragons and other outlandish creations.

Cinemas

Documentaries, retrospectives and thematic series are screened at the centre's **cinemas** (tickets €6/4): check the website for upcoming sessions.

Shows

Regular **shows** (tickets €14/10) of widely varying genres, from pop rock concerts to contemporary dance performances, take to the stage within the Centre Pompidou – the website's Agenda section has updated programs and booking info.

Temporary Exhibitions

The centre's diverse temporary exhibitions are a huge draw; some stay open on Thursdays to 11pm. Temporary exhibitions are included in the ticket price – check the Agenda section of the website to find out what's on.

Children's Gallery

Interactive art exhibitions fill the children's gallery, located on the 1st floor. There are also regular workshops for kids (in French only; check the website for costs and registration details), and a great new website, www.junior. centrepompidou.fr (in English and French), which is loaded with inspirational activities to fire kids' creativity.

Local Life
A Heads-Up on the Haut Marais

The lower Marais has long been fashionable but the haut Marais (upper, ie northern Marais, sometimes referred to as NoMa) is rapidly becoming a hub for up-and-coming fashion designers, art galleries and vintage, accessories and homewares boutiques, alongside long-established enterprises enjoying a renaissance. Keep tabs via http://hautmarais.blogspot.com, which lists new openings, exhibitions, events and pop-up shops.

❶ Juice Fix

Combinations of apple, lemon, carrot and ginger are among the detoxifying juices at **Rose Bakery** (30 Rue Debelleyme, 3e; dishes €7-17; ⊙ 9am-5pm Tue-Sun; Ⓜ St-Sébastien Froissart), whose organic fare also includes salads, quiches and hot dishes like tofu roti as well as its locally revered carrot cake.

2 Groundbreaking Fashion

Among the first boutiques to put the haut Marais on the fashion map, **Shine** (15 rue de Poitou, 3e; 11am-7.30pm Tue-Sat, 2-5pm Sun; M Filles du Calvaire) stocks hand-picked pieces from the current crop of young designers.

3 Recycled Fashion

Vic Caserta creates 'genetic vintage' fashions for his boutique **MadeinUsed** (www.madeinused.com; 36 rue de Poitou, 3e; 11-7pm; M Filles du Calvaire) by revamping vintage clothes and materials for a never-imagined new lease of life.

4 Discounted Fashion

Savvy Parisians grab last season's men's and women's designerwear (Dries van Noten et al) at up to 70% off original prices at **L'Habilleur** (44 rue de Poitou, 3e; noon-7.30pm Mon-Sat; M St-Sébastien Froissart).

5 Street-Smart Shoes

Strappy, spangly stilettos and wedges in inspired styles adorn the showroom of shoe designer **Pring** (www.pringparis. com; 29 rue Charlot, 3e; 10am-7pm Mon-Sat; M St-Sébastien Froissart).

6 Market Lunch

Hidden behind an inconspicuous green metal gate, **Marché aux Enfants Rouges** (39 rue de Bretagne, 3e; 8.30am-1pm & 4-7.30pm Tue-Fri, 4-8pm Sat, 8.30am-2pm Sun; M Filles du Calvaire) has produce stalls and dishes from bento boxes to crêpes to eat at communal tables.

7 Handbag Heaven

All of the super-soft, super-stylish handbags at **Pauline Pin** (www.pauline pin.com; 51 rue Charlot, 3e; 11am-7.30pm Tue-Sat; M Filles du Calvaire) are made here at founder and designer Clarisse's flagship store and workshop.

8 Fibre Fashion

Clothing and textile artworks crafted from natural and rare animal fibres are exhibited and sold at **La Boutique Extraordinaire** (www.laboutiqueextraordinaire. com, in French; 67 rue Charlot, 3e; 11am-8pm Tue-Sat, 3-7pm Sun; M Filles du Calvaire).

9 Coffee Break

The sunlit, art deco–tiled cafe **Le Progrès** (1 rue de Bretagne, 3e; 8am-10pm Mon-Sat; M St-Sébastien Froissart or Filles du Calvaire) is a sociable spot to chat with locals over strong coffee, inexpensive bistro fare and pitchers of wine.

10 Conscience-Clear Fashion

Profits from the cutting-edge fashions, homewares, gifts, books and organic canteen at concept shop **Merci** (www.merci-merci.com, in French; 111 bd Beaumarchais, 3e; 10am-7pm Mon-Sat; M St-Sébastien Froissart) go to children's charities.

11 Happy Hour

Head to hipster bar **Panic Room** (www.panicroomparis.com, in French; 101 rue Amelot, 11e; 6.30pm-1.45am Mon-Sat; M St-Sébastien Froissart) for wildly flavoured cocktails like gin, strawberries and basil during happy hour (6.30pm to 8.30pm).

For reviews see

◉	Top Sights	p90
◎	Sights	p98
✕	Eating	p101
🅐	Drinking	p105
☆	Entertainment	p107
🅐	Shopping	p108

0   400 m
0   0.2 miles

St-Ambroise

R St-Ambroise

R St-Maur

Square
Maurice
Gardette

Av Parmentier

R St-Sébastien

Bd Voltaire

R Duranti

R Merlin

Square
de la
Roquette

Richard
Lenoir

Bd Richard Lenoir

R Pelée

R Moufle

11e

R du Chemin Vert

R de la Roquette

R Amelot

R Bréguet

Square
Denis
Poulot

R de la Roquette

R Léon Frot

Chemin
Vert

Square
Bréguet
Sabin

R Froment

R Sedaine

Pl Léon
Blum

Voltaire

R Godefroy Cavaignac

R de Belfort

Bd Beaumarchais

Bréguet
Sabin

R du Cadet Lamy

R de la Roquette

30

R Basfroi

Charonne

17

R St-Sabin

R Daval

Passage Thiéré

R des Taillandiers

R Keller

Passage Charles Dalery

R Jules Vallès

Bastille

13

R de Lappe

41

20

R de Charonne

R Faidherbe

28

R Chanzy

R Titon

Place de la
Bastille

R du Faubourg St-Antoine

R Charles Delescluze

Bastille

40

R de Charenton

Ledru–Rollin

R Trousseau

R de Prague

R de Lyon

R Moreau

Av Ledru–Rollin

Square
Trousseau

R de Cotte

R d'Aligre

Place
Dr Antoine
Béclère

R de
Montreuil

Faidherbe
Chaligny

R de Chaligny

R de Reuilly

Jules César

Av Daumesnil

12e

48

9

R Émilio Castelar

29

27

47

Pl
d'Aligre

R Crozatier

R Crételx

St-Antoine

Promenade
Plantée

Sights

Musée Carnavalet
MUSEUM

1 ◉ Map p96, D3

Housed in a pair of sumptuous private mansions dating from the 16th and 17th centuries, Paris' history museum weaves together the city's story from the Gallo-Roman period through the French Revolution to its art nouveau epoch. Among the 140 rooms, don't miss Marcel Proust's cork-lined bedroom transplanted from his former home on bd Haussmann. (www.carnavalet.paris.fr; 23 rue de Sévigné, 3e; admission free; ⏱10am-6pm Tue-Sun; Ⓜ St-Paul or Chemin Vert)

Maison de Victor Hugo
MUSEUM

2 ◉ Map p96, D3

One of the symmetrical houses on the place des Vosges is this former home of Victor Hugo. The museum offers an evocative insight to the writer's life, featuring drawings, portraits and furnishings preserved just as they were when he wrote much of *Les Misérables* here. (www.musee-hugo.paris.fr; 6 place des Vosges, 4e; admission free; ⏱10am-6pm Tue-Sun; Ⓜ St-Paul or Bastille)

Maison Européenne de la Photographie
MUSEUM

3 ◉ Map p96, C3

Contemporary prints, pages, documentaries and films all feature in the light-filled photography centre housed in an early-18th-century Marais mansion. Regular temporary exhibitions spotlight major French and international photographers. (www.mep-fr.org, in French; 5-7 rue de Fourcy, 4e; admission €7/4; ⏱11am-8pm Wed-Sun; Ⓜ St-Paul or Pont Marie)

Musée d'Art et d'Histoire du Judaïsme
MUSEUM

4 ◉ Map p96, B2

Documents from the Dreyfus Affair, famously championed by Parisian novelist Émile Zola in his open letter to the government, *J'accuse...!* (*I Accuse...!*, 1898) and works by Jewish artists including Chagall and Modigliani are the highlights of this mansion-housed Jewish Art and History Museum tracing Jewish communities throughout Europe from the Middle Ages to today. (www.mahj.org; 71 rue du Temple, 3e; admission €6.80/4.50; ⏱11am-6pm Mon-Fri, 10am-6pm Sun; Ⓜ Rambuteau)

◉ Local Life

Place des Vosges

The stone cloisters of this 1612-built ensemble of mansions resonate with busking violinists and cellists, who provide an atmospheric soundtrack for sipping tea in one of several elegant cafes or browsing the arcaded galleries and antique shops. In the centre of **Place des Vosges** (Map p96, D3) you'll see au pairs playing with their charges in the little gated park.

Garden at Place des Vosges

Musée Cognacq-Jay MUSEUM

5 ◉ Map p96, C2

The paintings, pastels, sculpture, *objets d'art,* jewellery, porcelain and 18th-century furniture amassed by the founder of the (now defunct) La Samaritaine department store are a great excuse to see inside the Hôtel de Donon, the private mansion in which it's housed. (www.cognacq-jay.paris.fr, in French; 8 rue Elzévir, 3e; admission free; ◷10am-6pm Tue-Sun; Ⓜ St-Paul or Chemin Vert)

Hôtel de Ville TOWN HALL

6 ◉ Map p96, A3

Paris' beautiful neo-Renaissance town hall, completed in 1882, is adorned with 108 statues of illustrious Parisians. Temporary exhibitions here usually have a Paris theme, such as the photography of Robert Doisneau (who snapped his world-famous *Kiss at the Hôtel de Ville* here in 1950). An ice-skating rink sets up outside from December to early March. (www.paris.fr; place de l'Hôtel de Ville, 4e; exhibitions free; ◷10am-7pm Mon-Sat; Ⓜ Hôtel de Ville)

Pavillon de l'Arsenal MUSEUM

7 ◉ Map p96, C5

Scale models of Paris from different eras are the focal point of the city's town-planning and architectural centre, housed in glass-and-iron-roofed art nouveau premises. A comprehensive history of Paris' built environment, from its beginnings to the present day, is laid out along with models of upcoming buildings. (www.pavillon-arsenal.com; 21 bd Morland, 4e; admission free; ⊘10.30am-6.30pm Tue-Sat, 11am-7pm Sun; Ⓜ Sully Morland)

Mémorial de la Shoah

MUSEUM, MEMORIAL

8 Map p96, B3

Housing the largest collection of documents on the Holocaust in Europe, this important centre presents poignant footage and interviews. The actual memorial to the victims of the Shoah, a Hebrew word meaning 'catastrophe' and synonymous in France with the Holocaust, stands at the entrance, where a wall is inscribed with the names of 76,000 deportees. (www.memorialdelashoah.org, in French; 17 rue Geoffroy l'Asnier, 4e; admission free; ⊘10am-6pm Sun-Wed & Fri, to 10pm Thu; Ⓜ St-Paul)

 Local Life

Pletzl

The Jewish community around the Marais' rue des Rosiers and rue des Écouffes was traditionally known as the Pletzl, and you'll still find *cacher* (kosher) butchers, delis and take-away falafel windows here. The Pletzl's **Guimard synagogue** (Map p96, C3; 10 rue Pavée, 4e) was designed in 1913 by Hector Guimard (who also designed Paris' art nouveau metro entrances). The interior is closed to the general public.

Promenade Plantée

PARK

9 Map p96, F5

A disused 19th-century railway viaduct has been turned into this pioneering four-storey-high park planted with a fragrant profusion of cherry trees, maples, rosebushes and lavender. (www.promenade-plantee.org, in French; 12e; admission free; ⊘8am-sunset Mon-Fri, from 9am Sat & Sun)

Galerie Yvon Lambert

GALLERY

10 Map p96, C2

Marais gallery scene mover-and-shaker Yvon Lambert has been exhibiting and promoting international artists for over four decades while exploring new media such as video art. (www.yvon-lambert.com; 108 rue Vieille du Temple, 3e; admission free; ⊘10am-7pm Tue-Sat; Ⓜ St-Sébastien Froissart)

Musée de la Poupée

MUSEUM

11 Map p96, B1

The 500-or-so antique dolls at this doll museum are arranged in scenes representing Paris through the centuries. Admission for under 12s is free between 10am and noon on Sunday. (www.museedelapoupeeparis.com; impasse Berthaud, 3e; admission €8/6, free 2nd Fri of month; ⊘10am-6pm Tue-Sun; Ⓜ Rambuteau)

Musée Picasso

MUSEUM

12 Map p96, C2

This 17th-century mansion is an extraordinary insight into one of the world's most celebrated artists, with some 3500 pieces of his work, plus Picasso's personal art collection, including prized works by Braque, Cézanne, Matisse and Degas. (www.musee-picasso.fr, in French; 5 rue de Thorigny, 3e; ⊙closed for renovation until spring 2013; MSt-Sébastien Froissart, St-Paul or Chemin Vert)

Place de la Bastille SQUARE

13 Map p96, E4

Nothing remains of the former prison that was mobbed on 14 July 1789, igniting the French Revolution, but you can't miss the 52m-high green-bronze column topped by a gilded, winged Liberty. Revolutionaries from the uprising of 1830 are buried beneath. Now a skirmishly busy roundabout, it's still Paris' most symbolic destination for political protests. (MBastille)

Tour St-Jacques SQUARE

14 Map p96, A3

Along rue de Rivoli (near Châtelet metro station) you'll spot the Tour St-Jacques. This Flamboyant Gothic, 52m-high bell tower is all that remains of the Église St-Jacques la Boucherie, which was built by the butchers guild in 1523. The church was demolished shortly after the French Revolution in 1797, but the tower was spared so that it could be used to drop molten lead in the manufacture of shot. (Square de la Tour St-Jacques, 4e; MChâtelet).

Local Life
Rollers & Coquillages

Suitable for all levels of ability, mass inline skate **Rollers & Coquillages** (www.rollers-coquillages.org, in French; admission free; ⊙Sun 2.30-5.30pm, arrive 2pm) sets off on routes of 21km or so from **Nomades** (Map p96, E4; www.nomadeshop.com, in French; 37 bd Bourdon, 4e; weekday/weekend blade hire per half-day from €5/6; ⊙11.30am-7.30pm Tue-Fri, 10am-7pm Sat, noon-6pm Sun; MBastille), where you can buy or rent inline skates and protective equipment. See also p153.

Eating

Le Loir dans la Théière CAFE €

15 Map p96, C3

Filled with retro toys and comfy couches, the *Alice in Wonderland*–named the Dormouse in the Teapot is a wonderful space for a coffee, a towering lemon meringue pie or dishes such as vegetable couscous. Its farm-style wooden tables are laden at brunchtime on weekends. (3 rue des Rosiers, 4e; mains €10.50-13.50; ⊙9am-7pm; MSt-Paul)

Chez Marianne JEWISH €

16 Map p96, C3

There's often a wait for a table at vine-covered, black-and-white-tiled restaurant, but it's worth it for the phenomenal mix-and-match platters,

Understand

Parisian History: the 20th Century to Today

- -

WWI & WWII
The belle époque's advances (including the art nouveau movement and the first metro line) were cut short by France's involvement in WWI. Out of the conflict came increased industrialisation, confirming Paris' place as a major commercial and artistic centre. This was halted by WWII and Nazi occupation (see p32); Paris remained under direct German rule until 1944.

Uprisings & Advances
After WWII, Paris regained its position as a creative nucleus and nurtured a revitalised liberalism that peaked with the student-led uprisings of May 1968 – the Sorbonne was occupied, the Latin Quarter blockaded, and a general strike paralysed the country. After stability was restored the government made immediate reforms (such as lowering the voting age to 18, enacting an abortion law and increasing workers' self-management), creating, in effect, the modern society that is France today.

The second half of the century saw major architectural additions, many at the behest of its presidents, known as *grands projets* (great projects; see p174). In 2001, during the at times protest-charged presidency of (former Paris mayor) Jacques Chirac, socialist Bertrand Delanoë was elected mayor of Paris and became widely popular for making Paris more liveable through improved infrastructure and increased green spaces. Delanoë was elected for a second six-year term in 2008.

Ongoing Change
In 2007, Nicolas Sarkozy succeeded fellow conservative Union for a Popular Movement (UMP; Union pour un Mouvement Populaire) president Chirac. Sarkozy married model, actress and singer Carla Bruni within months of winning the presidency, and enacted constitutional reform whereby staff and employers can negotiate individual working hours (though the 35-hour week is retained as a standard). At the time of research, Sarkozy was expected to be a contender in the 2012 presidential election. His *grand project* is a national history museum, the Maison de l'Histoire de France (www.maison-histoire.fr). Despite protests, it's due to open in the Marais in 2015.

Pastry shop, rue des Rosiers

with choices including olives, hommus, eggplant and much more. Otherwise you can pack a picnic from the deli to take to the place des Vosges or pick up felafel sandwiches from the takeaway window. Note that food served here is not Beth Din kosher. (2 rue des Hospitalières St-Gervais, 4e; platters €12-16; ⏱noon-midnight; ⓂSt-Paul)

Marché Bastille   MARKET €

17 🍴 Map p96, E3

If you only get to one open-air market in Paris, this one – stretching between the Bastille and Richard Lenoir metro stations – is among the very best. (bd Richard Lenoir, 11e; ⏱7am-2.30pm Thu, to 3pm Sun; ⓂBastille or Richard Lenoir)

Pozzetto   ICE CREAM €

18 🍴 Map p96, B3

This gelato maker opened several years ago when a group of friends from northern Italy couldn't find their favourite ice cream in Paris, and imported the ingredients to create it here from scratch. Authentic Piedmontese flavours include *gianduia* (hazelnut chocolate) and *fiordilatte* (milk). (http://pozzetto.biz, in French; 39 rue du Roi de Sicile, 4e; ice cream from €4; ⏱11.30am-9.30pm Mon-Thu, to 11.30pm Fri-Sun; ⓂSt-Paul)

Apparemment Café

CAFE €

19 Map p96, C2

A snug little spot to cocoon on a chilly day, this lamp-lit cafe has sea-, countryside- and dairy-based *menus*, along with create-your-own salads where you tick off the ingredients you want on a checklist. (18 rue des Coutures St-Gervais, 3e; salads from €8, menus €18-24; ⏱noon-2am Mon-Sat, to midnight Sun; MSt-Sébastien Froissart)

Crêperie Bretonne

BRETON, CRÊPERIE €

20 Map p96, G4

Authentic down to its buckwheat *galettes* and perfectly buttered sweet crêpes – which in true Breton style are served flat on the plate and eaten with cutlery – this charmer is filled with emotive photos of Brittany and joy of joys serves brut Val de Rance cider. *Yec'hed mat* (cheers)! (67 rue de Charonne, 12e; crêpes €2.60-10.20; ⏱lunch & dinner Mon-Fri; MCharonne)

Le Potager du Marais

VEGETARIAN €€

21 Map p96, B2

A cut above most of Paris' vegetarian restaurants (not that there's much competition), the 'Vegetable Garden' serves organic fare in leafy surrounds, including vegan options. (☎01 42 74 24 66; 22 rue Rambuteau, 3e; menu €25; ⏱lunch & dinner Wed-Mon; MRambuteau)

L'As du Felafel

JEWISH €

22 Map p96, C3

L'As du Felafel's flawlessly textured fried chickpea balls are better value to take away than to eat in. Be prepared to queue at the takeaway window midweek, when local workers make a beeline here during their lunch break (though the queues move pretty quickly thanks to staff taking orders and money while you're lining up in the street). (34 rue des Rosiers, 4e; takeaway dishes €5-7.50; falafel sandwiches €7.50-9.50; mains €12-18; ⏱noon-midnight Sun-Thu, to 5pm Fri; MSt-Paul)

Le Clown Bar

BISTRO €

23 Map p96, E1

A riot of frescoes and mosaics of clowns and circus memorabilia (the evil-themed clowns will scare the pants off kids and coulrophobes!), Le Clown Bar is adjacent to the century-old Cirque d'Hiver winter circus, where flying trapeze artists, animal tamers and clowns perform from late October to early March. Traditional French *menus* are brilliant value. (114 rue Amelot, 11e; lunch/dinner menus €14/19; ⏱lunch Wed-Sat, dinner Mon-Sat; MFilles du Calvaire)

La Boutique Jaune

JEWISH €

24 Map p96, C3

Since 1946 this bright yellow-fronted *traiteur* (delicatessen) has been purveying fantastic cakes, breads, charcuterie and its famous 'Yiddish sandwich', filled with the flavours of Eastern Europe and served hot. There's a tiny sit-down area. (www.laboutiquejaune.com, in French; 27 rue des Rosiers, 4e; sandwiches €6.50; ⏱10am-7pm Wed-Mon; Ⓜ St-Paul)

Brasserie Bofinger
BRASSERIE €€

 25   Map p96, E4

Try for a seat beneath the glass cupola of this art nouveau brasserie, which has first-rate food and genuine service. Past diners span Mikhail Gorbachev to Madonna, but it's the little snippets of Parisian life around you that make a meal here unforgettable. (☎01 42 72 87 82; www.bofingerparis.com; 5-7 rue de la Bastille, 4e; 2-/3-course menus €28.50/33.50; ⏱lunch & dinner; Ⓜ Bastille)

Le Petit Bofinger
FRENCH €€

26   Map p96, E4

If you're on a budget, Brasserie Bofinger's splendidly tiled little brother across the street, Le Petit Bofinger, is a cheaper but still-atmospheric alternative serving fresh market fare. (6 rue de la Bastille, 4e; 2-/3-course menus €24.50/28.50; ⏱lunch & dinner; Ⓜ Bastille)

Marché Beauvau
MARKET €

27   Map p96, G5

Adjacent to the place d'Aligre flea market, this covered market sells fresh produce in addition to Arab and North African food specialities such

Ⓠ Local Life
Rue St-Martin

Close to the Centre Pompidou but away from the tourist crowds, **Café La Fusée** (Map p96, A1; 168 rue St-Martin, 3e; dishes €5-9; ⏱9am-2am; Ⓜ Rambuteau), strung with coloured lights, is a hip local hangout serving stylish salads and sandwiches. Along the same stretch of rue St-Martin you'll find other funky spots to eat, drink or hunt for obscure vinyl records and superhero comics. Be sure to peek too at the shops in **Passage Molière** (Map p96, A1; enter from 157 rue St-Martin).

as couscous and sweet pastries. (place d'Aligre, 12e; ⏱9am-1pm & 4-7.30pm Tue, 4-7.30pm Wed, 9am-1pm Thu-Sat; Ⓜ Ledru-Rollin)

Drinking

Le Pure Café
CAFE

 28   Map p96, H4

A classic Parisian haunt, this rustic, cherry-red corner cafe featured in the art-house film *Before Sunset*, but it's still a refreshingly unpretentious spot for a drink or well-crafted fare like veal with chestnut purée. (14 rue Jean Macé, 11e; ⏱7am-2am Mon-Fri, from 8am Sat, from 10am Sun; Ⓜ Charonne or Faidherbe Chaligny)

Understand
Getting Philosophical

Grappling with such concepts as existentialism is required for Parisians to pass the *baccalauréat* (school certificate) – hence the popularity of *philocafés* (philosophy cafes), where wide-ranging, brain-teasing discussions like 'what is a fact?' take place. The original (and arguably best), the Café des Phares, was established by late philosopher and Sorbonne professor Marc Sautet (1947–98). Most *philocafé* sessions are in French, but there's a popular English-language version at St-Germain des Prés' Café de Flore (p155) on the first Wednesday of every month from 7pm to 9pm. Entry's free but you need to buy a drink. To sign up, visit http://philosophy.meetup.com/274.

Le Baron Rouge   WINE BAR

29 Map p96, G5

Amid big wooden barrels and bottles lining its walls, this spirited wine bar serves superb wines by the glass. It takes on something of a party atmosphere on Sundays after the Marché aux Puces d'Aligre wraps up. (1 rue Théophile Roussel, 12e; ⏰10am-2pm & 5-10pm Mon-Thu, 10am-10pm Fri & Sat, 10am-4pm Sun; Ⓜ Ledru-Rollin)

La Fée Verte   BAR

30 Map p96, G3

You guessed it, the 'Green Fairy' specialises in absinthe (served traditionally with spoons and sugar cubes), but this fabulously old-fashioned neighbourhood bar also serves terrific food including Green Fairy cheeseburgers. (108 rue de la Roquette, 11e; ⏰8am-2am; Ⓜ Voltaire)

Andy Wahloo   BAR

31 Map p96, B1

Its name means 'I have nothing' in Arabic, but although this clubby bar has refined its '70s-style Moroccan decor, it still owes a greater debt to its almost-namesake, Andy Warhol. (http://andywahloo-bar.com; 69 rue des Gravilliers, 3e; ⏰6pm-2am Tue-Sat; Ⓜ Arts et Métiers)

Mariage Frères   SALON DE THÉ

32 Map p96, B3

Established in 1854, and incorporating its own tea museum, Paris' first-ever tea shop sells over 500 varieties of tea from 35 countries, which you can sip in the genteel tearoom. (www.mariagefreres.com; 30 rue du Bourg Tibourg, 4e; ⏰shop & museum 10.30am-7.30pm, tearooms noon-7pm; Ⓜ Hôtel de Ville)

Duplex Bar   GAY & LESBIAN

33 Map p96, B1

This relaxed gay bar also incorporates an art gallery with edgy exhibitions.

(www.duplex-bar.com; 25 rue Michel le Comte, 3e; 8pm-2am Sun-Thu, to 4am Fri & Sat; Rambuteau)

Café des Phares
CAFE

34 Map p96, E4

Even if your French isn't up to following the convoluted philosophy exchanges at this *philocafé* (philosophy cafe; see p106), it still offers a fascinating cultural insight and is a convivial spot for a drink anytime. (www.cafe-philo-des-phares.info, in French; 7 place de la Bastille, 4e; 7.30am-3am Sun-Thu, to 4am Fri & Sat, philosophy debates 10.30am-12.15pm Sun; Bastille)

Le Cox
GAY & LESBIAN

35 Map p96, B2

The name of Paris' gay bar-of-the-moment says it all. Happy hour (6pm to 9pm) is prime cruising time. (www.cox.fr; 15 rue des Archives, 4e; 5.30pm-2am Mon-Thu, from 4.30pm Fri-Sun; Hôtel de Ville)

3W Kafé
GAY & LESBIAN

36 Map p96, C3

Men are welcome, but rare, at this sleek lesbian lounge. (www.3wkafe.com, in French; 8 rue des Écouffes, 4e; 5.30pm-2am; St-Paul)

Café Baroc
BAR

37 Map p96, B3

Baroc's old cinema seats and vintage sofas are ideal for sipping beers with a twist of syrup in flavours such as lem-

on or peach. Normally a chilled little place, things get hyper during events like DJ sets and open mic sessions. (37 rue du Roi de Sicile, 4e; 5pm-2am Tue-Sat, from 3pm Sun; St-Paul)

Le Quetzal
GAY & LESBIAN

38 Map p96, B3

This house- and dance-spinning bar aptly sits opposite rue des Mauvais Garçons (Bad Boys' Street; named after the brigands who congregated here in 1540). (10 rue de la Verrerie, 4e; 5pm-2am Sun-Tue, to late Wed-Sat; Hôtel de Ville)

Open Café
GAY & LESBIAN

39 Map p96, B2

The wide, white-seated terrace at this perennially popular bar is a prime spot to survey the scene or strike up a conversation, with a predominantly social rather than cruisey vibe. (www.opencafe.fr; 17 rue des Archives, 4e; 11am-2am Sun-Thu, to 4am Fri & Sat; Hôtel de Ville)

Entertainment

Opéra Bastille
OPERA HOUSE

40 Map p96, E4

Instigated by former president Mitterrand as the city's second opera house, this 1989-built monolith seats 3400 people. Bargain-priced opera seats are available only from the box office, as are €5 standing-only tickets (available

Local Life
Rue de Lappe

Quiet during the day, at night little rue de Lappe comes alive when its string of bars are in full swing. Catch music at the 1936-opened dance hall **Le Balajo** (Map p96, E4;www.balajo.fr, in French; 9 rue de Lappe, 11e; ⏱vary; MBastille), which still pulls in the crowds for everything from salsa (including lessons) to rock, DJs, R&B and *musettes* (accordion gigs) from 2pm to 7pm Monday and Thursday with old-time tea dancing. Or you could try **La Chapelle des Lombards** (Map p96, F4; www.la-chapelle-des-lombards. com, in French; 19 rue de Lappe, 11e; ⏱11.30pm-late Tue-Sun; MBastille), which usually has concerts at 8.30pm on Friday and Saturday.

90 minutes prior to performances). (☎08 92 89 90 90; www.operadeparis.fr; 2-6 place de la Bastille, 12e; ⏱box office 10.30am-6.30pm Mon-Sat; MBastille)

La Scène Bastille   LIVE MUSIC

41 ⭐ Map p96, F4

The laidback 'Bastille Scene' puts on a mixed bag of concerts from Tuesday to Saturday, mostly revolving around electro, funk and hip hop. It also hosts various club nights – check the website for upcoming events. (www. scenebastille.com; 2bis rue des Taillandiers, 11e; ⏱concerts from 7.30pm, club nights from midnight; MBastille or Ledru-Rollin)

Shopping
Village St-Paul   ANTIQUES, CRAFTS

42 🔒 Map p96, C4

On the site of an ancient convent, this delightful 'village' brings together over 60 antiques dealers (18th-century through to art deco) and arts and crafts boutiques. Unusual items found here range from old postcards of Paris through to wacky new homewares inventions. (http://village-saint-paul.com, in French; rue St-Paul, 4e; ⏱most shops 11am-7pm Wed-Mon; MSt-Paul)

Bazar de l'Hôtel de Ville (BHV)   DEPARTMENT STORE

43 🔒 Map p96, B3

Parisians renovating their apartments head to this department store's basement hardware section for hammers, nails, drill bits and even DIY and decorating workshops (bookable online). You'll also find a wide range of clothes, accessories and stationery, plus kid-friendly eateries on the 5th floor. (www.bhv.fr, in French; 14 rue du Temple, 4e; ⏱9.30am-7.30pm Mon, Tue, Thu & Fri, to 9pm Wed, to 8pm Sat; MHôtel de Ville)

Chocolaterie Joséphine Vannier   FOOD & DRINK

44 🔒 Map p96, D3

Chocolate is an art form at this extraordinary shop, with edible creations including musical instruments (saxophones, pianos, violins and electric guitars) and shoes (high heels, flats and brogues) that look good enough to wear and far too good to eat. (www.chocolats-vannier.com, in French; 4 rue du Pas de la Mule, 3e; ⏰11am-7pm Tue-Sat, from 2.30pm Sun; Ⓜ Chemin Vert)

Red Wheelbarrow Bookstore

BOOKS

45 🔒 Map p96, C4

Brimming with quality English-language literature, this much-loved North American–run bookshop also has adorable kids' books and info on literary events. (22 rue St-Paul, 4e; ⏰10am-7pm Mon-Sat, 2-6pm Sun; Ⓜ St-Paul)

Un Chien dans le Marais

FASHION

46 🔒 Map p96, B3

This little boutique stocks nothing but dog outfits in all sizes. You can pick out a design from the latest autumn/winter and spring/summer collections from casual T-shirts, hoodies, pants, skirts and dresses through to evening-wear and fancy-dress costumes, plus raingear, bathrobes and pyjamas. (www.unchiendanslemarais.com; 35bis rue du Roi de Sicile, 4e; ⏰noon-7pm; Ⓜ St-Paul)

Marché aux Puces d'Aligre

MARKET

47 🔒 Map p96, G5

Rummage through boxes and racks jammed with vintage fashions at Paris'

most central flea market. The Marché Beauvau food market is next door. (http://marchedaligre.free.fr, in French; place d'Aligre, 12e; ⏰8am-1pm Tue-Sun; Ⓜ Ledru-Rollin)

Viaduc des Arts

ARTS & CRAFTS

48 🔒 Map p96, F5

Located beneath the Promenade Plantée, in the brick arches of its 19th-century viaduct, traditional crafts-men and women carry out antique renovations and repairs, and create new items using traditional methods. The 51 artisans include furniture and tapestry restorers, interior designers, cabinet makers, violin- and flute-makers, embroiderers and jewellers. (www.viaducdesarts.fr; av Daumesnil, 12e; ⏰vary; Ⓜ Bastille or Gare de Lyon)

Le Mots à La Bouche

BOOKS

49 🔒 Map p96, B3

'On the Tip of the Tongue' is Paris' premier gay and lesbian bookshop, with English-language books and reams of info about gay Parisian life. (www.motsbouche.com, in French; 6 rue Ste-Croix de la Bretonnerie, 4e; ⏰11am-11pm Mon-Sat, 1-9pm Sun; Ⓜ Hôtel de Ville).

Explore

Notre Dame
& the Islands

Paris' geographic and historic heart is situated here, in the Seine.
The city's watery beginnings took place on the Île de la Cité, the larger of the two inner-city islands. To its east, the serene Île St-Louis is
graced with elegant, exclusive apartments, along with a handful of
intimate hotels and charming eateries and boutiques.

The Sights in a Day

☀ The city's landmark cathedral, **Notre Dame** (p112), dominates the Île de la Cité, so where better to start your explorations? (Heading here first also means you'll beat the crowds.) In addition to viewing its stained-glass interior, allow around an hour to visit the top and another to explore the archaeological crypt. For even more beautiful stained-glass, don't miss nearby **Ste-Chapelle** (p120).

☀ Place Dauphine has a sprinkling of lunch spots with sunny terraces including **Ma Salle à Manger** (p122). From here it's a few footsteps to the French Revolution prison, the **Conciergerie** (p120). Cross the **Pont St-Louis** (p120) to the enchanting Île St-Louis to browse its **boutiques** (p124) and buy a **Berthillon** (p122) ice cream.

☽ After a traditional French meal at **L'Ilot Vache** (p122), stroll back over the Pont St-Louis, where you're likely to catch buskers, for a nightcap at the Île de la Cité's **Taverne Henri IV** (p123). If you're still going strong, cross the **Pont Neuf** (p120) for entertainment options on either side of the Seine.

 Top Sights

Notre Dame (p112)

💜 **Best of Paris**

History
Notre Dame (p112)

Ste-Chapelle (p120)

Conciergerie (p120)

Drinking
Taverne Henri IV (p123)

Parks & Gardens
Square du Vert Galant (p120)

Churches
Notre Dame (p112)

Ste-Chapelle (p120)

Gourmet Shops
La Petite Scierie (p124)

Getting There

Ⓜ **Metro** Cité (line 4) on the Île de la Cité is the islands' only metro station, and the most convenient for Notre Dame.

Ⓜ **Metro** Pont Marie (line 7) on the Right Bank is the Île St-Louis' closest station.

⛴ **Boat** The hop-on, hop-off Batobus (p204) stops opposite Notre Dame on the Left Bank.

Top Sights
Notre Dame

The mighty Cathédrale de Notre Dame de Paris (Cathedral of Our Lady of Paris) is a masterpiece of French Gothic architecture. Built on the site of earlier churches and, a millennium before that, a Gallo-Roman temple, it was largely completed by the early 14th century. The cathedral was badly damaged during the French Revolution, and extensive restorations were finished in 1864. Today, it's the city's most visited unticketed site, with over 13 million people crossing its threshold each year.

◉ Map p118, D3

www.notredamedeparis.fr

6 place du Parvis Notre Dame, 4e

admission to interior free

🕑 8am-6.45pm Mon-Fri, to 7.15pm Sat & Sun

Ⓜ Cité

Don't Miss

The Scale
The single most impressive aspect of Notre Dame is its sheer size: the interior alone is 130m long, 48m wide and 35m high, and can accommodate more than 6000 worshippers.

The Rose Windows
Exceptional features of Notre Dame include three spectacular rose windows, the most renowned of which are the 10m-wide window over the western façade (partly obscured by the organ), and the window on the northern side of the transept, which has remained virtually unchanged since the 13th century.

The Flying Buttresses
Square Jean XXIII, the little park behind the cathedral, has the best views of the forest of ornate flying buttresses. One of the world's first buildings to use them, Notre Dame wasn't originally designed to include flying buttresses around the choir and nave but exterior supports were necessary after stress fractures occurred as the walls pushed outwards.

The Treasury
The **Trésor** (Treasury; admission €3/2; ⏱9.30am-6pm Mon-Fri, 9.30am-6.30pm Sat, 1.30-6.30pm Sun) contains relics including the Ste-Couronne (Holy Crown), allegedly the wreath of thorns placed on Jesus' head before he was crucified. It's exhibited between 3pm and 4pm on the first Friday of each month, 3pm to 4pm every Friday during Lent and 10am to 5pm on Good Friday.

The Towers
The **Tours de Notre Dame** (Towers; www.monuments-nationaux.fr; rue du Cloître Notre Dame, 4e; admission

☑ Top Tips

▶ Pick up an audio-guide (€5) from Notre Dame's **information desk** (⏱9.30am-6pm Mon-Fri, from 9am Sat & Sun). Audioguide rental includes admission to the treasury.

▶ Join a free 90-minute English-language tour at 2pm on Wednesday and Thursday and 2.30pm on Saturday.

▶ Admission to the towers is free on the first Sunday of the month from November to March.

▶ Remember that Notre Dame is a place of worship – see p192 for tips on etiquette.

✕ Take a Break

Appealing eateries ring place Dauphine at the western end of the Île de la Cité, including Ma Salle à Manger (p122).

The adjacent Île St-Louis is scattered with places selling Berthillon (p122) ice cream.

€8/5; ⊙10am-6.30pm Mon-Fri, 10am-11pm Sat & Sun Jun-Aug, 10am-6.30pm daily Apr, May & Sep, to 5.30pm daily Jan-Mar & Oct-Dec; Ⓜ Cité) entrance is via the North Tower; limber up to climb the 422 spiralling steps (there's no lift/elevator) to the top.

The Gargoyles
Arriving at the top of the western façade brings you face to face with the cathedral's most frightening gargoyles. These grotesque statues divert rainwater from the roof to prevent masonry damage, with the water exiting through the elongated, open mouth; and, purportedly, to ward off evil spirits. Although they appear medieval, they were installed by Eugène Viollet-le-Duc in the 19th century.

The Chimera Gallery
From the Galerie des Chimères (Chimera Gallery), named for Viollet-le-Duc's mythical creatures and monsters, at the top of the western façade you will find a spectacular panorama of the Parisian skyline including the Latin Quarter's ancient streets and the Eiffel Tower.

The Bells
The top of the western façade offers an impressive view of the South Tower's 13-tonne bourdon bell, Emmanuel (all of the cathedral's bells are named). During the night of 24 August 1944, when the Île de la Cité was retaken by French, Allied and Resistance troops, the tolling of the Emmanuel announced Paris' approaching liberation.

The Portals
On the western façade, check out the exquisite detail of its three 13th-century portals: the Portal of the Virgin, on the left, depicting Mary's ascension to heaven; the Portal of the Last Judgement, in the centre, representing the Last Judgement according to the Gospel of Saint Matthew; and the oldest, the Portal of Saint Anne, on the right.

The Organ
Notre Dame's immense organ is one of the largest in the world, with 7800 pipes (900 of which have historical classification), 111 stops, five 56-key manuals and a 32-key pedalboard. It's played during Sunday services, at guest organist recitals on Sunday afternoons before the Vespers service (except during Lent) and at sacred music concerts.

Sacred Music Concerts
Check the program for **sacred music concerts** (www.musique-sacree-notredamedeparis.fr; tickets €18/10). The season generally runs from early October to late June, with an additional series of summer concerts in July and August. Tickets can be prepurchased at the information desk or online, or you can buy them at Notre Dame on concert evenings at 8pm.

Understand

Notre Dame Timeline

- -

1160 The Bishop of Paris, Maurice de Sully, ordered the demolition of the original cathedral, the 4th-century Saint-Étienne (St Stephen's).

1163 Notre Dame's cornerstone was laid and construction began on the new cathedral.

1182 The apse and choir were completed.

Early 1200s Work commenced on the western façade.

1225 The western façade was completed.

1250 Work finished on the western towers and north rose window.

Mid-1200s To 'modernise' the cathedral, the transepts were remodelled in the Rayonnant style.

1345 The cathedral was completed.

1548 Huguenots stormed and damaged the cathedral following the Council of Trent.

1793 Damage during the most radical phase of the French Revolution saw many of Notre Dame's treasures plundered or destroyed.

1845–64 Following petitions to save the by then derelict cathedral from demolition (see p116), architect Eugène Viollet-le-Duc carried out extensive repairs and architectural additions.

1991 A lengthy maintenance and restoration program was initiated.

2013 Notre Dame celebrates 850 years since construction began.

Services

All religious services are conducted in French except the 'international' Mass held at 11.30am on Sunday, which includes some readings and prayer in English; there are no English-only services. Midnight Mass on Christmas Eve is a particularly popular occasion. Service times are posted on the cathedral's website.

Night Shows

On Thursdays and Saturdays from May to October, Notre Dame presents free night shows – one-hour music-accompanied 'operas' with images

Understand
Saved by the Hunchback of Notre Dame

The damage inflicted on Notre Dame during the French Revolution saw it fall into ruin, and it was destined for demolition. Salvation came with the widespread popularity of Victor Hugo's 1831 novel, *The Hunchback of Notre Dame*, which sparked a petition to save it. The novel opens on the Epiphany (6 January), 1482, the day of the 'Feast of Fools', with the eponymous hunchback, Quasimodo, the deafened bell-ringer at Notre Dame, crowned the King of Fools. Much of the ensuing action takes place in and around the cathedral (such as the scene where the dancer Esmeralda is being led to the gallows and Quasimodo swings down by a bell rope to rescue her), which effectively becomes another 'character' in the novel. Subsequently, in 1845, architect Eugène Emmanuel Viollet-le-Duc began the cathedral's grand-scale renovations. Likewise, Hugo's novel has gone on to achieve immortality of its own, with numerous film, TV, theatre and ballet adaptations, including the hugely successful 1996 Disney animation incorporating faithfully recreated architectural detail.

projected on a 100-sq-metre near-invisible tulle screen, making them appear as floating apparitions. Check the website for upcoming shows and schedules.

Landmark Occasions

Historic events that have taken place at Notre Dame include Henry VI of England's 1431 coronation as King of France, the 1558 marriage of Mary, Queen of Scots, to the Dauphin Francis (later Francis II of France), the 1804 coronation of Napoleon I by Pope Pius VII and the 1909 beatification and 1920 canonisation of Joan of Arc.

Point Zéro

Notre Dame is the heart of Paris – so much so that distances from Paris

to the rest of mainland France are measured from place du Parvis Notre Dame, the square in front of the cathedral. A bronze star marks the exact location of *point zéro des routes de France*.

Archaeological Crypt

The archaeological crypt beneath place du Parvis Notre Dame, the **Crypte Archéologique du Parvis Notre Dame** (http://crypte.paris.fr; 7 Parvis Notre Dame, 4e; admission; €4/3; ⏱10am-6pm Tue-Sun; Ⓜ Cité) reveals, layer by layer, the Île de la Cités history from the Gallo-Roman town of Lutetia to the 20th century. To fully appreciate it, rent an audioguide (€3).

NOTRE DAME

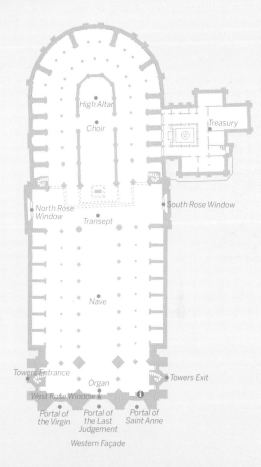

High Altar

Choir

Treasury

North Rose Window

South Rose Window

Transept

Nave

Towers Entrance

Towers Exit

Organ

West Rose Window

Portal of the Virgin

Portal of the Last Judgement

Portal of Saint Anne

Western Façade

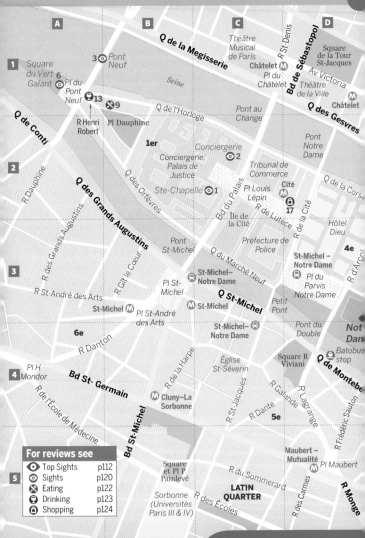

A
B
C
D

1

Square du Vert Galant

6 Pl du Pont Neuf

3 Pont Neuf

Q de la Megisserie

Seine

Théâtre Musical de Paris

R St-Denis

Bd de Sebastopol

Square de la Tour St-Jacques

Châtelet Ⓜ

Av Victoria

Pl du Châtelet

Théâtre de la Ville

Châtelet Ⓜ

13
9

Q de l'Horloge

Pont au Change

Q des Gesvres

Q de Conti

R Henri Robert

Pl Dauphine

1er

Conciergerie

Pont Notre Dame

Conciergerie; Palais de Justice

2

Tribunal de Commerce

Q de la Cors

R Dauphine

Q des Grands Augustins

Q des Orfèvres

Ste-Chapelle **1**

Bd du Palais

Pl Louis Lépin

R de Lutèce

Île de la Cité

Cité

17

R de la Cité

Hôtel Dieu

4e

R d'Arco

R des Grands Augustins

R Gît le Coeur

Pont St-Michel

Préfecture de Police

St-Michel – Notre Dame

R St-André des Arts

Pl St-Michel

Q du Marché Neuf

St-Michel– Notre Dame

Pl du Parvis Notre Dame

2

3

St-Michel Ⓜ

Pl St-André des Arts

St-Michel Ⓜ

Q St-Michel

Petit Pont

St-Michel– Notre Dame

Pont du Double

Not Dam

6e

R Danton

Batobus stop

Pl H Mondor

Bd St-Germain

Bd St-Michel

R de la Harpe

Église St-Séverin

Square R Viviani

Q de Montebe

4

R de l'École de Médecine

R St-Jacques

R Galande

R Lagrange

R Frédéric Sauton

Cluny–La Sorbonne Ⓜ

R Dante

5e

Maubert – Mutualité Ⓜ

Pl Maubert

R Monge

5

Square et Pl P Painlevé

R du Sommerard

R des Carmes

For reviews see

⊙	Top Sights	p112
⊙	Sights	p120
✕	Eating	p122
⊕	Drinking	p123
⊕	Shopping	p124

Sorbonne (Universités Paris III & IV)

R des Écoles

LATIN QUARTER

E · F · G

R du Renard

R du Temple

R des Archives

M Hôtel de Ville **M**

Bazar de l'Hôtel de Ville (BHV)

R de la Verrerie

R Vieille du Temple

R des Rosiers

r de la outellerie

Pl de l'Hôtel de Ville

R de Rivoli

Pl du Bourg Tibourg

R des Écouffes

M Hôtel de Ville

Hôtel de Ville

R de Lobau

Pl St-Gervais

R du Roi de Sicile

Pl Baudoyer

Église St-Gervais – St-Protais

R du Pont Louis-Philippe

R François Miron

4e

R de Jouy

M St-Paul

Pont d'Arcole

Q de l'Hôtel de Ville

R de l'Hôtel de Ville

Square A Schweitzer

R Charlemagne

Q aux Fleurs

Pont Louis-Philippe

Pl du Bataillon Français de l'ONU en Corée

R de Fourcy

3

Chanoinesse

M Pont Marie

u Cloître Notre Dame

Pont St-Louis

11 R Jean du Bellay

Q de Bourbon

Q des Célestins

Square Jean XXIII

4 ⊙

12 **20**

18

R Boutarel

Pont Marie

10

16

Île St-Louis

R le Regrattier

Q d'Anjou

Square de l'Île de France

R Budé

8

R des Deux Ponts

19

4

Pont de Archevêché

5 ⊙

Mémorial des Martyrs de la Déportation

Q d'Orléans

15

7 Église St-Louis en l'Isle

14 R St-Louis en l'île

R Poulletier

Q de la Tournelle

Q de Béthune

R des Bernardins

Pont de la Tournelle

Seine

Bd Henri IV

Square Barye

Bd St-Germain

R du Cardinal Lemoine

Musée de la Sculpture en Plein Air

Pont de Sully

5

N 0 — 200 m
0 — 0.1 miles

Sights

Ste-Chapelle
CHURCH

1 ◎ Map p118, C2

The luminous stained-glass windows of this 'Holy Chapel', consecrated in 1248, are a particularly ethereal backdrop for classical concerts, which allow you to spend extended time in these glorious surroundings and offset much of the entry price – see p192. Combined tickets with the Conciergerie cost €11/7.50. (www.monuments-nationaux.fr; 4 bd du Palais, 1er; admission €8/5; ◎9.30am-6pm Mar-Oct, 9am-5pm Nov-Feb; MCité)

Conciergerie
HISTORIC SIGHT

2 ◎ Map p118, C2

This cross-vaulted 14th-century palace was turned into a prison and torture chamber where 2780 *condamnés* (condemned) who had been brought before the Revolutionary Tribunal in the adjoining Palais de Justice – notably Marie-Antoinette – were incarcerated before being sent to the guillotine. (www.monuments-nationaux.fr; 2 bd du Palais, 1er; admission €7/4.50; ◎9.30am-6pm; MCité)

Pont Neuf
BRIDGE

3 ◎ Map p118, A1

Paris' oldest and most famous bridge (ironically named 'new bridge') was inaugurated in 1607, linking the Île de la Cité with the Seine's left and right banks. Its semicircular benches, recessed into the sparkling white stone, are a picturesque spot to watch Paris' riverboats pass by. (MPont Neuf)

Pont St-Louis
BRIDGE

4 ◎ Map p118, F4

The Île de la Cité and Île St-Louis are connected by the postcard-perfect Pont St-Louis. (MPont Marie)

Mémorial des Martyrs de la Déportation
MONUMENT

5 ◎ Map p118, E4

The Memorial to the Victims of the Deportation is a haunting monument to the 160,000 residents of France deported to and murdered in Nazi concentration camps during WWII. The walls of the Tomb of the Unknown Deportee are etched with inscriptions from celebrated writers and poets. (square de l'Île de France, 4e; ◎10am-noon & 2-7pm Apr-Sep, to 5pm Oct-Mar; MSt-Michel)

Square du Vert Galant
PARK

6 ◎ Map p118, A1

One of the most romantic spots in Paris, this triangular-shaped park sits at the western tip of the Île de la Cité. (1er; MPont Neuf)

Understand

The French Revolution

By the late 1780s, the extravagance of Louis XVI and his queen, Marie-Antoinette, had alienated virtually every segment of society and the king became increasingly isolated as unrest and dissatisfaction reached boiling point. When he tried to neutralise the power of the more reform-minded delegates at a meeting of the États-Généraux (States-General), the masses took to the streets. On 14 July 1789, a mob raided the Hôtel des Invalides for rifles, seizing 32,000 muskets, and then stormed the prison at Bastille. The French Revolution had begun.

At first, the Revolution was in the hands of moderate republicans called the Girondins. France was declared a constitutional monarchy and reforms were introduced, including the adoption of the Déclaration des Droits de l'Homme et du Citoyen (Declaration of the Rights of Man and of the Citizen). But as the masses armed themselves against the external threat to the new government by Austria, Prussia and the exiled French nobles, patriotism and nationalism combined with extreme fervour, and popularised and radicalised the Revolution. It was not long before the Girondins lost out to the extremist Jacobins, who abolished the monarchy and declared the First Republic in 1792. The Assemblée Nationale (National Assembly) was replaced by an elected Revolutionary Convention.

Louis XVI, who had unsuccessfully tried to flee the country, was convicted of 'conspiring against the liberty of the nation' and guillotined at today's place de la Concorde. Marie-Antoinette was executed later in 1793.

The Jacobins set up the notorious Committee of Public Safety to deal with national defence and to apprehend and try 'traitors'. This body had dictatorial control over the city and the country during the Reign of Terror (September 1793 to July 1794), which saw thousands beheaded, most religious freedoms revoked and churches closed to worship and desecrated.

After the Reign of Terror faded, moderate republicans set themselves up to rule the republic. A group of royalists bent on overthrowing them were led by Napoleon, whose victories would soon turn him into an independent political force.

Eating

Maison Berthillon SALON DE THÉ, ICE CREAM €

7 Map p118, G4

This esteemed *glacier* (ice-cream maker) was founded here in 1954, and is still run by the same family today. In typical Parisian style, its ice cream isn't slathered onto the cone but is meticulously set in place in a petite, perfectly rounded scoop. The 70 all-natural, chemical-free flavours include fruit sorbets such as blackcurrant and pink grapefruit, and much richer ice creams, made from fresh milk and eggs, like salted caramel, whisky and white chocolate. No credit cards. See also p122. (www.berthillon-glacier.fr; 31 rue St-Louis en l'Île, 4e; ice cream from €4; ⊙10am-8pm Wed-Sun, closed mid-Jul–early Sep; Ⓜ Pont Marie)

Local Life
An Island & its Ice Cream

The Île St-Louis' most famous foodstuff is Berthillon ice cream, which is sold at outlets around the island including Maison Berthillon's own premises (p122). But it's not the only *glacier* here. Some places sell other ice cream brands that people mistake for Berthillon – check the sign. And gelato maker Amorino opened its inaugural shop (47 rue St-Louis en l'Île, 4e) on the Île St-Louis and now has outlets as far afield as the South Pacific.

L'Ilot Vache FRENCH €€€

8 Map p118, G4

This traditional French restaurant is named for one of the Île St-Louis' two previous islands (see p123) and decorated with cow statuettes. Its candles give exposed stone and wooden beams a romantic glow. (☎01 46 33 55 16; http://restaurant-ilotvache.com; 35 rue St-Louis en l'Île, 4e; menu €37; ⊙dinner; Ⓜ Pont Marie)

Ma Salle à Manger FRENCH €€

9 Map p118, B1

Spilling onto a terrace on tucked-away Place Dauphine, this cute little pink-and-red-decorated bistro and wine bar chalks its changing menu on the blackboard. Its name means 'my dining room'; with simple yet inspired dishes like foie gras with mango chutney, you'll wish it was yours. (☎01 43 29 52 34; 26 place Dauphine, 1er; mains €15-25; ⊙lunch & dinner Mon-Fri; Ⓜ Cité)

Mon Vieil Ami FRENCH €€€

10 Map p118, F4

You're treated like an old friend – hence the name – from the moment you enter this sleek black bistro. Vegetables are the star of the menu, including starters like warm seasonal salads with raisins, almonds and tapenade-topped toast. (☎01 40 46 01 35; www.mon-vieil-ami.com; 69 rue St-Louis en l'Île, 4e; menu €41; ⊙lunch & dinner Wed-Sun; Ⓜ Pont Marie)

Brasserie de l'Île St-Louis
BRASSERIE €€

11 Map p118, F3

Renowned for its Alsatian cuisine, with various dishes doused in Riesling, you might just as easily be in a Strasbourg *winstub* (tavern) were it not for the Seine views from the terrace. (55 quai de Bourbon, 4e; mains €18-30; ⏱6pm-1am Thu, noon-midnight Fri-Tue; Ⓜ Pont Marie)

Café le Flore en l'Île
BRASSERIE, ICE CREAM €€

12 Map p118, F4

Beneath green-and-gold awnings, Le Flore en L'Île's takeaway window does a roaring trade in Berthillon ice cream. But, while brasserie fare is decent and service friendly, if you're just stopping by for a Berthillon cone, be aware that it charges up to a euro more than other establishments around the island. (42 quai d'Orléans, 4e; mains €12-28; ⏱8am-1am; Ⓜ Pont Marie)

Drinking

Taverne Henri IV
WINE BAR

13 Map p118, A1

Popular with Paris' legal eagles from the Palais de Justice nearby, this small, old-fashioned wine bar serves inexpensive and tasty accompaniments such as quiches and cheese and

---

---

charcuterie platters, all of which go well with a glass of Beaujolais; or you can just stop by for a drink. Hours can vary. (13 place du Pont Neuf, 1er; ⏱11.30am-10pm Mon-Fri, noon-6pm Sat, closed Aug; Ⓜ Pont Neuf)

La Charlotte de l'Îsle
SALON DE THÉ

14 Map p118, G4

Fresh from a refit and filled with wooden tables, this tearoom serves old-fashioned hot chocolate along with dozens of varieties of tea. (www.lacharlottedelisle.fr; 24 rue St-Louis en l'Île; ⏱11am-7pm Wed-Sun; Ⓜ Pont Marie)

Shopping

Clair de Rêve
TOYS

15 Map p118, G4

Stringed marionettes bob from the ceiling of this endearing little shop. Papier-mâché and leather marionettes start at around €100; expect to pay around six times that for one made of porcelain. Wind-up toys are also for sale. (www.clairdereve.com, in French; 35 rue St-Louis en l'Île, 4e; 11am-1pm & 2-7pm Mon-Sat; Pont Marie)

La Petite Scierie
FOOD & DRINK

16 Map p118, G4

Strewn with stuffed ducks, this tiny shop specialises in small-scale-production foie gras (made by the family who run it), which you can taste in-store on chunks of baguette. (www.lapetitescierie.fr; 60 rue St-Louis en l'Île, 4e; 11am-7pm Thu-Mon; Pont Marie)

Marché aux Fleurs
MARKET

17 Map p118, D2

Blooms have been sold at this flower market since 1808, making it the oldest market of any kind in Paris. On Sunday, between 9am and 7pm, it

RICHARD I'ANSON/LONELY PLANET IMAGES ©

Maison Berthillon (p122)

transforms into a twittering **bird market**. (place Louis Lépin, 4e; ⏰8am-7.30pm Mon-Sat; Ⓜ Cité)

Il Campiello   CRAFTS

18 🔒 Map p118, F4

Venetian carnival masks – intricately crafted from papier mâché, ceramics and leather – are the specialty of this exquisite shop, which also sells jewellery made from Murano glass beads. It was established by a native of Venice, to which the Île St-Louis bears more than a passing resemblance. (www.ilcampiello.com, in French; 88 rue St-Louis en l'Île, 4e; ⏰11am-7pm; Ⓜ Pont Marie)

Librairie Ulysse   BOOKS

19 🔒 Map p118, G4

You can barely move in between this shop's antiquarian and new travel guides, *National Geographic* back-editions and maps. Opened in 1971 by the intrepid Catherine Domaine, this was the world's first travel bookshop. Hours often vary, but ring the bell and Catherine will open up if she's around. (www.ulysse.fr, in French; 26 rue St-Louis en l'Île, 4e; ⏰11am-1pm & 1.45-7.15pm Mon-Sat; Ⓜ Pont Marie)

○ Local Life
Bouquinistes

Lining both banks of the Seine through the centre of Paris (not on the islands themselves), the open-air *bouquiniste* stalls selling secondhand, often out-of-print, books, rare magazines, postcards and old advertising posters are a definitive Parisian sight. The name comes from *bouquiner,* meaning 'to read with appreciation'. At night, *bouquinistes'* dark-green metal stalls are folded down and locked like suitcases. Many open only from spring to autumn (and many shut in August), but even in the depths of winter, you'll still find somewhere to barter for antiquarian treasures.

Oliviers & Co   FOOD & DRINK

20 🔒 Map p118, F4

This olive oil shop was the first of a now-worldwide chain created by Olivier Baussan, who also founded natural cosmetic company L'Occitane. In addition to Baussan's native Provence, Oliviers & Co also stocks oils from Italy, Greece, Israel, Turkey and Portugal. (www.oliviersandco.com; 81 rue St-Louis en l'Île, 4e; ⏰11am-2pm & 3-7.30pm Mon-Fri, 11am-7.30pm Sat & Sun; Ⓜ Pont Marie)

Explore

Latin Quarter

So named because international students communicated in Latin here until the French Revolution, the Latin Quarter remains the hub of academic life in Paris. Centred on the Sorbonne's main university campus, graced by fountains and lime trees, this lively area is also home to some outstanding museums and churches, along with Paris' beautiful art deco mosque and botanic gardens.

The Sights in a Day

☼ The **Batobus** (p204) stops at Paris' botanic gardens, the **Jardin des Plantes** (p134), so consider cruising here first and exploring its **natural history museums** (p135) and **menagerie**(zoo; p134). Then, make your way to the **Mosquée de Paris** (p134) to enjoy a *hammam* (Turkish steambath), shopping at its souk, sipping sweet mint tea in its courtyard and eating delicious *tajines* for lunch.

☼ Check out amazing Arab art and ingenious architecture at the **Institut du Monde Arabe** (p134) and pay your respects to some of France's most illustrious thinkers and innovators at the **Panthéon** (p134) mausoleum. For the ultimate medieval history lesson (where you can also see the remains of Gallo-Roman baths), visit the **Musée National du Moyen Âge** (p128), which is right by the **Sorbonne** (p136) university campus.

☽ After dinner at **Le Coupe-Chou** (p136), browse late-night bookshops like the charming, cluttered **Shakespeare & Company** (p139) and perhaps attend a literary reading, then catch jazz at **Le Caveau de la Huchette** (p138) or head to lively bars like **Le Pantalon** (p138).

For a local's day exploring historic rue Mouffetard, see p130.

Top Sights

Musée National du Moyen Âge (p128)

Local Life

A Stroll Along Rue Mouffetard (p130)

Best of Paris

Architecture
Institut du Monde Arabe (p134)

History
Musée National du Moyen Âge (p128)

Sorbonne (p50)

Eating
La Tour d'Argent (p136)

Getting There

Ⓜ **Metro** St-Michel (line 4) and the connected St-Michel–Notre Dame (RER B and C) is the neighbourhood's gateway.

Ⓜ **Metro** Other handy metro stations include Cluny–La Sorbonne (line 10) and Place Monge (line 7).

⚓ **Boat** The hop-on, hop-off Batobus (p204) stops in the Latin Quarter opposite Notre Dame and outside the Jardin des Plantes.

Top Sights
Musée National du Moyen Âge

Medieval history comes to life at France's Musée National du Moyen Âge. This National Museum of the Middle Ages is often referred to as the Musée de Cluny (or just Cluny), due to the fact that it's partly – and atmospherically – housed in the 15th-century Hôtel de Cluny, Paris' finest civil medieval building.

Map p132, A2

www.musee-moyenage.fr

6 place Paul Painlevé, 5e

admission €8.50/6.50

9.15am-5.45pm Wed-Mon

M Cluny–La Sorbonne

Don't Miss

The Roman-Gallo Baths

Long before construction began on the Hôtel de Cluny, the Gallo-Romans built *thermes* (baths) here around AD 200. The Musée National du Moyen Âge now occupies not only the Hôtel de Cluny but also the *frigidarium* (cooling room), which holds remains of the baths. Look for the display of the fragment of the mosaic *Love Riding a Dolphin*.

The Hôtel de Cluny

Initially the residential quarters of the Cluny Abbots, Alexandre du Sommerard moved to the Hôtel de Cluny in 1833 with his collection of medieval and Renaissance objects. Bought by the state after his death, the museum opened a decade later, retaining the original layout and features.

The Lady and the Unicorn Tapestries

Room 13 on the 1st floor displays *La Dame à la Licorne* (The Lady with the Unicorn), a sublime series of late 15th-century tapestries from the southern Netherlands. Five are devoted to the senses; the sixth is the enigmatic *À Mon Seul Désir* (To My Sole Desire), a reflection on vanity.

Other Collections

Spectacular displays include illuminated manuscripts, weapons, suits of armour, furnishings and *objets d'art* made of gold, ivory and enamel.

The Gardens

Small gardens to the museum's northeast, including Jardin Céleste (Heavenly Garden) and Jardin d'Amour (Garden of Love), are planted with flowers, herbs and shrubs that appear in masterpieces hanging throughout the museum. To the west the Forêt de la Licorne (Unicorn Forest) is based on the illustrations in the tapestries.

☑ Top Tips

▶ Although it's a national museum, the Musée National du Moyen Âge doesn't attract the same volume of tourists as other major sights, so any time is generally good to visit. Tickets aren't available for prepurchase online but the Paris Museum Pass (p206) is valid here.

▶ Audioguides are included in the admission price except on the first Sunday of the month year round, when admission to the museum is free but audioguides cost €1.

▶ For medieval history buffs, the museum's **document centre** (📞01 53 73 78 09; ⊙by appointment) has thousands of references. There's also an excellent onsite bookshop.

✗ Take a Break

For heritage-listed surrounds and outstanding French fare at reasonable prices, nearby brasserie Bouillon Racine (p152) is a treat.

Local Life
A Stroll Along Rue Mouffetard

Originally a Roman road, the sloping, cobbled rue Mouffetard acquired its name in the 18th century, when the now-underground River Bievre became the communal waste-disposal for local tanners and wood-pulpers. The odours gave rise to the name Moffettes (literally 'skunk'), which evolved into Mouffetard. The street's now filled with market stalls, cheap eateries and lively bars.

❶ Market Shopping
Today the aromas on 'La Mouffe', as it's nicknamed by locals, are infinitely more enticing. Grocers, butchers, fishmongers and other food purveyors set their goods out on street stalls during the **Marché Mouffetard** (⊙8am-7.30pm Tue-Sat, to noon Sun; M Censier Daubenton).

2 Fine Cheeses

You won't even have to worry about the aromas if you're taking home the scrumptious cheeses from *fromagerie* **Androuet** (http://androuet.com; 134 rue Mouffetard, 5e; ⏱9.30am-1pm & 4-7.30pm Tue-Thu, 9.30am-7.30pm Fri & Sat, 9.30am-1.30pm Sun; Ⓜ Censier Daubenton) – all of its cheeses can be vacuum-packed for free. (Be sure to look up to see the beautiful murals on building's façade!)

3 Delicious Deli

Stuffed olives and capsicums and marinated eggplant are among the picnic goodies at gourmet Italian deli **Delizius** (134 rue Mouffetard, 5e; ⏱9.30am-8pm Tue-Fri, 9am-8pm Sat, 9am-2pm Sun; Ⓜ Censier Daubenton), which also sells ready-to-eat hot meals and fresh and dried pasta.

4 Sweet Treats

Light, luscious macaroons in flavours like jasmine, raspberry and blackcurrant, and a mouth-watering range of chocolates by three *maîtres chocolatiers* (master chocolate-makers) – Fabrice Gillotte, Jacques Bellanger and Patrice Chapoare – are laid out like jewels at **Chocolats Mococha** (www.chocolatsmococha.com, in French; 89 rue Mouffetard, 5e; Ⓜ Censier Daubenton).

5 Movie Time

Even locals find it easy to miss the small doorway leading to cinema **L'Epée de Bois** (www.cinema-epee-de-bois. fr, in French; 100 rue Mouffetard, 5e; Ⓜ Censier Daubenton), which screens art-house flicks such as Julie Delpy–directed films.

6 Apéro at Le Vieux Chêne

Hosting revolutionary meetings in 1848, these days **Le Vieux Chêne** (69 rue Mouffetard, 5e; ⏱9am-2am Sun-Thu, to 5am Fri & Sat; Ⓜ Place Monge) is a student favourite, especially during happy 'hour' (4pm to 9pm Tuesday to Sunday, and from 4pm until closing on Monday). Resident DJs mix it up on Friday and Saturday nights.

7 Homewares Shopping

From rue Mouffetard, step down into the basement housing colourful homewares shop **Mouffetard Folie's** (51 rue Mouffetard, 5e; ⏱11am-8.30pm; Ⓜ Censier Daubenton), crammed with cute, kitsch, inexpensive new items such as battery-powered flying Fresian-cow mobiles and gumdrop-coloured lamps.

8 Crêpes at Chez Nicos

The signboard outside crêpe artist Nicos' unassuming little shop **Chez Nicos** (44 rue Mouffetard, 5e; crêpes €3.50-6; ⏱10am-2am; Ⓜ Place Monge) chalks up dozens of fillings, but ask by name for his masterpiece, 'La Crêpe du Chef', stuffed with eggplant, feta, mozzarella, lettuce, tomatoes and onions. There's a handful of tables inside; otherwise head to a nearby park.

R Charlemagne

R St-Paul

4e

Sully M Bd Henri IV
Morland

Bd Morland

Q Henri IV

Q St-Bernard

Square A
Schweitzer

Q des Célestins

Musée de la
Sculpture en
Plein Air

Jardin des
Plantes

Q de l'Hôtel
de Ville

M Pont Marie

Pont
Marie

Q d'Anjou

Square
Pont Barye
de Sully

Batobus
stop.

4

Ménagerie
du Jardin
des Plantes

3

Q de Bourbon

R St-Louis en l'île

Île
St-Louis

Institut du
Monde Arabe

Mohammed V

2

Universités
Paris VI & VII

R Cuvier

Pont
Louis-
Philippe

Pont
Marie

Q d'Orléans

Q de Béthune

Pont de
la Tournelle

12

R Linné

Pl Jussieu

M Jussieu

R Jussieu

Seine

Pl

R du Cardinal Lemoine

R des Fossés

St-Bernard

Bd St-Germain

Q de la Tournelle

Cardinal
Lemoine

R des
Boulangers

13

R Lacepède

Place Monge

Pont
Louis-
Philippe

Q aux Fleurs

Île de
la Cité

Pont de
l'Archevêché

R de Poissy

M

7

R Rollin

M

R Linné

Arènes
de Lutèce

14

R Ortolan

R Mouffe

B d'Arcole

R du Cloître
Notre Dame

Square
Jean XXIII

Q de
Montebello

R des Bernardins

R Monge

Square
Paul
Langevin

Église St-Étienne

Jardin
Carré

R Clovis

R Thouin

R Tournef

R Lhom

St-Michel –
Notre Dame

R de la Bûcherie

Notre
Dame

Batobus
stop.

18

R Lagrange

R de la Montagne
Ste-Geneviève

16

Pl Maubert
Maubert
Mutualité

8

Pl Ste-
Geneviève
du Mont

10

Pl du
Panthéon

5e

R Pierre et

Pont
St-Michel

Pl St-
Michel

M St-Michel

R de la Harpe

St-Michel

R St-Jacques

R Danton

17

R Dante

23

Square
R Viviani

24

21

M St-Michel

R de la Huchette

Pl Maubert

R de Lanneau

R Valette

R des Écoles

R de la
Sorbonne

Église

Panthéon

R Soufflot

R Gay Lussac

6e

Carrefour
de l'Odéon

Cluny–La
Sorbonne

Musée
National du
Moyen Âge

25

Eurolines

R du Sommerard

22

Sorbonne

Square F
A Mariette

9

R des Écoles

R Cujas

R St-Jacques

11

20

LATIN
QUARTER

15

Luxembourg

R des Fossés
St-Jacques

19

R Racine

R Danton

Bd St-Michel

R de l'Estrapade

R Clotilde

R de la Sorbonne

R Pierre et
Marie Curie

For reviews see

○	Top Sights	p128
○	Sights	p134
⊗	Eating	p136
⊗	Drinking	p138
✿	Entertainment	p138
⊕	Shopping	p139

Square Marie Curie

Ⓜ St-Marcel

Hôpital de la Pitié-Salpêtrière

R Jenner

R Jeanne d'Arc

R Esquirol

R Poliveau

Bd de l'Hôpital

R Pinel

National

Ⓜ ○5 Muséum d'Histoire Naturelle

Mosquée de Paris

R Geoffroy St-Hilaire

Campo Formio Ⓜ

13e

R Rubens

R Coypel

Bd Vincent Auriol

R Daubenton

R Mirbel

R Mor

R de la

rrey

R du Fer à Moulin

R Scipion

Bd St-Marcel

R Lebrun

R Fer à Moulin

R Candolle

LATIN QUARTER

Pl B

Halpern

Ⓜ Censier Daubenton

Square St-Médard

R Censier

Les Gobelins Ⓜ

Av des Gobelins

R Abel Hovelacque

Pl d'Italie

Ⓜ Place d'Italie

R Berbier du Mets

R Broca

R Pascal

Square René Le Gall

R de Croulebarbe

R de la Cordelière

400 m

0.2 miles

olette

R de l'Arbalète

R Vauquelin

R Claude Bernard

Bd de Port Royal

R St-Hippolyte

10 ⊗

R Pascal

R de Croulebarbe

Ⓝ

0

0

R des Feuillantines

R St-Jacqu

Val de Grâce

Cochin

R de la Santé

14e

Bd Arago

R de la Glacière

R Corvisart

R Vulpian

R Léon Maurice Nordmann

Bd Auguste Blanqui

Glacière Ⓜ

A | B | C | D | E

5 | 6 | 7 | 8

Sights

Panthéon
MAUSOLEUM

1 ◎ Map p132, B3

Commissioned by Louis XV as an abbey, this domed neoclassical building had the misfortune of reaching completion in 1789. The revolutionary climate saw it converted into a mausoleum, housing leading lights including Victor Hugo, Voltaire, Louis Braille and Émile Zola. Its first female resident, Marie Curie (accompanied by husband Pierre), arrived only in 1995. (www.monum.fr; place du Panthéon; admission €8/5; ◷10am-6.30pm Apr-Sep, to 6pm Oct-Mar; Ⓜ Maubert-Mutualité or RER Luxembourg)

Institut du Monde Arabe
MUSEUM

2 ◎ Map p132, D2

This innovative Jean Nouvel–designed building incorporates photo-sensitive apertures in the glass walls, inspired by latticed wooden windows. Exhibits encompass 9th- to 19th-century Arab arts, while incredible views stretch across the Seine, as far as Sacré-Cœur, from the 9th floor. Also here is a cinema, library, cafe, cafeteria and restaurant. (www.imarabe.org; place Mohammed V, 5e; admission €6/4; ◷10am-6pm Tue-Sun; Ⓜ Cardinal Lemoine or Jussieu)

Jardin des Plantes
GARDENS

3 ◎ Map p132, E4

Founded in 1626 as Louis XIII's herb garden, Paris' botanical gardens are a serious institute rather than a leisure destination, but fascinating all the same. Sections include a winter garden, tropical greenhouses and an alpine garden, as well as the school of botany, and a zoo. (www.jardindesplantes.net, in French; 57 rue Cuvier, 5e; admission free to €6/4, depending on section; ◷most sections 7.30am-7.45pm Apr-Oct, 8.30am-5.30pm Oct-Mar; Ⓜ Gare d'Austerlitz, Censier Daubenton or Jussieu)

Ménagerie du Jardin des Plantes
ZOO

4 ◎ Map p132, E4

Like the Jardin des Plantes in which it's located, this 1000-animal zoo is more than a tourist attraction, doubling as a research centre for the reproduction of rare and endangered species. During the Prussian siege of 1870, almost all of the animals at the zoo were eaten by the starving Parisians. (www.mnhn.fr; 57 rue Cuvier & 3 quai St-Bernard, 5e; admission €9/7 ◷9am-5pm; Ⓜ Gare d'Austerlitz, Censier Daubenton or Jussieu)

Mosquée de Paris
MOSQUE

5 ◎ Map p132, D5

A *hammam* (Turkish steam bath; women only on Mondays, Wednesdays, Thursdays and Saturdays, and men only on Tuesdays and Sundays), body scrub, massage, mint tea and couscous or *tajine* (North African stew) at Paris' art deco–Moorish mosque are cheapest as a €58 'Oriental' package, but you can take any of the above separately. (☎01 45 35 97 33; www.la-mosquee.com; 2bis place du Puits de l'Ermite, 5e; admission

Dining near 'La Sorbonne' (p136)

€3/2; mosque 9am-noon & 2-6pm Sat-Thu, tearoom 9am-11.30pm daily, restaurant lunch & dinner daily, hammam 10am-9pm Mon, Wed, Thu, Sat & Sun, 2-9pm Tue & Fri, souk 11am-7pm daily; M Censier Daubenton or Place Monge)

Musée National d'Histoire Naturelle   MUSEUM

6 ◉ Map p132, D5

France's National Museum of Natural History incorporates three separate centres that each adjoin the Jardin des Plantes: the **Galerie de Minéralogie et de Géologie** (closed for renovation at the time of research); the **Galerie d'Anatomie Comparée et de Paléontologie** (admission €7/5; 10am-5pm Wed-Mon), covering anatomy and fossils; and the topical **Grande Galerie de l'Évolution**

(admission €7/5; 10am-6pm Wed-Mon), highlighting humanity's effect on the ecosystem. (www.mnhn.fr; 57 rue Cuvier, 5e; M Censier Daubenton or Gare d'Austerlitz)

Arènes de Lutèce   HISTORIC SIGHT

7 ◉ Map p132, C4

The 2nd-century Roman amphitheatre, Lutetia Arena, once sat around 10,000 people for gladiatorial combats and other events. Found by accident in 1869 when rue Monge was under construction, it's now used by neighbourhood youths for playing football, and by old men for *boules* and *pétanque* (similar to the game of bowls). (49 rue Monge, 5e; admission free; 9am-9.30pm Apr-Oct, 8am-5.30pm Nov-Mar; M Place Monge)

Église St-Étienne du Mont
CHURCH

8 Map p132, B3

Built between 1492 and 1655, this bell-tower-topped church contains Paris' only surviving rood screen (1535), separating the chancel from the nave; the others were removed during the late Renaissance because they prevented the faithful assembled in the nave from seeing the priest celebrate Mass. In the nave's southeastern corner, a chapel contains the tomb of Ste Geneviève, patroness of Paris. (1 place Ste-Geneviève, 5e; ⏰8am-noon & 2-7pm Tue-Sat, 9am-noon & 2.30-7pm Sun; MCardinal Lemoine)

Sorbonne
UNIVERSITY

9 ⦿ Map p132, A2

One of the world's most prestigious universities, 'La Sorbonne' was founded in 1253 by Robert de Sorbon as a theological college for just 16 pupils, and went on to establish its own government and laws. The campus is undergoing a series of renovations until 2015. (www.sorbonne.fr, in French; 12 rue de la Sorbonne, 5e; MCluny-La Sorbonne)

Eating

L'Ourcine
BISTRO €€

10 ✕ Map p132, B7

A perfect example of a 'neo bistro', this intimate place may be casual (no dress code), but it takes its food seriously. The focus of the superb menu is on the flavours of the French Basque Country, including succulent pan-fried baby squid with fiery Espelette peppers. (☎01 47 07 13 65; 92 Rue Broca, 13e; lunch/dinner menus €26/34; ⏰lunch & dinner Tue-Sat; MLes Gobelins)

Le Coupe-Chou
FRENCH €€

11 ✕ Map p132, B3

This maze of candlelit rooms in a vine-clad 17th-century townhouse is overwhelmingly romantic, with beamed ceilings, antique furnishings, background classical music and dishes that capture the essence of the French countryside. (☎01 46 33 68 69; www.lecoupechou.com, in French; 9 & 11 rue de Lanneau, 5e; lunch/dinner menus from €13/26.50; ⏰lunch & dinner to 11.30pm Mon-Sat; MMaubert-Mutualité)

La Tour d'Argent
GASTRONOMIC €€€

12 ✕ Map p132, D2

Since it opened in 1582 (yes, 1582!), the 'Silver Tower' has refined every facet of fine dining. Its signature pressed duck still mesmerises diners, as do its glimmering views over Notre Dame and the Seine. Book well ahead. (☎01 43 54 23 31; www.latourdargent.com; 15 quai de la Tournelle, 5e; lunch menu €65, mains €70-140; ⏰lunch & dinner Tue-Sat; MCardinal Lemoine or Pont Marie)

Le Buisson Ardent
BISTRO €€

13 ✕ Map p132, C3

Classy fare at this rose-toned bistro includes roasted quail, pan-fried veal kidneys, and scorpion fish. (01 43 54

Understand
Local Lingo

Parisians have long had a reputation for being unable or unwilling to speak English, but this has changed dramatically, particularly since the internet became commonplace, and signposts, menus, establishment names and buzz words increasingly incorporate English.

Addressing people in French makes a *huge* difference, even simply '*Bonjour/bonsoir, parlez-vous anglais?*' (Good day/evening, do you speak English?). Often what is mistaken for Parisian arrogance is the equivalent of someone addressing you in a foreign language in your home country. On detecting an accent, many Parisians will switch to English to facilitate conversation (feel free to say if you prefer to converse in French).

Another potential cause for misunderstanding is the cut-to-the-chase directness of French communication. Whereas in English it's common to say, for example, 'Can I have a coffee, please?', the French '*Un café, s'il vous plaît*' (A coffee, please) can sound abrupt to an anglophone ear. Likewise, the French tendency to frame a question 'You would like a coffee?' rather than 'Would you like a coffee?' may seem forward, though it's not intentional.

93 02; www.lebuissonardent.fr; 25 rue Jussieu, 5e; lunch/dinner menus from €16.90/19.90; ⊘lunch daily, dinner Mon-Sat; M Jussieu)

Marché Monge
MARKET €

14 Map p132, C4

This open-air market is laden with wonderful cheeses, baked goods and a host of other temptations. (place Monge, 5e; ⊘7am-2pm Wed, Fri & Sun; M Place Monge)

Le Comptoir du Panthéon
BRASSERIE, BAR €

15 Map p132, A3

Beef carpaccio, salmon tartare and tagliatelle with vegetables are among the dishes served all day at this superbly situated spot, which has Eiffel Tower views from its terrace. (5 rue Soufflot, 5e; mains €10-14; ⊘7am-2am; M Cardinal Lemoine or RER Luxembourg)

Marché Maubert
MARKET €

16 Map p132, B2

The Left Bank's bohemian soul lives on at this colourful market. (place Maubert, 5e; ⊘7am-2.30pm Tue, Thu & Sat; M Maubert-Mutualité)

Pho 67
VIETNAMESE €€

17 Map p132, B1

Tuck into delicious Vietnamese dishes such as fried boned eel, crusty lacquered duck and rare tender goat with ginger, all cooked to order. Hidden in a small backstreet, it's fortunately located away from the

Figs at market on rue Mouffetard (p130)

over-touristy little maze of restaurants that surrounds rue de la Huchette. No credit cards. (☑ 01 43 25 56 69; 59 rue Galande, 5e; menu €23; ⏱ lunch & dinner; Ⓜ Maubert-Mutualité)

Drinking

Café Panis   CAFE

18 Map p132, B1

This rather elegant-looking cafe might seem an unlikely spot to find studenty-types scribbling in note-books, but it's close to Shakespeare & Company bookshop and waiters benevolently let impoverished writers sit with a coffee or warming soup for an hour or two. (21 quai de Montebello, 5e; ⏱ 7am-midnight; Ⓜ St-Michel)

Le Pantalon   BAR

19 Ⓟ Map p132, A3

Ripped vinyl seats, coloured-glass light fittings and old stickers plastered on the walls make this bar a favourite hangout of Parisian musicians. (7 rue Royer-Collard, 5e; ⏱ 5.30pm-2am; Ⓜ Cluny-La Sorbonne or RER Luxembourg)

Le Pub St-Hilaire   PUB

20 Ⓟ Map p132, B3

This pulsating student hangout keeps 'em coming back with extended happy hours, pool, board games, upbeat music and hearty bar food. (www.pub-sainthilaire.com, in French; 2 rue Valette, 5e; ⏱ 3pm-2am Mon-Thu, 3pm-4am Fri, 4pm-4am Sat, 4pm-midnight Sun; Ⓜ Maubert-Mutualité)

Entertainment

Le Caveau de la Huchette   JAZZ

21 ⭐ Map p132, B1

Count Basie, Memphis Slim and Sacha Distel are among the greats who have played in this former medieval cellar (later French Revolution torture chambers). It now hosts a diverse line-up of swing bands, South American jazz and more. No bookings. (www.caveaudelahuchette.fr; 5 rue de la Huchette, 5e; ⏱ 9.30pm-late; Ⓜ St-Michel)

Le Champo
CINEMA

22 Map p132, A2

Behind its art deco façade you can catch retrospectives of Hitchcock and Woody Allen, as well as films by French directors. (www.lechampo.com, in French; 51 rue des Écoles, 5e; Ⓜ St-Michel or Cluny-La Sorbonne)

Shopping

Shakespeare & Company
BOOKS

23 🔒 Map p132, B1

A kind of spell descends on you as you enter this charming bookshop, where nooks and crannies overflow with new and secondhand English-language books. Fabled for nurturing writers, at night its couches turn into beds where writers stay in exchange for stacking shelves. Readings by emerging to illustrious authors take place at 7pm most Mondays; it also hosts workshops and literary festivals. (www.shakespeare andcompany.com; 37 rue de la Bûcherie, 5e; ⏲ 10am-11pm Mon-Fri, from 11pm Sat & Sun; Ⓜ St-Michel)

Abbey Bookshop
BOOKS

24 🔒 Map p132, A1

In a heritage-listed townhouse, this welcoming Canadian-run bookshop

 Local Life

Café de la Nouvelle Mairie

Just around the corner from the Panthéon but hidden away on a small square with a fountain, the narrow wine bar **Café de la Nouvelle Mairie** (Map p132, A3; 19 rue des Fossés-Saint-Jacques, 5e; ⏲ 9am-8pm Mon-Fri; Ⓜ Cardinal Lemoine) is a neighbourhood secret, serving blackboard-chalked wines by the glass, as well as bottles.

serves free coffee (sweetened with maple syrup) to sip while you browse tens of thousands of new and used books, and organises literary events and countryside hikes. (rue de la Parcheminerie, 5e; ⏲ 10am-7pm Mon-Sat; Ⓜ St-Michel or Cluny-La Sorbonne)

Album
BOOKS, TOYS

25 🔒 Map p132, B2

Serious comic collectors – and anyone excited by Harry Potter wands, Star Wars, Superman and other superhero figurines and T-shirts (you know who you are!) – shouldn't miss this shop. (www.album.fr, in French; 67 bd St-Germain, 5e; ⏲ 10am-8pm Mon-Sat, noon-7pm Sun; Ⓜ Cluny-La Sorbonne)

Explore

Musée d'Orsay & St-Germain des Prés

Literature lovers, antique collectors and fashionistas flock to this mythological part of Paris. Legendary writers such as Sartre, de Beauvoir, Camus, Hemingway and Fitzgerald hung out here, and – after its gentrification – further south at Montparnasse where (despite late 20th-century eyesores like the '70s smoked-glass Tour Montparnasse skyscraper) you'll find surviving brasseries and re-energised backstreets.

The Sights in a Day

☀ Get your bearings from the panoramic observation deck of **Tour Montparnasse** (p152), before paying homage to writers Sartre and de Beauvoir and singer Serge Gainsbourg in the **Cimetière du Montparnasse** (p151) and getting a contemporary art fix at the **Fondation Cartier Pour l'Art Contemporain** (p150).

☀ After lunch at **Bouillon Racine** (p152) or a picnic in the **Jardin du Luxembourg** (p144), stroll through this beautiful park en route to viewing Delacroix's works in the **Église St-Sulpice** (p150) and **Musée National Eugène Delacroix** (p150). Stop by **Église St-Germain des Prés** (p151) before people-watching over a *café crème* at famous literary cafes like **Les Deux Magots** (p155) and browsing designer boutiques.

☾ Entry to the **Musée d'Orsay** (pictured left; p142) is cheaper in the late-afternoon, so it's an ideal time to check out its breathtaking collections. Dine at St-Germain des Prés' superb restaurants, such as **Le Salon d'Hélène** (p153), then return to Montparnasse's late-night cafes like **La Ruche** (p156).

To discover St-Germain des Prés' storied shops, see p146.

◉ Top Sights

Musée d'Orsay (p142)

Jardin du Luxembourg (p144)

◯ Local Life

St-Germain des Prés' Storied Shops (p146)

♥ Best of Paris

Architecture

Fondation Cartier Pour l'Art Contemporain (p150)

Museums

Musée d'Orsay (p142)

Eating

Poilâne (p147)

Grom (p154)

Getting There

Ⓜ **Metro** St-Germain des Prés (line 4), Mabillon (line 10) and Odéon (lines 4 and 10) are in the heart of the action.

Ⓜ **Metro** Montparnasse Bienvenüe (lines 4, 6, 12 and 13) is Montparnasse's hub.

⚓ **Boat** The hop-on, hop-off Batobus (p204) stops outside the Musée d'Orsay and at quai Malaquais in St-Germain des Prés.

Top Sights
Musée d'Orsay

Fresh from renovations that incorporate richly coloured walls, a reorganised layout and increased exhibition space, the home of France's national collection from the impressionist, postimpressionist and art nouveau movements is, appropriately, the glorious former Gare d'Orsay railway station, itself an art nouveau showpiece, where a roll-call of masters and their world-famous works are on display.

◉ Map p148, B1

www.musee-orsay.fr

62 rue de Lille, 7e

admission €8/5.50;

◷9.30am-6pm Tue, Wed & Fri-Sun, to 9.45pm Thu

Ⓜ Assemblée Nationale or RER Musée d'Orsay

Don't Miss

The Building
Built for the 1900 Exposition Universelle, by 1939 the Gare d'Orsay's platforms were too short for trains, and in few years all rail services ceased. In 1962 Orson Welles filmed Kafka's *The Trial* in the then-abandoned building before the government set about transforming it into the country's premier showcase for art from 1848 to 1914.

Painting Collections
Masterpieces include Manet's *On the Beach;* Monet's gardens at Giverny and *Rue Montorgueil, Paris, Festival of June 30, 1878;* Cézanne's card players, *Green Apples* and *Blue Vase;* Renoir's *Ball at the Moulin de la Galette* and *Girls at the Piano;* Degas' ballerinas; Toulouse-Lautrec's cabaret dancers; Pissarro's *The Harvest;* Sisley's *View of the Canal St-Martin;* and Van Gogh's *Starry Night.*

Decorative Arts Collections
Household items from 1848 to 1914, such as hat and coat stands, candlesticks, desks, chairs, bookcases, vases, silk-printed screens, water pitchers, decorated plates, goblets, bowls – and even soup terrines, kettles and cutlery – are true works of art and incorporate exquisite design elements.

Sculptures
Sculptures by Degas, Gaugin, Camille Claudel, Renoir and Rodin are housed in the museum.

Graphic Arts Collections
Drawings, pastels and sketches from major artists are another of the Musée d'Orsay's lesser-known highlights. Look for Georges Seurat's crayon on paper work *The Black Bow* (c 1882) and Paul Gaugin's poignant self-portrait (c 1902–03), which he drew near the end of his life.

☑ Top Tips

▶ Save money by purchasing a combined ticket with the nearby Musée Rodin (p26; €12 if you visit both on the same day); or a combined ticket with the Musée de l'Orangerie (p58; €13 for both within four days).

▶ Musée d'Orsay admission costs €5.50 for entry after 4.30pm (after 6pm on Thursday).

▶ Admission is free on the first Sunday of the month year round.

▶ Save time by prepurchasing tickets online.

✗ Take a Break

The stylised new **Café Campana** (dishes €9-18; ⏱10am-5pm Tue, Wed & Fri-Sun, to 9pm Thu) looks out through the former station's giant glass clockface.

Time has scarcely changed the station's **Restaurant Musée d'Orsay** (☎01 45 49 47 03; lunch/dinner menus €16.50/55; ⏱lunch Tue-Sun, dinner Thu, afternoon tea 2.45-5.45pm Tue-Sun).

Top Sights
Jardin du Luxembourg

An inner-city oasis of formal terraces, chestnut groves and lush lawns, the 23 gracefully laid-out hectares of the Luxembourg Gardens have a special place in the hearts of Parisians. Napoleon dedicated the park to the children of Paris, and many residents spent their childhoods enjoying old-fashioned activities that are still here today, in addition to the modern facilities.

👁 Map p148, D5

numerous entrances, 6e

🕐 between 7.30am and 8.15am to between 5pm and 10pm

Ⓜ St-Sulpice, Rennes or Notre Dames des Champs, or RER Luxembourg

Palais du Luxembourg

Don't Miss

Puppet Shows

You don't have to be a kid and you don't have to speak French to be delighted by marionette shows, which have entertained audiences in France since the Middle Ages. The lively puppets perform in the Jardin du Luxembourg's little **Théâtre du Luxembourg** (http://guignolduluxembourg. monsite-orange.fr; tickets €4.50; ☺3.15pm Wed, 11am & 3.15pm Sat & Sun, daily during school holidays).

Grand Bassin

All ages love the octagonal Grand Bassin, a serene ornamental pond that adults can lounge around while kids prod 1920s toy sailboats with long sticks. Nearby, littlies can ride ponies or the carousel (merry-go-round), or romp around the playgrounds. Small charges apply for all activities.

The Orchards

Dozens of apple varieties grow in the orchards in the gardens' south. Bees have produced honey in the nearby apiary, the Rucher du Luxembourg, since the 19th century; the annual Fête du Miel (Honey Festival) offers two days of tasting and buying its sweet harvest in late September.

Musée du Luxembourg

Prestigious temporary art exhibitions take place in this beautiful former *orangerie* (greenhouse) in the Jardin du Luxembourg, the **Musée du Luxembourg** (www.museeduluxembourg.fr, in French; 19 rue de Vaugirard, 6e; most exhibitions around €13.50/9; ☺10am-8pm Sun-Thu, to 10pm Fri & Sat).

Palais du Luxembourg

Built in the 1620s and now housing the French senate, the Palais du Luxembourg is occasionally open to visitors by guided tour – call ☎01 44 54 19 49.

☑ Top Tips

▶ Park opening hours vary seasonally; times are posted at entrance gates.

▶ If you're planning on picnicking, forget bringing a blanket – the elegantly manicured lawns are off-limits apart from a small wedge on the southern boundary. Instead, do as Parisians do, and corral one of the iconic 1923-designed sage-green metal chairs and find your own favourite part of the park.

▶ Arrive at least half an hour ahead of time for puppet shows.

✗ Take a Break

Kiosks and cafes are dotted throughout the park, including places selling fairy (candy) floss.

Polidor (Map p148, E4; ☎01 43 26 95 34; www. polidor.com, in French; 41 rue Monsieur le Prince, 6e; menus from €22; ☺lunch & dinner; Ⓜ Odéon) and its decor date from 1845, and it still serves family-style French cuisine.

Local Life
St-Germain des Prés' Storied Shops

While St-Germain des Prés spills over with chic fashion and interior design boutiques, it's also filled with locally patronised antique and vintage dealers, small shops specialising in everything from handmade umbrellas to tiny tin soldiers, and the city's oldest department store, the Gustave Eiffel–designed Le Bon Marché, which all provide an insight into the neighbourhood's history.

❶ Arcade Exploration

Browse the shops in the enchanting 1735-built, glass-roofed passageway **Cour du Commerce St-André**, and duck through the arcade entrance to have lunch at the world's oldest cafe, the 1686-founded **Le Procope** (www. procope.com; 13 rue de l'Ancienne Comédie, 6e; 2-/3-course menus from €20.90/27.90; ⏱11.30am-midnight; Ⓜ Odéon).

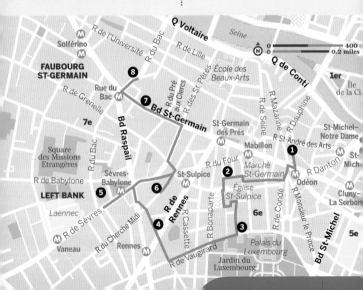

❷ Soldiering On

Miniature tin and lead soldiers have been sold at the tiny shop **Au Plat d'Étain** (http://auplatdetain.com, in French; 16 rue Guisarde, 6e; ⏱11am-12.30pm & 2-7pm Tue & Thu-Sat; Ⓜ Odéon) since 1775.

❸ Doll's House

Opposite the residence of the French Senate's president, the teensy shop **La Maison de Poupée** (☎06 09 65 58 68; 40 rue de Vaugirard, 6e; ⏱2.30-7pm Mon-Sat, by appt Sun; Ⓜ Odéon or RER Luxembourg) sells its namesake doll's houses as well as *poupées anciennes* (antique dolls).

❹ Bathroom Beauty

The antique and retro mirrors (hand-held and on stands), perfume spritzers, soap dishes and even basins and tapware at the long-established shop **Le Bain Rose** (www.le-bain-rose.fr; 11 rue d'Assas, 6e; ⏱10am-7pm Mon-Sat; Ⓜ Rennes) can transform your bathroom into a belle époque sanctum.

❺ Department Store Decadence

The 1852-established department store **Le Bon Marché** (www.bonmarche.fr; 24 rue de Sèvres, 7e; ⏱10am-8pm Mon-Wed & Fri, to 9pm Thu & Sat; Ⓜ Sèvres-Babylone) houses fabulous fashion, homewares and the glorious food hall, **La Grande Épicerie de Paris** (www.lagrandeepicerie.fr; 36 rue de Sèvres, 7e; ⏱8.30am-9pm Mon-Sat), with fantastical displays of chocolates, pastries, biscuits, cheeses and more.

❻ Bakery Treats

Pierre Poilâne opened his *boulangerie* (bakery) **Poilâne** (www.poilane.fr; 8 rue du Cherche Midi, 6e; ⏱7.15am-8.15pm Mon-Sat; Ⓜ Sèvres-Babylone) upon arriving from Normandy in 1932. Today his granddaughter runs the company, which still turns out wood-fired, rounded sourdough loaves made with stone-milled flour and Guérande sea salt. The cafe next door uses the loaves for fabulous gourmet *tartines* (open sandwiches).

❼ Rainy Day Style

Parapluies (parasols) and *ombrelles* (umbrellas) have been handcrafted at **Alexandra Sojfer** (www.alexandrasojfer.fr, in French; 218 bd St-Germain, 7e; ⏱9.30am-6.30pm Tue-Sat; Ⓜ St-Germain des Prés) since 1834.

❽ A Menagerie of Sorts

Overrun with creatures including lions, tigers, zebras and storks, taxidermist **Deyrolle** (www.deyrolle.com; 46 rue du Bac, 7e; ⏱10am-7pm Tue-Sat; Ⓜ Rue du Bac) opened in 1831. In addition to stuffed animals (for rent and sale), it stocks minerals, shells, corals and crustaceans, stand-mounted ostrich eggs and pedagogical storyboards.

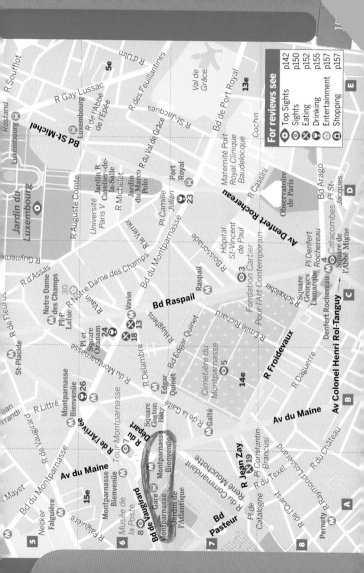

For reviews see

⊙	Top Sights	p142
⊙	Sights	p150
⊗	Eating	p152
⊗	Drinking	p155
⊙	Entertainment	p157
⊙	Shopping	p157

5e

13e

14e

15e

R Soufflot

R Gay Lussac

Bd St-Michel

Jardin du Luxembourg

Bd du Montparnasse

Bd Raspail

Av du Maine

Bd du Montparnasse

Av du Maine

Bd de Vaugirard

Bd Pasteur

R Froidevaux

Av Colonel Henri Rol-Tanguy

Av Denfert Rochereau

Val de Grâce

Observatoire de Paris

Cimetière du Montparnasse

Tour Montparnasse

Jardin de l'Atlantique

R Jean Zay

Sights

Église St-Sulpice
CHURCH

1 Map p148, D4

Until Dan Brown set a murderous scene of *The Da Vinci Code* around the Rose Line (to the right of the middle of the nave), the few visitors to this stately church, constructed over 150 years from 1646, were fans of artist Eugène Delacroix, who painted the frescoes in the Chapelle des Stes-Agnes. (www.paroisse-saint-sulpice-paris.org, in French; place St-Sulpice, 6e; ☉7.30am-7.30pm; Ⓜ St-Sulpice)

Musée National Eugène Delacroix
MUSEUM

2 Map p148, D3

The father of French romanticism lived at this courtyard studio off a magnolia-shaded square until his death in 1863. Although his most famous works are at the Louvre, Musée d'Orsay and St-Sulpice, this much more intimate museum's collection includes oils, watercolours, pastels and drawings. (www.musee-delacroix.fr; 6 rue de Furstemberg, 6e; admission €5/free; ☉9.30am-5pm Wed-Mon; Ⓜ Mabillon or St-Germain des Prés)

Fondation Cartier Pour l'Art Contemporain
EXHIBITIONS

3 Map p148, C7

Designed by Jean Nouvel, this light-flooded space is worth checking out for the building alone, but it also hosts temporary exhibits spanning all facets of contemporary art from the 1980s on, including paintings, photography, video and fashion. (www.fondation.cartier.fr; 261 bd Raspail, 14e; admission €9.50/6.50, free 2-6pm Wed; ☉11am-10pm Tue, to 8pm Wed-Sun; Ⓜ Raspail)

Catacombes
CATACOMBS

4 Map p148, C8

Paris' most macabre sight is its series of underground passages lined with skulls and bones exhumed from the city's overflowing cemeteries and packed in here in 1785. From the belle époque building on av Colonel Henri Roi-Tanguy (adjacent to place Denfert Rochereau), descend 130 steps to prowl 2km of chilly tunnels. (www.catacombes.paris.fr; 1 av Colonel Henri Rol-Tanguy, 14e; admission €8/6; ☉10am-5pm Tue-Sun; Ⓜ Denfert Rochereau)

Local Life

Antique Shopping

Art and antique dealers congregate within the **Carré Rive Gauche** (Map p148, C1; www.carrerivegauche.com; Ⓜ Rue du Bac or Solférino). Bounded by quai Voltaire and rues de l'Université, des St-Pères and du Bac, this 'Left Bank square' is home to more than 120 specialised merchants. Antiques fairs are usually held in spring, while exhibitions take place throughout the year.

Vault, Église St-Germain des Prés

Cimetière du Montparnasse
CEMETERY

5 ⊙ Map p148, B7

Celebs laid to rest here include writers Charles Baudelaire, Guy de Maupassant, Jean-Paul Sartre and Simone de Beauvoir; playwright Samuel Beckett; singer Serge Gainsbourg; and photographer Man Ray. Free maps are available from the conservation office. (bd Edgar Quinet & rue Froidevaux, 14e; admission free; ⊙btwn 8am and 9am-btwn 5.30pm and 6pm; Ⓜ Edgar Quinet or Raspail)

Église St-Germain des Prés
CHURCH

6 ⊙ Map p148, D3

Built in the 11th century on the site of an abbey, this charming Romanesque church is Paris' oldest and was the city's main centre of Catholic worship until it was eclipsed by Notre Dame. It's the (rumoured) resting place of its namesake, St Germain (AD 496–576), the city's first bishop. (www.eglise-sgp. org, in French; 3 place St-Germain des Prés; ⊙8am-7pm Mon-Sat, 9am-8pm Sun; Ⓜ St-Germain des Prés)

Tour Montparnasse
TOWER

7 ⊙ Map p148, B6

In low-rise Paris, this early '70s 210m-high skyscraper sticks out like a sore thumb. On the upside, its 56th-floor exhibition centre and bar (reached in 38 seconds in Europe's fastest lift/elevator) and 59th-floor observation terrace (reached by stairs) offer stupendous views and are about the only spots in Paris where you can't see this unsightly smoked-glass office block. (www.tourmontparnasse56.com; rue de l'Arrivée, 15e; admission €11.50/8.50; ☺9.30am-11.30pm Apr-Sep, to 10.30pm Sun-Thu, to 11pm Fri & Sat Oct-Mar; Ⓜ Montparnasse Bienvenüe)

Musée de la Poste
MUSEUM

8 ⊙ Map p148, A6

Anyone inspired by travel and communications will enjoy this postal museum. Exhibits span antique postal equipment and early French stamps and telecommunication. Imaginative temporary exhibitions could be anything from artistic letter boxes to wartime postal services. (www.musee delaposte.fr, in French; 34 bd de Vaugirard, 15e; admission €5/3.50; ☺10am-6pm Mon-Wed & Fri-Sat, to 8pm Thu; Ⓜ Montparnasse Bienvenüe or Pasteur)

Musée de la Monnaie de Paris
MUSEUM

9 ⊙ Map p148, D2

Extensive renovations of the 18th-century former royal mint the Hôtel de la Monnaie are due to incorporate Michelin-starred chef Guy Savoy's restaurant. Stay tuned... (www.mon naiedeparis.fr, in French; 11 quai de Conti, 6e; ☺closed for renovation until 2013; Ⓜ Pont Neuf)

Eating

Bouillon Racine
BRASSERIE €€

10 ✕ Map p148, E4

Secluded in a quiet street, this heritage-listed 1906 art nouveau brasserie has magnificent mirrored walls, floral motifs and ceramic tiling. The food is by no means an afterthought, with superbly executed dishes such as stuffed, spit-roasted suckling pig, pork shank in Rodenbach red beer, and scallops and shrimps with lobster coulis. (✆01 44 32 15 60; www.bouillonracine.com; 3 rue Racine, 6e; mains €16.40-22.90☺noon-11pm; Ⓜ Cluny-La Sorbonne)

Brasserie Lipp
BRASSERIE €€

11 ✕ Map p148, C3

Elegantly poured beers in tall glasses and brasserie fare such as pork knuckle are served by waiters in black waistcoats, bow ties and long white aprons at this historic haunt. Hemingway sang its praises in *A Moveable Feast* and today its faded glamour is neither too faded nor too glamorous but simply perfect. (✆01 45 48 53 91; 151 bd St-Germain, 6e; mains €17-24; ☺11.45am-12.45am; Ⓜ St-Germain des Prés)

L'Atelier de Joël Robuchon

INTERNATIONAL €€€

12 Map p148, C2

Within the Hôtel Pont Royal, Joël Robuchon's contemporary cuisine is served at long counters rather than separate tables, reflecting the increasing numbers of Parisians dining alone who still want to eat *very* well. The

 Local Life

On a Roll: Paris' Mass Skates

Paris is home to the world's largest inline mass skate, **Pari-Roller** (Map p148, A6; www.pari-roller.com; to/from place Raoul Dautry, 14e; admission free; ⏱Fri 10pm-1am, arrive 9.30pm; Ⓜ Montparnasse Bienvenüe), which regularly attracts over 10,000 bladers and covers a different 30-odd-km route each week. Dubbed 'Friday Night Fever', routes incorporate cobblestones and downhill stretches, and are geared for experienced bladers only (for your safety and everyone else's).

Less feverish are the courses covered by **Rollers & Coquillages** (p101), though you'll still need basic proficiency (ie knowing how to brake!).

Both of Paris' mass-skates are accompanied by yellow-jersey-clad volunteer marshals, along with police (some on inline skates) and ambulances. Wear bright clothes to make yourself visible to drivers and other skaters.

hotel's mahogany-panelled bar (once the hangout of Aldous Huxley, Henry Miller, Truman Capote and TS Eliot) is ideal for pre- or post-meal drink. (📞01 42 22 56 56; www.hotel-pont-royal.com; 5 rue de Montalembert, 7e; mains €32-67; ⏱lunch & dinner; Ⓜ Rue du Bac)

Le Dôme

SEAFOOD €€€

13 Map p148, C6

So the story goes, it was here that Gertrude Stein allegedly persuaded Henri Matisse to open his artists' academy – only for Matisse to later add his voice to the *Testimony against Gertrude Stein* over her 1933 *Autobiography of Alice B Toklas*. Le Dôme is still one of the swishest places around for a seafood extravaganza. (📞01 43 35 25 81; 108 bd du Montparnasse, 14e; mains €37.20-49.30, seafood platter €54; ⏱lunch & dinner; Ⓜ Vavin)

Le Salon d'Hélène

FRENCH €€€

14 Map p148, C4

Female star chefs are a rarity in Paris, but Hélène Darroze is a stellar exception. These premises house both her elegant Michelin-starred restaurant upstairs and this relaxed salon downstairs. Renowned for its multicourse tasting menus, Le Salon d'Hélène's dishes reflect Darroze's native southwestern France, such as wood-grilled foie gras. (📞01 42 22 00 11; www.helenedarroze.com; 4 rue d'Assas, 6e; lunch/dinner menus from €28/85; ⏱lunch & dinner Tue-Sat; Ⓜ Sèvres-Babylone)

Local Life

Rue de Seine & Rue de Buci

Food shops and street-market stalls cluster around the intersection of rues de Seine and de Buci, including France's only outlet of Turin gelato-maker **Grom** (Map p148, D3; www.grom.fr; 81 rue de Seine; ice cream from €3.50; ⏰1-10.30pm Mon-Wed, 1pm-midnight Thu-Sat, noon-10.30pm Sun) serving flavours made from high-grade ingredients like Syrian pistachio nuts and Venezuelan chocolate chips.

Roger La Grenouille   FRENCH €€

15   Map p148, E3

Nine varieties of frogs' legs are served at the time-worn institution 'Roger the Frog', with dozens more frog sculptures and statues scattered about. If you're squeamish about devouring Roger and his mates, roast pheasant with dried figs and cod with roast vegetables are also on the menu. Service is head and shoulders above many of the neighbourhood's restaurants. (☎01 56 24 24 34; 26-28 rue des Grands Augustins, 6e; lunch/dinner menus from €19/24; ⏰lunch Tue-Sat, dinner Mon-Sat; Ⓜ St-Michel)

Marché Raspail   MARKET €

16   Map p148, B4

A traditional open-air market on Tuesday and Friday, Marché Raspail is especially popular on Sundays when it's filled with organic produce. (bd Raspail btwn rue de Rennes & rue du Cherche Midi, 6e; ⏰regular market 7am-2.30pm Tue & Fri, organic market 9am-3pm Sun; Ⓜ Rennes)

Pères et Filles   CAFE, RESTAURANT €€

17   Map p148, D3

Retractable timber-framed glass doors opening on to the street make this a good spot for people-watching while dining on French fare with fusion elements or stopping by for a drink and banter with the fun-loving staff. Inside black-and-white photos and books line the walls of the spacious ground floor and mezzanine. (☎01 43 25 00 28; 81 rue de Seine, 6e; mains €18-24; ⏰noon-midnight; Ⓜ Mabillon)

La Coupole   BRASSERIE €€

18   Map p148, C6

This art deco brasserie's muraled columns were painted by artists including Chagall; and Simone de Beauvoir worked on *L'Invitée (The Guest)* here in 1940. Classic brasserie fare includes seafood; it's a great option if you're travelling with kids, who are given pencils and game-filled notebooks and can choose from waffles, fruit cocktails and more on their own menu. (www.lacoupole-paris.com, in French; 102 bd du Montparnasse, 14e; 2-/3-course menus €28/33.50; ⏰8.30am-midnight Sun-Wed, to 1am Thu-Sat; Ⓜ Vavin)

Marché Brancusi

MARKET €

19 Map p148, A7

Overdose on organic produce at this weekly open-air market. (place Constantin Brancusi, 14e; ⊙9am-3pm Sat; MGaîté)

Drinking

Les Deux Magots

CAFE

20 Map p148, C3

If ever there were a cafe that summed up St-Germain des Prés' early 20th-century literary scene, it's this former hangout of anyone who was anyone. You will need to spend *beaucoup* to sip a coffee or hot chocolate in a wicker chair on the terrace, shaded by dark-green awnings and geraniums spilling from window boxes, but it's an undeniable piece of Parisian history. (www.lesdeuxmagots.fr; 170 bd St-Germain, 6e; ⊙7.30am-1am; MSt-Germain des Prés)

Les Deux Magots

Café de Flore

CAFE

21 Map p148, C3

A St-Germain des Prés landmark, this 1880s cafe is where Sartre and de Beauvoir essentially set up office, writing in its warmth during the Nazi occupation. (www.cafedeflore.fr, in French; 172 bd St-Germain, 6e; ⊙7am-2am; MSt-Germain des Prés)

Bistro des Augustins

BAR, BISTRO

22 Map p148, E3

Plastered with old advertising posters from the *bouquiniste* (booksellers) stalls opposite, this authentic bistro and bar is a cosy spot for a glass of red or scrumptious bistro fare. (www.bistrodesaugustins.com; 39 quai des Grands Augustins, 6e; ⊙10am-1am; MSt-Michel)

La Closerie des Lilas

BRASSERIE, BAR

23 Map p148, D7

With a legacy stretching back to Baudelaire, 'the Lilac Enclosure' is where Hemingway wrote much of *The Sun Also Rises*. Brass plaques tell you where he and such luminaries as Picasso, Apollinaire and Samuel Beckett imbibed. In addition to the bar, there's a hedged terrace adjoining the brasserie and an upmarket

Top Tip

Discounted Theatre Tickets

For cheap tickets head to **Kiosque Théâtre Montparnasse** (Map p148, A6; www.kiosquetheatre.com, in French; parvis Montparnasse, 15e; ⏱12.30-8pm Tue-Sat, to 4pm Sun; Ⓜ Montparnasse Bienvenüe) – see also p186.

restaurant. (www.closeriedeslilas.fr; 171 bd du Montparnasse, 6e; ⏱bar 11pm-1.30am, brasserie noon-1am, restaurant lunch & dinner; Ⓜ Port Royal)

Le Select   CAFE

24 🍷 Map p148, C6

This Montparnasse institution was the first of the area's grand cafes to open late into the night in its 1920s heyday, and still draws everyone from beer-swigging students to whisky-swilling politicians. (99 bd du Montparnasse, 6e; ⏱7am-2am Sun-Thu, to 4am Fri & Sat; Ⓜ Vavin)

Les Etages St-Germain   BAR

25 🍷 Map p148, D3

Spilling from its dark-red interior, Les Etages' terrace wraps around two bustling streets in the heart of St-Germain des Prés and is positively hopping on a sunny afternoon or balmy night. (5 rue de Buci, 6e; ⏱noon-2am; Ⓜ Odéon)

La Ruche   CAFE

26 🍷 Map p148, B6

Even when other cafes in the Montparnasse area are quiet, this cherry-red, split-level cafe with funky light fittings buzzes with a young, fun crowd. (73 bd du Montparnasse, 14e; ⏱6am-2am; Ⓜ Montparnasse Bienvenüe)

La Palette   CAFE

27 🍷 Map p148, D2

One of Henry Miller's favourites, this mirror-lined cafe, which opens to a covered terrace, was also a haunt of Cézanne and Braque, and these days is popular with art dealers. (www.cafelapaletteparis.com; 43 rue de Seine, 6e; ⏱6.30am-2am Mon-Sat; Ⓜ Mabillon)

Le Pré   BAR

28 🍷 Map p148, D3

Mauve-and-orange wicker chairs line the terrace of this groovy drinking spot, while inside the chrome-and-laminex bar resembles a '50s Airstream trailer. (www.cafelepreparis.com, in French; 4-6 rue du Four; ⏱24hr; Ⓜ Mabillon)

Le Wagg   NIGHTCLUB

29 🍷 Map p148, D3

Although it's not as hip as many Right Bank party spots, this Terrence Conran club (associated with the popular Fabric in London) isn't as hard to get into, either, and has slick fixtures and a contemporary design. The dance floor starts filling up in the wee hours; check the website for parties and events. (www.wagg.fr, in French; 62 rue Mazarine, 6e; ⏱11pm-6.45am Thu-Sat, 5.30pm-midnight Sun; Ⓜ Odéon)

Entertainment

Le Lucernaire
CULTURAL CENTRE

30 ⭐ Map p148, C5

Sunday-evening concerts – from *chansons* to classical guitar – are a permanent fixture on the impressive repertoire of this dynamic arts centre, which also has exhibitions, theatre and films. (www.lucernaire.fr, in French; 53 rue Notre Dame des Champs, 6e; ⏱restaurant & bar 10am-10pm or later Mon-Fri, from 3pm Sat & Sun; Ⓜ Notre Dame des Champs)

Théâtre du Vieux Colombier
THEATRE

31 ⭐ Map p148, C3

One of the three venues of the **Comédie Française** (p65), France's oldest theatre company, staging classic works. (www.comedie-francaise.fr; rue du Vieux Colombier, 6e; Ⓜ St-Sulpice)

Shopping

A La Recherche de Jane
ACCESSORIES

32 🔒 Map p148, E3

This *chapelier* (milliner) has literally thousands of handcrafted hats on hand for both men and women, and

also makes them to order. Hours can vary. (http://alarecherchedejane. wordpress.com, in French; 41 rue Dauphine, 6e; ⏱11.30am-7.30pm Tue-Sat, 12.30-7pm Sun; Ⓜ St-Germain des Prés)

Plastiques
HOMEWARES

33 🔒 Map p148, C4

Lollypop-coloured tableware (trays, serving bowls, dinner settings etc) and cookware (whisks, mixing bowls and much more) fill this original, inexpensive boutique. (www.plastiques-paris.fr; 103 rue de Rennes, 6e; ⏱10.15am-7pm Mon-Sat; Ⓜ Rennes)

Max Maroquinerie Bagagerie et Accessoires
ACCESSORIES

34 🔒 Map p148, D3

Among the wares of this handbag boutique are small-run, limited-edition Frederic T totes for extremely reasonable prices. (45 rue Dauphine, 6e; ⏱noon-7pm Mon-Sat; Ⓜ Odéon)

Village Voice
BOOKS

35 🔒 Map p148, D3

On a quaint backstreet, this English-language bookshop specialises in North American literature (including obscure Hemingway novellas), and has an excellent range of French literature in translation. It hosts regular readings and literary events. (www. villagevoicebookshop.com; 6 rue Princesse, 6e; ⏱2-7.30pm Mon, 10am-7.30pm Tue-Sat, noon-6pm Sun; Ⓜ Mabillon)

Understand
Paris in Print & on Screen

Paris has been the inspiration for countless works of literature over the centuries, and is at least as much a star as the actors who compete with it on the big screen. Below is a selection of some of the best books and films set in the city.

Books

Les Misérables (Victor Hugo; 1862) Epic novel adapted to the stage and screen, tracing 20 years in the life of convict Jean Valjean through the battles and barricades of early 19th-century Paris.

Life: A User's Manual (Georges Perec; 1978) Intricately structured novel distilling Parisian life through a parade of characters inhabiting an apartment block between 1833 and 1975.

Down and Out in Paris and London (George Orwell; 1933) Eric Blair's (aka Orwell's) first published work is a no-holds-barred account of early 20th-century Paris, recounting his days as a downtrodden dishwasher in a Parisian hotel.

A Moveable Feast (Ernest Hemingway; 1964) Wry work recalling the author's early writing career in the 1920s with priceless vignettes depicting his contemporaries including F Scott Fitzgerald, Gertrude Stein and Ford Maddox Ford.

Films

Midnight in Paris (2011) Paris' timeless magic is palpable in Woody Allen's love letter to the city.

À Bout de Souffle (Breathless; 1960) Filmed with hand-held cameras, this new-wave story of a thief who kills a policeman revolutionised cinema.

La Haine (Hate; 1995) Raw, angst- and violence-ridden film shot in black and white. Three teenagers from Paris' *banlieues* (suburbs), trapped by crime, poverty and xenophobia, wait for a train overnight.

La Môme (La Vie en Rose; 2007) Acclaimed biopic of 'little sparrow' Édith Piaf, uncannily played by Marion Cotillard. Most songs in the soundtrack use Piaf's own voice.

Les Etages St-Germain (p156)

Gérard Durand
ACCESSORIES

36 Map p148, B3

Brightly coloured, boldly printed *col-lants* (tights) and *bas* (stockings) are the specialty of this boutique, which also stocks equally vibrant socks, scarves and gloves. (www.accessoires-mode.com, in French; 75-77 rue du Bac, 7e; 9am-7pm Mon-Sat; Rue du Bac)

Sonia Rykiel
FASHION

37 Map p148, C3

In the heady days of May 1968 amid Paris' student uprisings, Sonia Rykiel opened her inaugural Left Bank bou-tique here, and went on to revolution-ise garments with inverted seams, 'no hems' and 'no lining'. Her diffusion labels (including children's wear) are housed in separate boutiques nearby, with other outlets around Paris. (www.soniarykiel.com; 175 bd St-Germain, 6e; 10.30am-7pm Mon-Sat; St-Germain des Prés)

Cine Reflet
BOOKS

38 Map p148, E4

An old projector takes pride of place at this cinema-dedicated bookshop. (14 rue Monsieur-le-Prince, 6e; 1-8pm Mon-Tue & Thu-Sat, to 9.15pm Wed; Odéon)

Top Sights
Père Lachaise

Getting There

Père Lachaise is about 4.5km northeast of Notre Dame.

Ⓜ **Metro** Philippe Auguste (line 2), Gambetta (lines 3 and 3b) and Père Lachaise (lines 2 and 3).

Paris is a collection of villages and the 48 hectares of cobbled lanes and elaborate tombs, with a population (as it were) of more than a million, certainly qualifies as one in its own right. The world's most visited cemetery was founded in 1804, and initially attracted few funerals because of its distance from the city centre. The authorities responded by exhuming famous remains and resettling them here. Their marketing ploy worked and Cimetière du Père Lachaise has been Paris' most fashionable final address ever since.

Don't Miss

Édith Piaf's Grave
DIVISION 97

Songstress Édith Piaf (née Gassion) died in 1963, leaving behind a string of stirring classics like *Non, je ne regrette rien* and *La Vie en Rose*. Time-honoured tomb traditions at Père Lachaise include leaving red roses on Piaf's grave.

Jim Morrison's Grave
DIVISION 6

Père Lachaise's most venerated tomb belongs to the Doors' Jim Morrison, who died in a Marais apartment in 1971. Prior to his family's complaints, 'traditions' included fans taking drugs and having sex on his grave. There's now a permanent security guard and code-of-conduct leaflet.

Oscar Wilde's Grave
DIVISION 89

Topped by a naked winged angel, the flamboyant grave of Irish playwright and humorist Oscar Wilde, who died in Paris in 1900 (see p168), was plastered in lipstick kisses until a glass cover was installed in 2011.

Marcel Proust's Grave
DIVISION 85

Madeleine cakes are traditionally left on the tomb of Marcel Proust (1871–1922), author of *À la Recherche du Temps Perdu* (Remembrance of Things Past).

Georges Seurat's Grave
DIVISION 66

The tomb of pointillism pioneer Georges Seurat (1859–1891) is one of many that resemble a small house, adding to Père Lachaise's village-like feel.

---

www.pere-lachaise.com

main entrance bd de Ménilmontant, 20e

admission free

⊗ 8am-6pm Mon-Sat, 9am-6pm Sun mid-Mar–early Nov, 8.30am-5.30pm Mon-Sat, 9am-5.30pm Sun early Nov–mid-Mar

☑ Top Tips

▶ Père Lachaise has five entrances, including two on bd de Ménilmontant.

▶ Maps locating noteworthy graves are posted around the cemetery and on its website, or you could pick up a free map from the conservation office (16 rue du Repos, 20e).

▶ A visit to Père Lachaise fits well with a stroll along Canal St-Martin and around (p84) and/or exploring the Centre Pompidou and the Marais (p88) neighbourhood.

✕ Take a Break

▶ Boutique hotel **Mama Shelter** (p201) has a groovy restaurant, pizzeria and bar (all open to nonguests).

Top Sights
Versailles

Getting There

Versailles is about 22km southwest of Notre Dame.

🚇 **RER** Line C5 (€3.20, 45 minutes, frequent) from Left Bank RER stations travels to Versailles–Rive Gauche station.

When it comes to over-the-top opulence, the Château de Versailles is in a class of its own, even for France. Louis XIV transformed his father's hunting lodge into the colossal Château de Versailles in the mid-17th century. The baroque palace was the kingdom's political capital and the seat of the royal court from 1682 until the fateful events of 1789 when revolutionaries massacred the palace guard and dragged Louis XVI and Marie-Antoinette back to Paris, where they were ingloriously guillotined. The Unesco-listed estate sprawls over 900 hectares of fountain-graced gardens, pond-filled parks and woods.

Statue, Versailles

Don't Miss

The Château de Versailles in Numbers

Louis XIV ordered 700 rooms, 2153 windows, 352 chimneys and 28 acres of roof for the 580m-long main palace. It housed the entire court of 6000 (plus 5000 servants). The finest talent of the day installed some 6300 paintings, 2000 sculptures and statues, 15,000 engravings and 5000 furnishings and *objets d'art*.

The Hall of Mirrors

The palace's opulence peaks in its shimmering and sparkling Galerie des Glaces (Hall of Mirrors). This 75m-long ballroom with 17 giant mirrors on one side and an equal number of windows on the other has to be seen to be believed.

The King's and Queen's State Apartments

Luxurious, ostentatious appointments – frescoes, marble, gilt and woodcarvings, with themes and symbols drawn from Greek and Roman mythology – ooze from every last moulding, cornice, ceiling and door in the palace's Grands Appartements du Roi et de la Reine (King's and Queen's State Apartments).

Guided Tours

To access areas that are otherwise off limits and learn more about Versailles' history, take a 90-minute **guided tour** (€16, ⊘English-language tours 9.30am & 2pm Tue-Sun) of the Private Apartments of Louis XV and Louis XVI and the Opera House or Royal Chapel. Tours include access to the most famous parts of the palace; prebook online.

The Gardens

Celebrated landscape artist André Le Nôtre was commissioned by Louis XIV to design the château's magnificent **gardens** (admission free

www.chateau
versailles.fr

admission passport (estate-wide access) €18, with musical events €25, palace €15; ⊘8am-6pm Tue-Sat, 9am-6pm Sun Apr-Oct, 8.30am-5.30pm Tue-Sat, 9am-5.30pm Sun Nov-Mar

☑ Top Tips

▶ By noon queues for tickets and entering the château both spiral out of control: arrive early morning and avoid Tuesday and Sunday, the palace's busiest days.

▶ Save time by prepurchasing tickets online or at Fnac (www.fnac. com) branches and head straight to Entrance A.

▶ Hire an electric car, hop on the shuttle train or rent a bike or boat to see all of the vast estate.

✗ Take a Break

▶ Eateries dotted around the estate include **Angelina** (www. angelina-versailles.fr; Cour des Princes; mains €10-24; ⊘10am-6pm Tue-Sat Apr-Oct, to 5pm Tue-Sat Nov-Mar) – see also p63.

Louis XIV (1643–1715) ascended the throne in 1643 at the age of five. Throughout his long reign, Louis sought to project the power of the French monarchy – bolstered by claims of divine right – both at home and abroad. He involved France in a series of costly, almost continuous wars with Holland, Austria and England, which gained France territory but nearly bankrupted the treasury. State taxation to fill the coffers caused widespread poverty and vagrancy in Paris, by then a city of almost 600,000 people.

But Louis was able to quash the ambitious, feuding aristocracy and create the first truly centralised French state. By pouring huge sums of money into building his extravagant palace, he turned his nobles into courtiers, forcing them to compete with one another for royal favour and reducing them to ineffectual sycophants.

except during musical events; ⏰8am-8.30pm Apr-Oct, 8am-6pm Tue-Sat Nov-Mar). The best view over the rectangular pools is from the Hall of Mirrors. Pathways include the Royal Walk's verdant 'green carpet', with smaller paths leading to leafy groves.

The Canals
The Grand Canal, 1.6km long and 62m wide, is oriented to reflect the setting sun. It's traversed by the 1km-long Petit Canal, forming a cross-shaped body of water with a perimeter of over 5.5km.

Marie-Antoinette's Estate
Northwest of the main palace is the **Domaine de Marie-Antoinette** (Marie-Antoinette's Estate; admission €10; ⏰noon-6.30pm Tue-Sat Apr-Oct, to 5.30pm Tue-Sat Nov-Mar). Tickets include the Grand and Petit Trianon palaces, and

the **Hameau de la Reine** (a mock village of thatched cottages); admission is included in passport tickets.

The Trianon Palaces
The pink-colonnaded Grand Trianon was built in 1687 for Louis XIV and his family as a place of escape from the rigid etiquette of the court, and renovated under Napoleon I in the Empire style. The ochre-coloured, 1760s Petit Trianon was redecorated in 1867 by the consort of Napoleon III, Empress Eugénie, who added Louis XVI-style furnishings.

The Shows
Versailles mounts stirring *spectacles* (shows). Check the program and buy **tickets** (☎01 30 83 78 89; www.chateau versaillesspectacles.fr) in advance when possible.

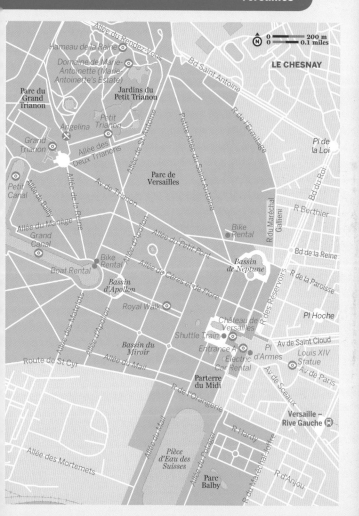

LE CHESNAY

Allée du Rendez-vous

Hameau de la Reine

Domaine de Marie-
Antoinette (Marie-
Antoinette's Estate)

Bd Saint Antoine

Parc du
Grand
Trianon

Jardins du
Petit Trianon

Petit
Trianon

Angelina

Grand
Trianon

Allée des
Deux Trianons

R de l'Hermitage

Pl de
la Loi

Bd du Roi

Petit
Canal

Allée de Bailly

Av de Trianon

Allée de la Reine

Petite Allée du Saint Antoine

Allée du Saint Antoine

Parc de
Versailles

R du Maréchal
Gallieni

R Berthier

Allée du Manege

Grand
Canal

Boat Rental

Bike
Rental

Allée du Petit Pont

Bike
Rental

Bassin
de Neptune

Bd de la Reine

R de la Paroisse

Allée de Cerès et de Flore

Allée des Matelots

Bassin
d'Apollon

Royal Walk

R des Réservoirs

Pl Hoche

Château de
Versailles

Allée d'Apollon

Bassin du
Miroir

Route de St Cyr

Allée du Mail

Shuttle Train

Entrance A

Electric
Car Rental

Pl
d'Armes

Av de Saint Cloud

Louis XIV
Statue

Av de Paris

Av de Sceaux

Parterre
du Midi

R de l'Orangerie

Versaille –
Rive Gauche

R Hardy

Allée du Mail

Allée des Mortemets

Pièce
d'Eau des
Suisses

Allée de l'Orangerie

Parc
Balby

R du Maréchal Joffre

R d'Anjou

0   200 m
0   0.1 miles

The Best of
Paris

Paris' Best Walks

Left Bank Literary Loop 168

Seine-Side Romantic
Meander 170

Right Bank Time Passages 172

Paris' Best...

Architecture.............................. 174

Cooking & Wine-Tasting
Courses 176

Markets 177

Museums 178

History.......................................180

Eating 182

Drinking 184

Literary Paris............................185

Nights Out 186

Gay & Lesbian Paris 188

Parks & Gardens.......................189

Fashion 190

Churches 192

Multicultural Paris....................193

Panoramas 194

For Free 195

Tours 196

Gourmet Shops 197

For Kids 198

Gargoyle, Notre Dame (p112)
JONATHAN SMITH/LONELY PLANET IMAGES ©

Best Walks
Left Bank Literary Loop

🏃 The Walk

It wasn't only Paris' reputation for liberal thought and relaxed morals that lured writers in the early 20th century – Left Bank Paris was cheap and, unlike Prohibition-era America, you could drink to your heart's content. This walk takes in pivotal places from the era. For more on Literary Paris, see p185.

Start Rue du Cardinal Lemoine; Ⓜ Cardinal Lemoine

Finish Rue Notre Dame des Champs; Ⓜ Port Royal

Length 6.5km; three hours

🍴 Take a Break

The route is littered with cafes and brasseries with literary associations, including favourites of Jean-Paul Sartre and Simone de Beauvoir Les Deux Magots (p155) and Café de Flore (p155), Hemingway's favoured Brasserie Lipp (p152) and La Closerie des Lilas (p155), and literary luminary magnets Le Dôme (p153) and Le Select (p156).

Shakespeare & Company

❶ Rue du Cardinal Lemoine

Walk southwest along rue du Cardinal Lemoine, peering down the passageway at **No 71**, where James Joyce finished *Ulysses* in apartment E. From 1922 to 1923, Ernest Hemingway lived at **No 74**.

❷ Paul Verlaine's Garret

Hemingway wrote in a top-floor garret of a hotel at **39 rue Descartes** – the very hotel where the poet Paul Verlaine died. Ignore the incorrect plaque.

❸ George Orwell's Boarding House

In 1928 George Orwell stayed in a boarding house above **6 rue du Pot de Fer**, which he called 'rue du Coq d'Or' in *Down and Out in Paris and London* (1933).

❹ Jack Kerouac's Hotel

The **Relais Hôtel du Vieux Paris** at 9 rue Gît le Cœur was a favourite of poet Allen Ginsberg and Beat writer Jack Kerouac in the 1950s.

❺ Shakespeare & Company

The original **Shakespeare & Company** bookshop stood at 12 rue de l'Odéon, where owner Sylvia Beach lent books to Hemingway and published *Ulysses* for Joyce in 1922. It was closed during WWII's Nazi occupation; see p139 for the present incarnation.

❻ Henry Miller's Room

Henry Miller stayed on the 5th floor of **36 rue Bonaparte** in 1930; he wrote about the experience in *Letters to Emil* (1989).

❼ Oscar Wilde's Hotel

The former Hôtel d'Alsace (now **L'Hôtel**), 13 rue des Beaux-Arts, is where Oscar Wilde died in 1900.

❽ Hemingway's First Night in Paris

Hemingway spent his first night in the city at the **Hôtel d'Angleterre**, 44 rue Jacob.

❾ Gertrude Stein's Home

Ezra Pound and Hemingway were among those entertained at **27 rue de Fleurus**, where Gertrude Stein lived with Alice B Toklas.

❿ Rue Notre Dame des Champs

Pound lived at **70bis rue Notre Dame des Champs**, while Hemingway's first apartment in this area was above a sawmill at **No 113**.

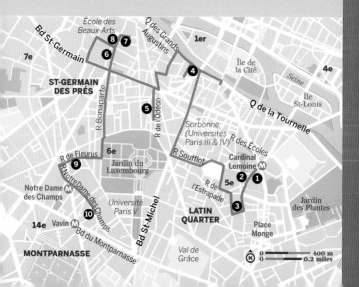

Best Walks
Seine-Side Romantic Meander

🏃 The Walk

The world's most romantic city has no shortage of beguiling spots, but the Seine and its surrounds are Paris at its most seductive. On this walk, you'll pass graceful gardens, palaces, intimate parks, a flower market and an enchanting bookshop. Descend the steps along the quays where it's possible to stroll along the river's edge.

Start Place de la Concorde; Ⓜ Concorde

Finish Jardin des Plantes; Ⓜ Gare d'Austerlitz

Length 7km; three hours

🍴 Take a Break

The Seine's islands – the Île de la Cité and the Île St-Louis – have plenty of enticing places to eat and/or drink, such as Ma Salle à Manger (p122), as well as some picturesque spots for a picnic. Or simply leave it to serendipity (which is, after all, the essence of every great romance).

OLIVER STREWE/LONELY PLANET IMAGES ©

Seine

❶ Jardin des Tuileries

After taking in the 'yes-we're-really-in-Paris' panorama from **place de la Concorde** (p60), stroll through the leafy **Jardin des Tuileries** (p58).

❷ Jardin du Palais Royal

Browse the colonnaded arcades flanking the peaceful **Jardin du Palais Royal** (p58), adjoining the 17th-century palace where Louis XIV once lived.

❸ Cour Carrée

Walk through the **Jardin de l'Oratoire** to the reflective Cour Carrée of the **Louvre** (p46) and exit at the **Jardin de l'Infante** (Garden of the Princess), which Monet painted in 1867.

❹ Square du Vert Galant

From the **Pont Neuf** (p120), take the steps to the park perched at the tip of the Île de la Cité, **Square du Vert Galant** (p120), before ascending to **place du Pont Neuf** and crossing **place Dauphine**.

❺ Marché aux Fleurs

Parisians have been buying bouquets at the **Marché aux Fleurs** (p124) for centuries. Choose carefully: tradition has it that chrysanthemums are only for cemeteries, carnations bring bad luck, and yellow roses imply adultery.

❻ Shakespeare & Company

Amid handpainted quotations, make a wish in the wishing well, leave a message on the 'mirror of love' or curl up with a volume of poetry in the attic-like reading library of the magical bookshop **Shakespeare & Company** (p139).

❼ Love Locks

Cross **Pont de l'Archevêché** – one of many Parisian bridges covered in padlocks (to the chagrin of city authorities). The locks are attached by couples who throw the key into the Seine as a symbol of eternal love.

❽ Berthillon

From the Île de la Cité take **Pont St-Louis** (p120) to the Île St-Louis, lined with quaint boutiques and tea-rooms, and share an ice cream from famous *glacier* (ice-cream maker) **Berthillon** (p122).

❾ Jardin des Plantes

End your romantic meander at the tranquil **Jardin des Plantes** (p134). For the ultimate denouement, cruise back along the Seine by Batobus (p204).

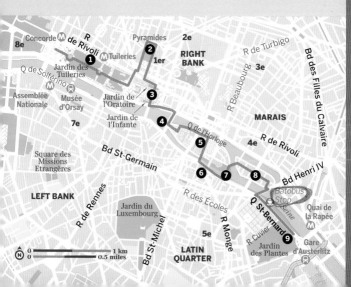

Best Walks
Right Bank Time Passages

🏃 The Walk

Stepping into the *passages couverts* (covered shopping arcades) of the Right Bank is the best way to get a feel for what life was like in early 19th-century Paris. Around half a century later, Paris had around 150 of these sumptuously decorated arcades; for more on their history, see p68. This walking tour is tailor-made for a rainy day, but it's best avoided on a Sunday when some arcades are shut tight.

Start Galerie Véro Dodat; Ⓜ Louvre–Rivoli

Finish Passage Verdeau; Ⓜ Le Peletier

Length 3km; two hours

✕ Take a Break

Like visitors 150 years ago, on this walk you can dine and drink within the arcades as well as shop and even attend the theatre. For a twin-Michelin-starred meal, book ahead to dine at Passage 53 (p61) inside the Passage des Panoramas.

Passages des Panoramas

❶ Galerie Véro Dodat

At 19 rue Jean-Jacques Rousseau, **Galerie Véro Dodat** retains its 19th-century skylights, ceiling murals, Corinthian columns, tiled floor, gas globe fittings (now electric) and shopfronts including furniture restorers.

❷ Galerie Vivienne

Built in 1826, **Galerie Vivienne** is decorated with floor mosaics and bas-reliefs on the upper walls. Don't miss wine shop **Legrand Filles & Fils** (p67), **Wolff et Descourtis**, selling silk scarves, and **Emilio Robba**, one of the most beautiful flower shops in Paris.

❸ Galerie Colbert

Enter this 1826-built passage, featuring a huge glass dome and rotunda, from rue Vivienne. Exit on rue des Petits Champs (and check out the fresco above).

❹ Passage Choiseul

This 1824-built, 45m-long passage has scores

of shops including those specialising in discount and vintage clothing, beads and costume jewellery as well as cheap eateries. Comedies are performed at the **Théâtre des Bouffes Parisiens**, which backs onto the passage's northern end.

⑤ Passage des Panoramas

From 10 rue St-Marc, enter Paris' oldest covered arcade (1800), the first to be lit by gas (1817). It was expanded in 1834 with four interconnecting passages – Feydeau, Montmartre, St-Marc and Variétés – and is full of eateries and unusual shops, such as autograph dealer **Arnaud Magistry**. Exit at 11 bd Montmartre.

⑥ Passage Jouffroy

Enter at 10-12 bd Montmartre into passage Jouffroy, Paris' last major passage (1847). There's a wax museum, the **Musée Grévin**, and wonderful boutiques including bookshops, silversmiths and **M&G Segas**, where Toulouse-

Lautrec bought his walking sticks. Exit at 9 rue de la Grange Batelière.

⑦ Passage Verdeau

Cross the road to 6 rue de la Grange

Batelière to the last of this stretch of covered arcades. There's lots to explore: vintage comic books, needlepoint, daguerreotypes and more. The northern exit is at 31bis rue du Faubourg Montmartre.

Best
Architecture

Several key eras are woven into Paris' contemporary architectural fabric. From the 11th century magnificent cathedrals and palaces were built. Baron Haussmann's demolition of the city's disease-ridden streets made way for boulevards, lined by neoclassical buildings. And, after the art nouveau movement, additions centred on French presidents' bold *grands projets* (great projects).

JOHN SONES/LONELY PLANET IMAGES ©

Haussmann's Renovation

Paris' appearance today is largely the work of Baron Georges-Eugène Haussmann (1809–91). Under Napoleon III, Haussmann completely rebuilt swathes of Paris between 1853 and 1870, replacing chaotic narrow streets (easy to barricade in an uprising) with arrow-straight, wide thoroughfares, including the 12 avenues radiating out from the Arc de Triomphe.

Art Nouveau Influence

Art nouveau swept through the Parisian cityscape from the mid-19th century until WWI, leaving its mark on architecture, interior design, furniture and graphics. Sinuous swirls, curls and floral tendrils characterise this 'new art' movement; materials that supported its signature motifs included wrought iron, glass, richly grained timbers and marble.

Rising Skyline

Strict height limits enforced following the outrage over the construction of the 1970s eyesore Tour Montparnasse (p152) prompted a clampdown on skyscrapers. However, in 2010, due to Paris' housing and office space shortage, the city council voted to raise height limits to 180m. Advocates include Pritzker Prize–winning French architect, Jean Nouvel (1945–).

Best Art Nouveau Splendours

Eiffel Tower Paris' 'iron lady' is art nouveau at its best. (p24)

Abbesses metro entrance Hector Guimard's finest remaining metro entrance. (p75)

Galeries Lafayette Beautiful department store topped by a stunning stained-glass dome. (p66)

Musée d'Orsay It's worth visiting this monumental museum just for the 1900-built former railway station that houses it. (p58)

Le Train Bleu Resplendent example of Paris' ornate brasseries. (p86)

Best Grands Projets

Centre Pompidou
Former President
Georges Pompidou's
now-beloved cultural
centre sparked a furore
when it was unveiled in
1977. (p90)

Louvre glass pyramid
IM Pei's pyramid, insti-
gated by former Presi-
dent François Mitterrand,
likewise created an
uproar in 1989. (p48)

Opéra Bastille Mitterrand oversaw a slew of
other costly *projets* including the city's second,
state-of-the-art opera
house. (pictured left with
Colonne de Juillet; p107)

**Bibliothèque Nation-
ale de France** Another
Mitterrand-instigated
landmark, housing the
national library in book-
shaped towers. (p87)

Best Jean Nouvel Buildings

Musée du Quai Branly
President Jacques
Chirac's pet *projet*, de-
signed by Nouvel. (p30)

**Institut du Monde
Arabe** The building that
established Nouvel's
reputation blends mod-
ern and traditional Arab
elements with Western
influences. (p134)

**Fondation Cartier Pour
l'Art Contemporain**
Stunning contemporary
art space. (p150)

Best Architectural Exhibits

**Cité de l'Architecture
et du Patrimoine** Huge
space with exhibits cov-
ering Paris' architectural
history and its future.
(p42)

Pavillon de l'Arsenal
Paris' town-planning and
architectural centre has
intriguing scale models.
(p99)

Worth a Trip
The futuristic glass-and-chrome urban jungle of the La Défense business district rises just northwest of the *Périphérique* (ring road), reached
by a regular metro ticket. Its dramatic gateway is the 110m-high Carrara-
marble-and-granite **Grande Arche** (www.grandearche.com; 1 Parvis de la Défense;
admission €10/8.50; 10am-8pm Apr-Aug, to 7pm Sep-Mar; La Défense); there's an
architecture museum and info centre nearby.

Best
Cooking & Wine-Tasting Courses

KRZYSZTOF DYDYŃSKI/LONELY PLANET IMAGES ©

If dining in the city's restaurants whets your appetite, there are stacks of cookery schools offering courses for all levels of ability and budgets, even if you're only here on a lightning-quick trip. Where there's food in Paris, wine is never more than an arm's length away; plenty of places offer wine tastings and instruction for beginners through to connoisseurs.

Best Culinary Classes

Les Coulisses du Chef Cours de Cuisine Olivier Berté (☎01 40 26 14 00; www.coursdecuisine paris.com; 2nd fl, 7 rue Paul Lelong, 2e; MBourse) These three-hour courses (€100) often specialise in a theme such as sauces or soufflés. Classes for children aged seven and up cost €30.

École Le Cordon Bleu (☎01 53 68 22 50; www.cordonbleu.edu; 8 rue Léon Delhomme, 15e; MVaugirard or Convention) Learn how to impress dinner party guests at this venerable 1895-established culinary school. Short courses start from €41 for two hours.

Best Wine Appreciation Sessions

O-Château (☎01 44 73 97 80; www.o-chateau.com; 68 rue Jean-Jacques Rousseau, 1er; MLouvre-Rivoli) Oliver Magny's courses are as entertaining as they are educational. Tastings start from €30 for one hour; there are also wine and cheese lunches and wine-tasting dinners, as well as tours. Don't miss Olivier's on-the-money blog, Stuff Parisians Like.

Musée du Vin (☎01 45 25 63 26; www.museedu vinparis.com; rue des Eaux, 5 square Charles Dickens, 16e; museum admission €11.90/9.90; ⏱10am-6pm Tue-Sun; MPassy) In addition to its displays, Paris' wine museum offers instructive tastings (€59 for two hours).

Best
Markets

Nowhere encapsulates Paris' village atmosphere more than its markets. Not simply places to shop, the city's street markets are also social gatherings for the entire neighbourhood. Residents toting quintessentially Parisian canvas shopping bags on wheels chat with neighbours, fellow shoppers and stallholders and pick up culinary tips. Flea markets are full of antique, vintage and new treasures.

Street Markets

Nearly every little quarter has its own street market held at least once a week (never Mondays), where tarpaulin-topped trestle tables bow beneath spit-roasted poultry, seafood on beds of crushed ice, fresh meat, huge wheels of cheese, sun-ripened fruit and vegetables, and pâtés, preserves and other delicacies. Many markets also sell clothes, accessories, homewares and more. *Marchés biologiques* (organic markets) are also sprouting up across Paris.

Flea Markets

Exquisite antiques, vintage and retro clothing, jewellery, bric-a-brac, cheap brand-name clothing, footwear, African carvings, DVDs and electronic items are laid out at the city's colourful flea markets. Watch out for pickpockets!

Marché Bastille One of the city's largest, liveliest street market. (p103)

Marché aux Enfants Rouges Paris' oldest covered market, with communal tables where you can eat lunch. (p95)

Marché aux Puces d'Aligre Central flea market. (p109)

Marché aux Fleurs Fragrant flower market. (p124)

Worth a Trip

Europe's largest flea market, the **Marché aux Puces de St-Ouen** (www.parispuces.com; 140 rue des Rosiers, St Ouen, 18e; 9am-6pm Sat, 10am-6pm Sun, 11am-5pm Mon; Porte de Clignancourt), has over 2500 stalls spread across 10 speciality 'villages'. Among them you'll find quality antique dealers and fabulous vintage treasures. It's liveliest on Sundays; Mondays can be very quiet.

Best
Museums

WILL SALTER/LONELY PLANET IMAGES ©

The cultured French capital has literally scores of museums, harbouring treasures from throughout the ages. There's everything from major national institutions to super-specialised museums highlighting a single – sometimes offbeat – subject. Temporary exhibitions take place in diverse venues – keep an eye out for what's on while you're in town.

Planning Your Visit

Most museums close one day a week, usually Monday or Tuesday; many open late one or more nights a week – usually the least crowded time to visit. You'll also save time by prepurchasing tickets online where possible. Remember that the cut-off for entry to museums is generally half an hour to an hour before the official closing times (including times listed in this book). Audioguides are sometimes included with admission, but often incur an extra charge.

Paris' best art and specialty museums are listed below. See p180 for the best history museums, and p193 for the best multicultural museums.

National Museums Free Entry

If you can, time your trip to be here on the first Sunday of the month when you can visit the *musées nationaux* (national museums; www.rmn.fr, in French) as well as a handful of monuments for free (some during certain months only – see also p195). Temporary exhibitions still incur a charge.

City Museums Free Entry

You can visit the permanent collections of selected *musées municipaux* (city-run museums; www.paris.fr) for free any time. Temporary exhibitions incur a charge.

☑ Top Tips

▶ Save money by investing in a museum pass (p206) or taking advantage of combo deals offered by some museums.

▶ Museum admission is often reduced at certain times or on certain days.

▶ Museums generally charge extra for temporary exhibitions but often offer a discounted combo rate for permanent and temporary exhibits.

Best Impressionist Collections

Musée d'Orsay France's national museum for impressionist and related

Horse statue outside Musée d'Orsay (p142)

artistic movements is a must. (p142)

Musée de l'Orangerie
Monet conceived a stunning cycle of his *Water Lilies* series especially for this building. (pictured left; p58)

Best Modern & Contemporary Art Museums

Musée National d'Art Moderne The country's national modern and contemporary art museum, located within the striking Centre Pompidou. (p90)

Musée d'Art Moderne de la Ville de Paris
Paris' modern art museum spans the 20th century to the present day. (p40)

Dalí Espace Montmartre Showcases the work

of the surrealist master. (p78)

Best Photography Museums

Jeu de Paume France's national photography centre. (p59)

Maison Européenne de la Photographie Excellent photography exhibits. (p98)

Best Specialised Museums

Musée du Vin Wine museum (with tastings, too). (p176)

Galerie Musée Baccarat Crystal museum. (p41)

Musée du Parfum Perfume museum; displays bottles and bottling in its annex. (p60)

Worth a trip

Secluded in the Duke of Valmy's former hunting lodge, the intimate **Musée Marmottan** (www.marmottan. com; 2 rue Louis Boilly, 16e; admission €10/5; ⏲10am-8pm Tue, to 6pm Wed-Sun; Ⓜ La Muette) houses the world's largest collection of Claude Monet's works, including his *Impression: Sunrise* (1872), after which impressionism was named, plus paintings by Gauguin, Sisley, Pissarro, Renoir, Degas and Manet.

Best
History

Paris' history is a saga of battles, bloodshed, grand-scale excesses, revolution, reformation, resistance, renaissance and constant reinvention. But this epic is not just consigned to museums and archives: reminders of the capital's and the country's history are evident all over the city.

Early Beginnings

Paris was born in the 3rd century BC, when the Parisii tribe of Celtic Gauls settled on Île de la Cité. Julius Caesar ended centuries of conflict between the Gauls and Romans in 52 BC. Christianity was introduced in the 2nd century AD; in 508 Frankish king Clovis I united Gaul and made Paris his seat.

Conflicts

In the 12th century, Scandinavian Vikings pushed towards Paris heralding the Hundred Years' War with Norman England, which resulted in England gaining control of France in 1420. In 1429 Joan of Arc rallied French troops to defeat the English.

Revolution

The excesses of Louis XIV (p164) and his heirs triggered an uprising of Parisians on 14 July 1789, which kick-started the French Revolution (see p121). The government was consolidated in 1799 under Napoleon Bonaparte, who then conquered most of Europe before his defeat at Waterloo.

Reformation & Beyond

At the behest of Napoleon III, Baron Haussmann (p174) reshaped the cityscape. However, when Parisians heard of Napoleon III's capture in the war with Prussia in 1870, they demanded a republic. It gave rise to the glittering belle époque ('beautiful era'), which advanced arts and sciences.

Best Roman Legacies

Musée National du Moyen Âge Incorporates the remains of Gallo-Roman baths c AD 200. (p128)

Crypte Archéologique du Parvis Notre Dame Remains of the Gallo-Roman town of Lutetia. (p116)

Best Medieval Milestones

Notre Dame Completed in the early 14th century. (p112)

Louvre Immense 12th-century fort-turned-palace-turned-museum. (p48)

Ste-Chapelle Consecrated in 1248. (p120)

Sorbonne University founded in 1253. (pictured above; p136)

Conciergerie (p120)

Musée National du Moyen Âge Partly housed in the 15th-century Hôtel de Cluny, this is Paris' finest civil medieval building. (p128)

Best Revolutionary Sights

Place de la Bastille Site of the former prison stormed on 14 July 1789, mobilising the Revolution. (p101)

Versailles The October 1789 March on Versailles forced the royal family to leave the château. (p162)

Place de la Concorde Louis XVI and his queen, Marie-Antoinette, were among thousands guillotined where the obelisk now stands. (p60)

Conciergerie Marie-Antoinette was one of the aristocratic prisoners tried and imprisoned here. (p120)

Parc du Champ de Mars This former military training ground was the site of revolutionary festivals. (p30)

Best Parisian History Attractions

Musée Carnavalet Chronicles the history of Paris. (p98)

Forum des Images Archive of films set in Paris, plus newsreels, documentaries and advertising. (p65)

Best Cemeteries

Père Lachaise The world's most visited cemetery, with famous graves and time-honoured tomb traditions. (p160)

Cimetière du Montparnasse More famous graves, south of St-Germain des Prés. (p151)

Cimetière de Montmartre Yet more famous graves, west of Sacré-Cœur. (p78)

Best
Eating

France pioneered what is still the most influential style of cooking in the Western world and Paris is its showcase *par excellence*. Colours, textures and garnishes are impeccably arranged everywhere from simple restaurants to *haute cuisine* establishments helmed by legendary chefs. The city doesn't have its own 'local' cuisine, but is the crossroads for France's regional produce and flavours.

Evolving Trends

In addition to classical French fare, look out for cuisines from around the globe. One of the most enduring culinary trends of recent times is *bistronomique* – bistros offering pared-down regional fare, often by big-name chefs, with lower prices, which are typically referred to as 'neo-bistros'. Exclusively vegetarian establishments are emerging but still rare.

Dining Times

Breakfast (usually a baguette with butter and jam and strong coffee) is seen as a mere precursor to lunch, the traditional main meal. Starting around 12.30pm with an aperitif, it is almost always washed down with wine. Most restaurants open for dinner around 7pm or 7.30pm. Some high-end restaurants close at weekends, and many places close in August.

Menus

Eateries usually serve a *plat du jour* (dish of the day) or *formule* (fixed main course plus starter or dessert) at lunch (and occasionally at dinner), as well as *menus* (fixed-price meals) of an *entrée* (starter), *plat* (main course) and *fromage* (cheese) or dessert or both. These offer infinitely better value than ordering à la carte. Meals are often considerably cheaper at lunch than dinner.

☑ Top Tips

▶ Tap water is safe and free of charge; ask for *une carafe de l'eau* (jug of water).

▶ Doggie bags or boxes of leftovers aren't 'done', as the dining experience and the food itself are considered inseparable.

▶ Booking ahead – up to a couple of months for popular and/or high-end places – is recommended.

Best Bistros

Frenchie Hidden alleyway bistro serving sensational *menus*. (p61)

Le Miroir Stylish, creative bistro fare. (p81)

Le Jules Verne (p31), Eiffel Tower

Le Tambour Lively insomniac's favourite, decorated with Parisian street furniture. (p55)

Le Hide Smart, affordable French cuisine including decadent desserts. (p43)

Best Gastronomic Extravaganzas

Le Jules Verne Sublime fine dining directed by Alain Ducasse on the 2nd level of the Eiffel Tower. (p31)

L'Arpège Exceptionally prepared produce, especially vegetables. (p31)

Yam'Tcha Exquisitely fused French and Asian flavours, paired with teas. (p60)

Passage 53 Exciting, intricately constructed dishes; inside the city's oldest arcade. (p61)

La Tour d'Argent Centuries-old establishment overlooking Notre Dame serving signature pressed duck. (p136)

Best Boulangeries

Poilâne Famed for its handcrafted sourdough loaves – and its *Punitions* (crispy butter biscuits). (p147)

Stohrer Historic patisserie baking fabulous bread and treats including its own invention, *baba rhum* (rum-drenched brioche). (p62)

Worth a trip

'Gastronomic' doesn't do justice to the twin-Michelin-starred creations of **Michel Rostang** (☎ 01 47 63 40 77; www.michel rostang.com; 20 rue Rennequin, 17e; lunch/ dinner menus from €78/169; ⏲ lunch Tue-Sat, dinner Mon-Sat; Ⓜ Pereire) like thin-sliced bleu duck breast in blood-thickened foie gras sauce. Seriously, wow.

Best
Drinking

For Parisians, drinking and eating go together like wine and cheese, and the line between a cafe, *salon de thé* (tearoom), bistro, brasserie, bar and even a *bar à vins* (wine bar) is blurred. The line between drinking and clubbing is often nonexistent – a cafe that's quiet in midafternoon might have DJ sets in the evening and dancing later on.

JEAN-BERNARD CARILLET/LONELY PLANET IMAGES ©

Cafe Culture

Paris' cafes have long been the city's communal lounge rooms: places to meet friends, read, write, philosophise, flirt and fall in – and out of – love.

Ordering Coffee

If you order *un café* (a coffee), you'll be served a single shot of espresso. A *café allongé* is lengthened with hot water, a *café au lait* comes with milk and a *café crème,* lengthened with steamed milk, is the closest to a latte.

Best Film-Set Cafes

Les Deux Moulins Starring in the film *Amélie* hasn't altered this local hangout. (p78)

Le Pure Café Still as quintessentially Parisian as Ethan Hawke's character found it in *Before Sunset*. (p105)

Best Wine Bars

Le Baron Rouge Rustic barrel-filled spot. (p106)

Taverne Henri IV Authentic wine bar serving cheese and charcuterie platters. (p123)

Best Bars

Bar à Champagne Sip champagne at the top of the Eiffel Tower. (p25)

Harry's New York Bar Knock-out cocktails from the inventor of the Bloody Mary. (p63)

Bar Hemingway Legendary showpiece of the Ritz. (p63)

☑ Top Tips

▶ Many establishments have a tiered pricing structure based on where you sit, with coveted terrace seats more expensive than perching at the counter.

▶ Most places serve at least light meals (sometimes full menus), and it's normally fine to order a coffee or alcohol if you're not dining.

Best
Literary Paris

ELLIOT DANIEL/LONELY PLANET IMAGES ©

Flicking through a street directory reveals just how much Paris honours its literary history, with listings including places Colette and Victor Hugo, avs Marcel Proust and Émile Zola, and rue Balzac to name just a few. The city has nurtured countless French authors over the centuries, who, together with expat writers from Dickens on, have sealed Paris' literary reputation.

Literary Experiences

You can leaf through Paris' literary heritage in atmospheric bookshops, browse *bouquiniste* (booksellers) stalls, hang out in cafes (p168) and swish literary bars, visit writers' former-homes-turned-museums or sleep in hotels where they holed up, pay your respects at cemeteries and even work on your own novel at cafes. We could go on, but as Hemingway wrote in *A Moveable Feast,* 'There is never any ending to Paris.' For a walking tour that takes in key literary sights, see p168.

Bookshops

Our pick of Paris' English-language bookshops (below) have details of literary events throughout the year, many of which are held at the shops themselves. They also sell stacks of books on Paris' literary connections.

Best Bookshops

Shakespeare & Company A 'wonderland of books', as Henry Miller described it. (p139)

Abbey Bookshop Welcoming biblioparadise. (p139)

Red Wheelbarrow Bookstore Delightful little shop with a good kids section. (p109)

Village Voice Popular bookshop specialising in North American literature. (p157)

Worth a Trip

Balzac fans will be fascinated by **Maison de Balzac** (www.balzac. paris.fr, in French; 47 rue Raynouard, 16e; admission free, temporary exhibitions €4/3; ⏲10am-6pm Tue-Sun; Ⓜ Passy or Kennedy–Radio France), the prolific French novelist's cottage (rented between 1840 and 1847 in his housekeeper's name to avoid his creditors) where he wrote for 18-hour days, fuelled by 'torrents' of coffee.

Best
Nights Out

From sipping cocktails in swanky bars to grooving at hip clubs, rocking to live bands, being awed by spectacular operas, ballets and classical concerts, entertained by films, dazzled by high-kicking cabarets, intrigued by avant-garde theatre productions or listening to smooth jazz or stirring *chansons*, a night out in Paris promises a night to remember.

Nightclubs

Paris' residential make-up means clubs aren't ubiquitous. Still, electronica, laced with funk and groove, remains its strong suit. DJs tend to have short stints in venues – look for flyers or check www.gogoparis. com. Salsa and Latino also maintain a huge following. Admission to clubs is free to around €20.

Jazz, Chansons & Cabarets

Paris has some fantastic jazz and *chansons* (heartfelt, lyric-driven music typified by Édith Piaf) venues. Tickets to major cabaret spectacles start from around €90 (€130 with lunch, €150 with dinner) and usually include a half-bottle of champagne.

Opera, Ballet, Theatre & Classical Music

France's Opéra National de Paris and Ballet de l'Opéra National de Paris perform at the Palais Garnier (p64) and Opéra Bastille (p107) opera houses. Virtually all theatre productions are in French but increasingly project English-language subtitles.

Cinema

Pariscope and *L'Officiel des Spectacles* list screening times; tickets cost around €10 per adult, with discounts on Wednesdays. Foreign films screened in their original language with French subtitles are labelled 'VO' (*version originale*); films labelled 'VF' (*version française*) are dubbed in French.

☑ **Top Tips**

▶ On the day of performance, tickets are often available at half price (plus commission of about €3) at Kiosque Théâtre Madeleine (p64) and Kiosque Théâtre Montparnasse (p156).

▶ Fnac (www.fnac. fr, in French) and Virgin Megastore (www.virginmega.fr, in French) sell a wide range of entertainment and sport tickets.

Moulin Rouge (p82)

Best Nightclubs

Point Éphemère Edgy
cultural centre, club and
performance venue book-
ing exceptional emerging
and established DJs,
artists and bands. Uber-
cool. (p85)

Rex Club Paris' first
dedicated techno club is
still cutting edge. Phe-
nomenal sound system.
(p66)

Social Club Subterra-
nean nightclub with su-
perb DJs and occasional
live bands. (p64)

Le Nouveau Casino
Intimate concerts and
top DJs playing electro,
pop, deep house and
rock. (p85)

Best Jazz Clubs

Sunset & Sunside
Respected double venue
on a street famed for its
jazz clubs. (p65)

**Le Caveau de la Hu-
chette** Always entertaining cellar venue. (pictured
above left; p138)

Best Cabarets

Moulin Rouge The
cancan creator is touristy
but spectacular all the
same. (p82)

Au Lapin Agile Historic
and authentic. (p75)

Worth a Trip

An abandoned
railway station has
been transformed
into the alterna-
tive club **La Flèche
d'Or** (www.flechedor.
fr, in French; 102bis
rue de Bagnolet, 20e;
⏰8pm-2am Mon-Thu,
to 6am Fri & Sat, noon-
2am Sun; Ⓜ Alexandre
Dumas or Gambetta),
hosting some of the
hottest DJs and live
music acts (espe-
cially reggae and
rock) in town.

Best
Gay & Lesbian Paris

The city known as 'gay Paree' lives up to its name. Paris was the first-ever European capital to vote in an openly gay mayor when Bertrand Delanoë was elected in 2001, and the city itself is very open – same-sex couples commonly display affection in public and checking into a hotel room is unlikely to raise eyebrows.

Finding the Scene

Paris is so open in fact that there's less of a defined 'scene' here than other cities where it's more underground. While the Marais – particularly around the intersection of rue Ste-Croix de la Bretonnerie and rue des Archives, and eastwards to rue Vieille du Temple – is the mainstay of gay and lesbian nightlife, you'll find venues right throughout the city attracting a mixed crowd.

Festivities

Gay pride peaks during late June's Gay Pride March (pictured above; www.gaypride.fr, in French), with over-the-top floats and festivities.

Resources

Good online resources in English include www.legayparis.fr, www.paris-gay.com, www.girlports.com and the Centre Gai et Lesbien de Paris Île de France (Lesbian, Gay, Bisexual and Transsexual Centre; www.cglparis.org).

Best Gay & Lesbian Bars

Duplex Bar Also houses an art gallery. (p106)

Le Queen Don't miss disco night. (p44)

Le Cox Many a Marais night starts here at happy hour. (p107)

3W Kafé The name of this cocktail bar and club stands for 'women with women'. (p107)

Worth a Trip

In the northwestern-most corner of the Marais in a historic 1930s dancehall, **Le Tango** (www.boite-afrissons.fr; 13 rue au Maire, 3e; ⏱10.30pm-5am Fri & Sat, 5-11pm Sun; Ⓜ Arts et Métiers) starts off with waltzing, salsa and tango until 12.30am or so, when DJs playing 'everything except techno' take over. There are often theme nights; Sunday's gay tea dance is legendary.

Best
Parks & Gardens

TRISH PUNCH/LONELY PLANET IMAGES ©

If Paris' cafes are the city's communal lounge rooms, its parks, gardens and squares are its backyards. The larger parks are idyllic for strolling or simply soaking up the sunshine, with plenty of seating as well as kiosks and cafes, while small, secreted gardens are tucked between gracious old buildings or even perched in the middle of the Seine.

Best Traditional Gardens

Jardin du Luxembourg Paris' most popular park. (p144)

Jardin des Tuileries Part of Paris' historic axis and as classical as it gets. (p58)

Versailles Designed by André Le Nôtre, the château's gardens are fit for a king. (p162)

Best Parks

Parc des Buttes Chaumont Hilly, forested haven. (p85)

Promenade Plantée The world's first elevated park. (p100)

Jardin des Plantes Some sections of Paris' botanic gardens are free. (pictured above; p134)

Best Squares

Place des Vosges Paris' prettiest square, ringed by cloisters, with a park at its centre. (p98)

Square du Vert Galant Romantically situated on the tip of the Île de la Cité. (p120)

Worth a Trip

At the 35-hectare pavilion-filled 'park of the future' **Parc de la Villette** (www.villette.com; admission free; ⊙6am-1am; M Porte de la Villette or Porte de Pantin) you can wander between 10 themed gardens and playgrounds including a Garden of Islands, Bamboo Gardens, Mirror Gardens and Dragon Garden. Adjacent are a kid-pleasing science museum, a music museum and new 2400-seat concert hall.

☑ Top Tips

▶ A comprehensive list of parks and gardens by *arrondissement* is available at www.paris-walking-tours.com/paris gardens.html.

▶ Watch this space: ecominded city initiatives will see Paris become even greener, with many more open areas being created.

Best
Fashion

Fashion shopping is Paris' forte. Yet although its well-groomed residents mean the city can look and feel like a giant catwalk, fashion here is about style and quality, rather than status or brand names. While some fashion shops open daily, most close at least one or two days a week.

Fashion Districts

Shopping spreads throughout the city but certain neighbourhoods are especially concentrated. Luxury Parisian labels are anchored by flagship stores, particularly in the Triangle d'Or (Golden Triangle; p44), bordered by avs Georges V, Champs-Élysées and Montaigne, and St-Germain des Prés (p146). The emerging 'haut Marais' (p94) and Canal St-Martin (p84) are fertile grounds for experimental designers.

Arcades & Department Stores

Paris' covered passages (see p172) are treasure chests of exquisite boutiques, while the city's *grands magasins* (department stores) sell high-quality wares.

Speciality Shops

What sets Paris apart is its incredible array of speciality shops selling food (p197) and goods ranging from hats, handbags, umbrellas, stockings and tights to chic children's wear. Even Parisian dogs are fashionably outfitted, with some shops selling only dog outfits and accessories.

Fashion Shows

Tickets for Paris' famed *haute couture* (high fashion) and prêt-à-porter (ready-to-wear) fashion shows (www.modeaparis.com) are like hen's teeth, even among fashion media. For some catwalk action, reserve ahead to attend free weekly fashion shows at Galeries Lafayette (p66).

☑ Top Tips

▶ Clothing sizes aren't standardised among European countries – head to a *cabine d'essayage* (fitting room), or check www.online-conversion.com/clothing.

▶ If you're happy browsing, tell sales staff *Je regarde* – 'I'm just looking'.

▶ Paris' *soldes* (sales) traditionally take place over six weeks in early summer and in winter.

Best Department Stores

Galeries Lafayette Quality men's, women's and kids' clothing. (p66)

Le Printemps Grand department store. (p66)

Le Bon Marché Incorporates a stellar array of designers. (p147)

Best Fashion Boutiques

Chloé The creator of Paris' first-ever luxury prêt-à-porter collection is still setting trends today. (p45)

Shine Stocks a discerning selection of up-and-coming designers' clothing. (p95)

Pring Stunning designer shoes. (p95)

MadeinUsed Designer creations made from recycled clothing. (p95)

Frivoli Quality second-hand clothing arranged on colour-coded racks. (p85)

Eres Stylish swimwear and seductive lingerie. (p66)

Un Chien dans le Marais Outfit your dog as fashionably as Paris' pampered pooches in this boutique's doggie designs. (p109)

Best Fashion Accessories

A La Recherche de Jane Handcrafted men's and women's hats. (p157)

Lancel Lancel's designer handbags are stealing thunder from its neighbour, Louis Vuitton. (p45)

Maroquinerie Saint-Honoré Well-made, well-priced handbags. (p69)

Best Concept Shops

Colette Hipster haven for limited edition fashion, accessories, homewares and more. (p69)

Merci Multilevel, multiproduct store with profits donated to charity. (p95)

Worth a Trip

For previous seasons' collections, surpluses and seconds by name-brand designers, save money on fashion shopping at the discounted outlet stores along **rue d'Alésia** (14e; M Alésia or Plaisance), particularly between av de Maine to rue Raymond-Losserand. Don't miss the cut-price men's, women's and children's wear from French label **Cacharel** (114 rue d'Alésia, 14e; 🕙10am-7pm Mon-Sat; M Alésia).

Best Churches

Some of the city's most magnificent buildings are its churches and other places of worship. Not only exceptional architecturally and historically, they also contain exquisite art, artefacts and other priceless treasures. And best of all, entry to general areas within them is in most cases free. Many Parisian churches are also the resplendent settings for classical music concerts.

Classical Concerts

Paris' beautiful, centuries-old stone churches have magnificent acoustics and provide a meditative backdrop for classical music concerts. Posters outside churches advertise upcoming events with ticket information, or you could visit www.ampconcerts.com, where you can make online reservations. Tickets cost around €23 to €30.

Etiquette

Bear in mind that although many of Paris' places of worship are also major tourist attractions, Parisians come here to pray and celebrate significant events on religious calendars as part of their daily lives. Be respectful, keep noise to a minimum, obey photography rules (check signs), dress appropriately and try to avoid key times (eg Mass) if you're sightseeing only.

Best Landmark Churches

Notre Dame (p112) The city's mighty cathedral is without equal.

Sacré-Cœur (p72) Paris' domed basilica lords it over the city.

Église St-Sulpice (p150) Featured in *The Da Vinci Code,* with frescoes by Eugène Delacroix.

Église St-Germain des Prés (p151) Built in the 11th century, this is Paris' oldest church.

Best Churches for Classical Concerts

Ste-Chapelle Concerts provide the perfect opportunity to truly appreciate Ste-Chapelle's beauty. (p120)

Église de la Madeleine Renowned for its monumental organ. (p58)

Église St-Eustache Concerts have long been a tradition at this central church. (p58)

Best Non-Christian Places of Worship

Mosquée de Paris Paris' 1920s art deco–Moorish tiled mosque has a wonderful tearoom and *hammam* (steam baths). (p134)

Guimard Synagogue Art nouveau synagogue. (p100)

Best
Multicultural
Paris

Paris might be the bastion of French culture but these days that definition incorporates myriad nationalities who call this cosmopolitan city home. Throughout the capital you'll find vibrant hubs of cultural life that make up *mondial* (multicultural) Paris. Visiting grocery stores, delis, markets, shops and places of worship as you explore the city offers a mini world-tour.

Multicultural Background

Waves of immigration over the centuries – including a large number of immigrants from France's former colonies since the middle of last century – have given rise to an exhilarating mix of ethnicities, cuisines and the arts – and to debates like the 2004 ban at state-run schools on Muslim headscarves (and all other religious symbols, such as crucifixes) in favour of secularism, and the controversial 2011 ban on women wearing burqas in public (France was the first European country to do so). Under French law, censuses can't ask questions regarding ethnicity or religion, but do collect country-of-birth statistics, which confirm Paris as one of the most multicultural cities in Europe.

Best Mondial Museums

Musée du Quai Branly Indigenous art, artefacts, music and more from every continent bar Europe. (p30)

Institut du Monde Arabe Arab arts are displayed in stunning surrounds. (p134)

Musée Guimet des Arts Asiatiques Exceptional collection of Asian art and artefacts. (p40)

Worth a Trip

Unlike many of Paris' ornate arcades, the dilapidated **Passage Brady** (46 rue du Faubourg St-Denis & 33 bd de Strasbourg, 10e; **M** Strasbourg St-Denis or Château d'Eau) isn't aesthetically beautiful. But aromatically, it's just as tantalising, crammed wall to wall with Indian, Pakistani and Bangladeshi cafes and grocery stores. You can get a fantastic lunch here for under €10 and dinner for only slightly more.

BETHUNE CARMICHAEL/LONELY PLANET IMAGES ©

Best
Panoramas

Paris is a photographer's dream. In addition to close-up shots of local street life, there are spectacular vantage points where you can snap vistas of the city – from the top of monuments, on hilltops, in vast squares and on bridges. Even without a camera, the views are unforgettable. Stroll around and you'll find your own favourite panoramas of Paris.

Best Buildings with a View

Eiffel Tower Not only the city's most iconic building but also its highest. (p24)

Tour Montparnasse The saving grace of this otherwise-hideous high-rise is its panoramic observation deck. (p152)

Arc de Triomphe Climb to the top for the best views along Paris' historic axis. (p36)

Grande Arche Great views of the Arc de Triomphe extend from La Défense's own arch. (p175)

Centre Pompidou Captivating views of Paris, including the Eiffel Tower. (p90)

Galeries Lafayette Incredible views of Paris unfold from this department store's rooftop – and they're free! (p66)

Le Printemps This magnificent department store also has mesmerising rooftop views for free. (p66)

Worth a Trip

The scenic, helium-filled **Le Ballon Air de Paris** (☎ 01 44 26 20 00; www.ballondeparis.com, in French; Parc André Citroën, 2 rue de la Montagne de la Fage, 15e; admission Mon-Fri €10/9, Sat & Sun €12/10; ☉9am-at least 4.30pm; Ⓜ Balard or Lourmel) remains tethered as it lifts you 150m. Confirm ahead as the balloon doesn't ascend in windy conditions.

☑ Top Tips

▶ For transport with a view, hop on a Batobus (p204) or regular bus. Scenic bus routes include lines 21 and 27 (Opéra–Panthéon), line 29 (Opéra–Gare de Lyon), line 47 (Centre Pompidou–Gobelins), line 63 (Musée d'Orsay–Trocadéro), line 73 (Concorde–Arc de Triomphe) and line 82 (Montparnasse–Eiffel Tower); see p204 for ticket info.

Best
For Free

JOHN SONES/LONELY PLANET IMAGES ©

Paris' national museums offer free entry on the first Sunday of the month and, what's more, permanent exhibits at city museums are free – see p178 for more information. A handful of Paris' national monuments also have free entry on the first Sunday of the month (in some cases certain months only), including those listed below.

Walking in Paris for Free

Paris is an eminently walkable city, with beautiful parks and gardens, awe-inspiring architecture, markets, buskers' performances and fashion shops (well, window shopping never goes out of style) to check out along the way. For a free walking tour, contact Paris Greeter (p196) in advance for a personalised excursion led by a resident volunteer.

Cycling in Paris (almost) for Free

If you'd rather freewheel around Paris, the Vélib' system costs next-to-nothing for a day's subscription, and the first 30 minutes of each bike rental is free – see p204 for details.

Arc de Triomphe Free entry to the top on the first Sunday of the month from November to March. (p36)

Notre Dame Free entry to the towers on the first Sunday of the month from November to March. (p112)

Père Lachaise This vast, village-like, celebrity-filled cemetery is free to wander. (p160)

Maison Européenne de la Photographie Free admission to superb photography displays from 5pm to 8pm every Wednesday year round. (p98)

Conciergerie Free entry to this Revolution site on the first Sunday of the month from November to March. (p120)

Panthéon Free entry to Paris' mighty mausoleum on the first Sunday of the month from November to March. (p134)

Pavillon de l'Arsenal Admission to the city's fascinating town-planning and architectural centre is free every day year round. (p99)

Best
Tours

Paris Greeter (www.parisiendunjour.fr; by donation) See Paris through local eyes with two- to three-hour city tours. Volunteers lead groups (maximum six people) to their favourite spots in the city. Minimum two weeks' advance notice needed.

Bateaux-Mouches (01 42 25 96 10; www.bateaux-mouches.com; Port de la Conférence, 8e; €11/5.50; Alma Marceau) Runs nine 1000-seat glassed-in tour boats, the largest on the Seine. Cruises (70 minutes) run frequently from 10.15am to 11pm April to September and 13 times a day between 11am and 9pm the rest of the year. Commentary in both French and English.

Paris Walks (01 48 09 21 40; www.paris-walks.com; walks from €12/10) Engaging and informative walking tours in English focusing on various quarters or themes.

Fat Tire Bike Tours (01 56 58 10 54; www.fattirebiketoursparis.com; 24 rue Edgar Faure, 15e; La Motte-Picquet Grenelle) Popular day- and night-time city tours. Bike tours start from €28/26. Ask about entertaining 'segway' tours on gyroscopic two-wheeled contraptions.

Canauxrama (01 42 39 15 00; www.canauxrama.com; €16/12, concession not valid Sat, Sun & public holidays; daily Mar-Oct, rest of yr by reservation; Bastille or Jaurès) Barges travel between Port de Plaisance de Paris−Arsenal, 12e, and Bassin de la Villette, 19e, (and vice-versa) along canals St-Martin and l'Ourcq, including an illuminated underground section, taking 2½ hours one way. Discounted online bookings.

L'Open Tour (01 42 66 56 56; www.parislopentour.com; 13 rue Auber, 9e; 1 day €29/15, 2 consecutive days €32/15; Havre Caumartin or Opéra) Hop-on, hop-off open-deck bus tour circuits (central Paris, Montmartre−Grands Boulevards, Bastille−Bercy and Montparnasse−St-Germain) operating daily year-round.

Eye Prefer Paris (06 31 12 86 20; www.eyepreferparistours.com; 3 people €195) New Yorker-turned-Parisian Richard leads offbeat 3-hour city tours. Cooking classes also available.

Best
Gourmet Shops

JOHN SONES/LONELY PLANET IMAGES ©

Instead of stocking up at a supermarket, Parisians will buy their bread at a *boulangerie* (bakery; p183), cheese at a *fromagerie* (cheese shop), meat at a *charcuterie* (specialist butcher), fruit and vegetables at street-market stalls (p177) and delectable items from speciality shops. It takes longer, but the goods are fresher and better, and the social interaction forms part of the city's village atmosphere.

Take-Home Treats

Pastries may not keep, but *patisserie* items you can take home (customs regulations permitting) include light-as-air macaroons. Other specialty items to squeeze into your suitcases range from honey and mustard to truffles and foie gras, as well as jam and preserves – even cheese.

Choosing Cheese

Cheese at the city's enticing *fromageries* are split into five main categories: *fromage de chèvre* (goat's cheese), *fromage à pâte persillée* (veined or blue cheese), *fromage à pâte molle* (soft cheese), *fromage à pâte demi-dure* (semihard cheese) and *fromage à pâte dure* (hard cheese).

Best Food & Drink Shops

Fauchon Beautifully wrapped jams, pâtes and much more. (p66)

La Grande Épicerie de Paris Gourmet emporium. (p147)

Hédiard Exclusive grocer. (p66)

La Maison de la Truffe Truffles. (p67)

Boutique Maille Mustard. (p68)

La Maison du Miel Honey. (p67)

Legrand Filles & Fils Wine. (p67)

La Petite Scierie Foie gras. (p124)

Mariage Frères Tea. (p106)

Worth a Trip

The only *fromagerie* in Paris with its own underground cellars, the heady **Fromagerie Alléosse** (☏ 01 46 22 50 45; www.alleosse.com; 13 rue Poncelet, 17e; ⏰9am-12.45pm & 4-7pm Tue-Thu, 9am-12.45pm & 3.30-7pm Fri & Sat, 9am-12.45pm Sun; Ⓜ Ternes) often has free tastings.

Best
For Kids

Parisians adore *les enfants* (children) and welcome them with open arms just about every where. You'll notice French kids are generally quiet and polite, and you'll be expected to make sure yours are, too. But kids can still burn off plenty of energy: central Paris' residential make-up means you'll find playground equipment in parks and squares throughout the city.

Dining with Kids

Many restaurants accept little diners (confirm ahead). Children's menus aren't widespread, however, and most restaurants don't have highchairs. Department store cafeterias and chain restaurants like Flunch (www.flunch.fr) offer kid-friendly fare. In fine weather, pick up sandwiches and crêpes from a street stall or pack a market-fresh picnic and head to the city's parks and gardens.

Accommodating Kids

Parisian buildings' premium on space often means premium-priced family-size accommodation – apartments (p200) may be more economical. Check availability and costs for a *lit bébé* (cot).

Best Activities for Kids

Le Grand Rex Kids can become movie stars on entertaining behind-the-scenes tours. (p65)

Cinéaqua State-of-the-art aquarium. (p41)

Jardin du Luxembourg Pony rides, puppet shows and more. (p144)

Worth a Trip

Littlies will love the **Jardin d'Acclimation** (☏ 01 40 67 90 82; www.jardindacclimatation.fr, in French; av du Mahatma Gandhi; admission €2.90, some attractions extra charge; ☉ 10am-7pm May-Sep, to 6pm Oct-Apr; Ⓜ Les Sablons), an amusement park filled with rides and activities. A cute narrow-gauge train (€2.70 return) runs to the park from Porte Maillot (Ⓜ Porte Maillot).

☑ Top Tips

▶ Children under four travel free on public transport and generally receive free admission to sights. Discounts vary for older kids (up to 18) – anything from a euro off to free.

▶ Be extra vigilant crossing roads as Parisian drivers frequently ignore green pedestrian lights.

Survival Guide

Before You Go   **200**

When to Go 200

Book Your Stay 200

Arriving in Paris   **202**

Air............................... .202

Train............................ .202

Bus.............................. .202

Getting Around   **203**

Bicycle.......................... .203

Boat 204

Bus............................. .204

Metro & RER..................... .204

Taxi............................. .205

Essential Information   **205**

Business Hours.................. .205

Discount Cards 206

Electricity 206

Emergency...................... 206

Money.......................... 206

Public Holidays................. .207

Safe Travel .... .207

Telephone 208

Toilets.......................... 208

Tourist Information............. 208

Travellers with Disabilities....... 209

Visas 209

Language   **210**

Survival Guide

Before You Go

When to Go

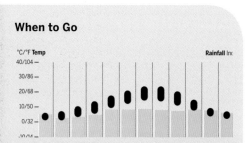

°C/°F Temp
Rainfall In(

40/104 —
30/86 —
20/68 —
10/50 —
0/32 —
-10/14 —

➡ **Winter (Nov–Feb)**
Cold and dark, occasional snow. Museums and attractions are quieter and prices lower.

➡ **Spring (March–May)**
Mild, wet and blustery. Major sights start getting busier; parks and gardens begin to come into their own.

➡ **Summer (June–August)** Warm to hot, generally sunny. Main tourist season. Some businesses close for August. Riverside beaches and outdoor festivals.

➡ **Autumn (Sep–Nov)**
Mild, generally sunny. Cultural life moving into top gear after the summer lull.

Book Your Stay

☑ **Top Tip**

Accommodation outside central Paris is marginally cheaper than within the city itself, but it's almost always a false economy, particularly as travelling into the city will eat up precious time. Choose somewhere within Paris' 20 *arrondissements* (city districts), where you can experience Parisian life from the moment you ste out the door.

➡ Paris' accommodation is often *complet* (full) we in advance. Reservations are recommended any time of year and are essential during the warme months (April to October and all public and school holidays.

➡ Even the best Paris hot rooms tend to be small. Cheaper hotels may not have lifts (elevators); air conditioning is rare.

➡ Paris levies a *taxe de sé jour* (tourist tax) of €0.2(up to €1.50 per person p(

ght (normally added to
ur bill).

Breakfast is almost
ver included; cafes
er the best breakfast
ue.

To live like a Parisian,
nsider renting a short-
ay apartment. The
st apartment-booking
rvices are listed in this
ction.

eful Websites

ris Hotel (www.hotels
ris.fr) Well-organised
e with lots of user
views.

ris Hotel Service
ww.parishotelservice.com)
pecialises in boutique
ms.

ris Hotels (www.paris
els.com) Loads of op-
ons and locations.

nely Planet (www.
nelyplanet.com/hotels)
uthor-penned reviews
Lonely Planet's top
oices.

ris Housing Scam
atch (http://parishousing
amwatch.wordpress.com/
g/housing-scams) Helpful
os to identify and avoid
sreputable apartment
ntals.

Best Budget

Hôtel du Nord – Le Pari-Vélo (www.hoteldunord
-leparivelo.com) Charming
and fantastic value.

Hôtel Henri IV (www.
henri4hotel.fr) Spruced up
and right on the Île de
la Cité.

Hôtel de Blois (www.
hoteldeblois.com) Simple
but stylish.

Hôtel Eldorado (www.
eldoradohotel.fr) Retro-style
place above a bistro and
wine bar.

Plug-Inn Hostel (www.
plug-inn.fr) Welcoming
boutique hostel.

Best Midrange

Mama Shelter (www.
mamashelter.com) Hipster
haven near Père Lach-
aise.

**Hôtel les Degrés de
Notre Dame** (http://les
degreshotel.monsite-orange.
fr) Quaint hotel near the
Seine.

The Five Hotel (www.
thefivehotel-paris.com)
Small, snazzy rooms.

Hôtel Amor (www.hotel
amourparis.fr) Artist-
designed rooms, groovy
bar and courtyard garden.

Hôtel du Petit Moulin
(www.paris-hotel-petitmoulin.
com) Verging on Top
End, but you'll often find
specials online.

Best Top End

Hôtel Ritz Paris (www.
ritzparis.com) The name
says it all.

**Four Seasons Hotel
George V Paris** (www.
crillon.com) Just off the
Champs-Élysées, with a
frescoed swimming pool.

**Hôtel Particulier
Montmartre** (www.hotel
-particulier-montmartre.com)
Fairy tale Montmartre
mansion.

Le Meurice (www.lemeurice.
com) Classical grandeur;
very family-friendly.

Le Six (www.hotel-le-six.
com) Ultracontemporary,
with an amazing spa bar.

Best Apartment Rental Agencies

Paris Attitude (www.paris
attitude.com) Thousands of
apartments, professional
service, reasonable fees.

Paris Stay (www.paristay.
com) Wide range of
properties.

**A La Carte Paris Apart-
ments** (www.alacarte-paris

-apartments.com) Designer apartments.

Paris Accommodation Service (www.paris-accommodation-service.com) Numerous apartments to choose from.

Feel Paris (www.feelparis.com) Good for discounted last-minute specials.

Arriving in Paris

☑ **Top Tip** For the best way to get to your accommodation, see p16.

Charles de Gaulle
Paris' largest international airport, **Aéroport Roissy Charles de Gaulle** (☎01 70 36 39 50; www.adp.fr), is 30km northeast of the city centre in the suburb of Roissy. Its terminals are linked by free *navettes* (shuttle buses) and free CDGVAL shuttle trains – check www.easycdg.com for info.

➡ Both terminals are served by **RoissyRail** (€9.10 one way) on RER line B3 (follow the signs 'Paris by Train'). Trains leave every 15 minutes from

5.30am to midnight and take 40 minutes to reach the centre of Paris.

➡ **Air France bus** (☎08 92 35 08 20; http://videocdn.airfrance.com/cars-airfrance; one-way tickets from €15) runs services to several locations in central Paris. Services generally run half-hourly or more frequentlyfrom around 5am to about 11pm – check the website for lines' individual hours of operation.

➡ **Noctilien night bus** (☎32 46; www.noctilien.fr; adult €7.60; ⏰12.30am-5.30pm) Bus 140 to/from Gare de l'Est links with Charles de Gaulle hourly.

➡ **Roissybus** (☎32 46; www.ratp.fr; one-way €10) Links the airport with rue Scribe, place de l'Opéra. Buses take 45 minutes and run from 5.45am to 11pm.

➡ Prebook private door-to-door shuttles such as **Paris Airports Service** (☎01 55 98 10 80; www.parisairportservice.com; from €26/42 day/night per person to/from Charles de Gaulle or Orly). Allow time for numerous pick-ups and drop-offs.

➡ The tariff for a **taxi** to the city is around €50 to €65. The journey

takes 30 to 50 minutes, depending on traffic.

Orly
Situated 18km south of Paris' city centre, **Aéroport d'Orly** (☎01 49 75 15 15; www.adp.fr) has two terminals – Ouest (West; mainly domestic flights) and Sud (South; mainly international flights), which are linked by the free Orlyval shuttle train.

➡ The **Orlyval shuttle train** (☎08 92 68 77 14; www.orlyval.com; €10.75 one way) links Aéroport d'Orly with RER line B at Antony (eight minutes) with frequent services from 6am to 11pm. From Antony it's a 35-minute trip to central Paris.

➡ **Air France Bus** (☎08 92 35 08 20; http://videocdn.airfrance.com/cars-airfrance; €11.50 one way) runs from the airport to several central Paris locations. Buses takes 30 to 45 minutes; they run every 30 minutes from 6.15am to 11.50pm from the airport and from 6am to 11.30pm to the airport.

➡ **Orlybus** (☎08 92 68 77 14; €6.90 one way) links place Denfert Rochereau 14e, with the airport. Buses take 30 minutes; they run every 15 to 20

inutes from 6am to
.50pm from the airport
nd from 5.35am to
.05pm to the airport.

The tariff for a **taxi** to
e city is €40 to €50
epending on time of
ay). The journey takes
owards of 30 minutes.

See p202 for door-to-
oor services.

eauvais

**éroport Paris Beauvais
illé** (☎03 44 11 46 86,
eneral enquiries 08 92 68 20
4; www.aeroportbeauvais.
m), served by budget
arriers including Ryanair,
80km north of Paris.

Express **bus** services
ave the airport about
0 to 30 minutes after
ach flight's arrival from
45am to 7.15pm and
rop passengers on Paris'
lace de la Porte Maillot.
uses leave Paris for the
rport three hours and
5 minutes before flight
epartures at **Parking
ershing** (1 bd Pershing, 17e;
15 one way; Ⓜ Porte Maillot)
om 5.15am to 7.55pm.
ickets for the 75-minute
ip can be purchased
t the sales point just
utside the terminal and
om a kiosk in the car
ark or at the bus station
t Parking Pershing at
orte Maillot.

➡ Between the city and
Beauvais, a **taxi** costs
from €140 (day) and
€180 (night and all day
Sunday).

Gare du Nord

➡ The highly civilised
Eurostar (☎08 92 35 35
39, UK 08 432 186 186; www.
eurostar.com) whisks you
between Paris' Gare du
Nord and London's St
Pancras Station in around
two hours, 20 minutes.
Through-ticketing is
available to/from many
regional UK stations.

➡ **Thalys** (☎36 35, 08 92 35
35 36; www.thalys.com) links
Paris' Gare du Nord to
Brussels–Midi, Amster-
dam CS and Cologne's
Hauptbahnhof.

Other Mainline
Train Stations

Paris has five other sta-
tions for long-distance
trains, each with its own
metro station: Gare
d'Austerlitz, Gare de
l'Est, Gare de Lyon, Gare
Montparnasse and Gare
St-Lazare; the station
used depends on the
direction from Paris.
Contact **SNCF** (Société
Nationale des Chemins de
Fer; ☎36 35, 08 92 35 35 35;
www.voyages.sncf.com) for
connections throughout

France and continental
Europe.

Gare Routière
Internationale de
Paris–Galliéni

The **Gare Routière
Internationale de Paris–
Galliéni** (☎08 92 89 90 91;
28 av du Général de Gaulle;
Ⓜ Gallieni), the city's international bus terminal,
is in the inner suburb of
Bagnolet. **Eurolines** (☎01
41 86 24 21; www.eurolines.
com; 55 rue St-Jacques, 5e;
Ⓜ Cluny-La Sorbonne) has
services throughout
Europe.

Getting
Around

Bicycle
☑ **Best for** sightseeing
and exercise.

Upwards of 370km of
permanent *pistes cycla-
bles* (cycling lanes) now
criss-cross the city. And,
under the scheme Paris
Respire ('Paris Breathes'),
cars are banned on Sun-
days and public holidays
in favour of pedestrians,
cyclists and skaters in
popular locations, including large sections around
the Seine, Montmartre,

Bastille and Canal St-Martin. For updated coverage of these areas and maps of every cycling path in Paris, visit www.velo.paris.fr. Guided bicycle tours are listed on p196.

➡ Paris has revolutionised pedal-powered transport via the **Vélib'** (☏ 01 30 79 79 30; www.velib.paris.fr; day/week subscription €1.70/8, bike hire up to 30min/60min/90 min/2hr free/€1/2/4) system. This pick-up, drop-off bicycle rental scheme operates across 1800 Vélib' stations citywide, spaced around 300m apart. Accessible 24 hours, each station incorporates about 20 bike stands – over 20,000 bikes in all. Using the Vélib' system is simple. Start by setting up a Vélib' account at any bike station's multilingual terminal using any major credit card, providing it has a microchip and PIN number, or presubscribe online. If the station where you're returning your bike is full, swipe your card across the terminal to get 15 free minutes to find another station. The multigeared bikes are designed for cyclists aged 14 and over, and are fitted with an antitheft lock and front

and rear lights but not helmets (bring your own).

➡ For longer rentals, try **Fat Tire Bike Tours** (p196) or **Paris A Velo, C'est Sympa!** (☏ 01 48 87 60 01; www.parisvelosympa.com; 22 rue Alphonse Baudin, 11er; half-/full-day/weekend/week €12/15/25/60; ⏱ 9.30am-1pm & 2-6pm Mon & Wed-Fri, 9.30am-1pm Tue, 9am-7pm Sat & Sun), which rents bikes and organises tours (you'll need to leave €250 deposit with a credit card or a passport).

Boat
☑ **Best for** scenery.

➡ Paris has numerous boat cruises – see p196. To combine Seine sightseeing with transportation, the **Batobus** (☏ 01 40 62 75 10; www.batobus.com; 1-/2-/5-day pass €14/18/21; ⏱ at least 10.30am-4.30pm, to 9.30pm in high summer) is a handy hop-on, hop-off service stopping at eight key destinations: the Eiffel Tower, Musée d'Orsay, St-Germain des Prés, Notre Dame, Jardin des Plantes, Hôtel de Ville, the Louvre and the Champs-Élysées.

Bus
☑ **Best for** sightseeing, parents with prams/

strollers and people with limited mobility.

➡ Frequent bus services run from around 5.30am to 8.30pm (some lines to 12.30am). The number of routes is reduced at night and on Sundays. Timetables and route information is available from Paris' transit authority, **RATP** (Régie Autonome des Transports Parisians; www.ratp.fr), which also runs the metro and RER.

➡ **Noctilien** (www.noctilien.fr) night buses operate after the metro closes; the website has information and maps. Routes cover most of the city; look for blue 'N' or 'Noctilien' signs at bus stops. Tickets cost the same as one metro/bus ticket for short journeys; longer journeys require two or more tickets.

Metro & RER
☑ **Best for** general travel throughout Paris. This book indicates the closest metro station after the Ⓜ in each listing.

➡ Paris' underground rail network has two separate but linked systems: the metro, with 16 lines and over 300 stations, spaced around 500m apart; and the RER (Réseau Express

Régional), a network of ve suburban services designated A to E) that ass through the city entre. RER stops are nore widely spaced, naking them good for rossing the city quickly.

Most metro and RER ervices begin about 5.20am with the last train eaving around 1.15am around 2.15am on Friday nd Saturday nights), depending on the line. The rst and last departure imes are displayed on each station's platforms.

Tickets for travel within Paris' city limits cost C1.70, or €12.50 for a arnet of 10.

A ticket (called a t+) an be used on the netro; on the RER for ravel within zone 1; on he bus; or on the tram. You can use a single icket to make unlimited nbroken metro/metro, RER/RER, metro/RER, nd bus/bus connections vithin central Paris for ½ hours from the first o final validations (no eturn journeys), but not or transfers between he metro and buses, or etween the RER and ouses. Transfers aren't lowed on Noctilien night ouses.

→ Keep your ticket until you exit the station or you risk a fine.

→ If you're staying in Paris for a week or more, ask at metro station offices about rechargeable **Navigo** (www.navigo.fr, in French) passes.

Taxi

☑ **Best for** travelling with luggage and for reaching destinations not located near public transport stops.

→ You'll find ranks around major intersections, or you can hail taxis in the street.

→ The *prise en charge* (flagfall) is €2.30. Within the city limits, it costs €0.92 per kilometre for travel between 10am and 5pm Monday to Saturday (*Tarif* A; white light on meter). At night (5pm to 10am), on Sunday from 7am to midnight and in the inner suburbs the rate is €1.17 per kilometre (*Tarif* B; orange light on meter). Travel in the outer suburbs is at *Tarif* C, €1.42 per kilometre.

→ There's a €3 surcharge for taking a fourth passenger, but drivers may refuse for insurance reasons. The first piece of baggage is free; ad-

ditional pieces over 5kg cost €1 extra.

→ Avoid 'freelance' – ie illegal – cabs.

→ To order a taxi, call Paris' **central taxi switchboard** (☎01 45 30 30 30, passengers with reduced mobility 01 47 39 00 91; ⏲24hr) or reserve online or by phone with **Taxis G7** (☎01 41 27 66 99; www.taxisg7.fr), which has English-speaking operators.

Essential Information

Business Hours

☑ **Top Tip** Final entry to attractions such as monuments and museums is generally half an hour to an hour before official closing times.

Opening hours fluctuate constantly, and some sights close later during summer and peak season. Check ahead to be sure.

→ **Shops & businesses** In general, closed on Sunday and either Monday or Tuesday; many also close for lunch (around 12.30pm to 2.30pm) and some close on Saturday afternoons.

➡ **Large shops** Often open to around 10pm once a week, usually Thursday.

➡ **Banks** Open from 9am to 4pm (some close for lunch), Monday to Friday.

➡ **Restaurants** Generally serve lunch from noon to 2.30pm or 3pm and dinner from 7pm or 7.30pm until at least 9.30pm; many serve late into the night.

➡ **Museums** The majority are closed one day a week; some open late one night a week.

Discount Cards

☑ **Top Tip** Concessions (usually 30% to 50%) abound for youth, students and seniors on everything from transport to museums. Bring whatever concession ID you have from home and flash it every time you pull out your wallet. Prices in this book are adult/concession.

If you plan to visit a lot of museums, your best bet is a Paris Museum Pass (www.parismuseum pass.fr; 2/4/6 days €35/50/65), which gives you entry to more than 60 museums and monuments, and allows you to skip the queues and head straight in. Pick it up from tourist offices, participating museums and monuments or branches of Fnac. (Preordering online will incur postage costs.) European citizens under 26 get free entry to national museums and monuments, so don't buy a museum pass if you qualify.

The Paris Visite (p206) pass offers some discounts. See p198 for information about reduced rates for kids.

Electricity

230V/50Hz

Emergency

Ambulance (☏15)
Fire Brigade (☏18)
Police (☏17)

Money

France uses the euro (€) For updated currency exchange rates, check www.xe.com.

Tickets & Passes

Paris Visite (www.parisvisite.com) gives users unlimited travel, as well as discounted entry to certain museums, and other discounts or bonuses. Passes are valid for either three, five or eight zones. The zone 1-3 pass costs €9.30/15.20/20.70/29.90 for one/two/three/five days. Passes are sold online, at larger metro and RER stations, Paris' SNCF offices and airports. They're valid on the metro, RER, SNCF's suburban lines, buses, night buses, trams and Montmartre's funicular railway – though if you're not using public transport frequently each day, a regular *carnet* (book) of transport tickets may work out cheaper.

Visa is the most widely accepted credit card, followed by MasterCard. American Express and Diners Club cards are accepted only at more exclusive establishments. Some restaurants don't accept credit cards.

Many automated services, such as ticket machines, require a chip-and-PIN credit card. Ask your bank for advice before you leave.

Public Holidays

New Year's Day (*Jour de l'An*) 1 January

Easter Sunday (*Pâques*) late March/April

Easter Monday (*Lundi de Pâques*) late March/April

May Day (*Fête du Travail*) 1 May

Victory in Europe Day (*Victoire 1945*) 8 May

Ascension Thursday (*L'Ascension*) May

Whit Sunday/Whit Monday (*Pentecôte/Lundi de Pentecôte*) May/June

Bastille Day (*Fête Nationale*) 14 July

Assumption Day (*L'Assomption*) 15 August

All Saints' Day (*La Toussaint*) 1 November

Money-saving Tips

➤ Many museums are free on at least the first Sunday of the month – see p178.

➤ Consider investing in a transport (p206) or museum (p206) pass.

➤ Stock up on fresh food at the markets and food shops and head to a park for a picnic.

➤ See p186 to save on theatre tickets.

➤ Short-stay apartments (p200) can work out to be considerably cheaper than a hotel room.

➤ Head to one of the city's 400 free wi-fi points (some time-limited) at popular locations including parks, libraries, local town halls and tourist hotspots. Locations are mapped at www.paris.fr (in French).

Armistice Day (*Le Onze Novembre*) 11 November

Christmas Day (*Noël*) 25 December

Safe Travel

➤ Pickpockets prey on busy places; *always* stay alert to the possibility of someone surreptitiously reaching for your pockets or bags.

➤ In an increasingly common ruse, scammers pretend to 'find' a gold ring (by subtly dropping it on the ground) then offer it to you as a diversionary tactic for pickpocketing, or an opening to get money.

➤ Paris has a high incidence of beggars; if someone approaches you and you're not willing or able to give money, simply say '*désolé*' ('sorry').

➤ The metro is safe to use until it closes, including for women travelling alone, but stations best avoided late at night include the long passageways of Châtelet–Les Halles and Montparnasse–Bienvenüe, as well as Château Rouge, Gare du Nord, Strasbourg St-Denis, Réaumur–Sébastopol and Stalingrad. *Bornes d'alarme* (alarm boxes) are located in the centre of each metro

Dos and Don'ts

➡ Greet or farewell anyone you interact with, such as shopkeepers, with '*Bonjour (bonsoir* at night)/*Au revoir*'.

➡ Particularly in smaller shops, staff may not appreciate you touching the merchandise until invited to do so.

➡ *Tu* and *vous* both mean 'you' but *tu* is used only with people you know very well, children or animals. Use *vous* until you're invited to use *tu*.

➡ Talking about money (eg salaries or spending outlays) is generally taboo in public.

➡ You'll have a much more rewarding experience if you address locals in French, even if all you say is '*Parlez-vous anglais*?' (Do you speak English?)

and RER platform and in some station corridors.

Telephone

Check with your service provider to make sure your mobile phone will work in France and find out what the roaming costs will be.

Public telephones generally require a phonecard (*télécarte*), which can be purchased at post offices, *tabacs* (tobacconists) and anywhere displaying a blue '*télécarte en vente ici*' ('phonecards sold here') sticker. Cards start from €7.50.

France doesn't use separate area codes –

you always dial the full 10-digit number. Drop the initial 0 if calling France from abroad.

Country code ☎ 33

International access code (from France) ☎ 00

Toilets

☑ **Top Tip** Take advantage of the toilets before you leave any monument or museum – they're well maintained and incur no extra charge.

➡ Public toilets in Paris are signposted *toilettes* or WC.

➡ Tan-coloured, self-cleaning cylindrical toilets on Parisian pavements

are open 24 hours and are free of charge. Look for the words *libre* (available; green-coloured) or *occupé* (occupied; red-coloured).

➡ Cafe staff don't appreciate you using their facilities if you're not a paying customer (a coffee can be a good investment). Fast-food chains usually require door codes, which are printed on receipts. In older cafes and bars, you may find a *toilette à la turque* (Turkish-style toilet), the French term for a squat toilet.

➡ There are free public toilets in front of Notre Dame cathedral, near the Arc de Triomphe, east down the steps at Sacré Cœur, at the northwestern entrance to the Jardins des Tuileries and in some metro stations.

➡ Other good bets are major department stores or big hotels.

Tourist Information

The main branch of the **Paris Convention & Visitors Bureau** (Office de Tourisme et de Congrès de Paris; Map p56; ☎ 08 92 68 30 00; www.parisinfo.com; 25-27 rue des Pyramides, 1er; ⏰ 9am-7pm; Ⓜ Pyramides) is 500m

orthwest of the Louvre.
lsewhere in Paris, the
elephone number and
ebsite is the same as for
he main office.

Anvers (Map p76; 72 bd
ochechouart, 18e; ⏰10am-
pm; Ⓜ Anvers)

Gare de l'Est (Place du 11
Novembre 1918, 10e; ⏰8am-
pm Mon-Sat, closed public
olidays; Ⓜ Gare de l'Est) In
he arrivals hall for TGV
rains.

Gare de Lyon (20 bd
Diderot, 12e; ⏰8am-6pm
Mon-Sat, closed public holi-
ays; Ⓜ Gare de Lyon) In the
rrivals hall for mainline
rains.

Gare du Nord (18 rue de
unkerque, 10e; ⏰8am-6pm;
Ⓜ Gare du Nord) At the sta-
on's eastern end.

**Syndicate d'Initiative
le Montmartre** (Map
76; ☎01 42 62 21 21; www.
montmartre-guide.com; 21
lace du Tertre, 18e; ⏰10am-
pm, closed 1-2pm Sat & Sun;
Ⓜ Abbesses) Locally run
ffice.

Travellers with Disabilities

Paris' antiquated architecture, including much of the metro, means unfortunately that *fauteuil roulent* (wheel-chair) access is severely limited, and ramps are rare. Newer hotels, muse-ums and public facilities must (by law) provide access. Many restaurants may have only partial access and restaurant bathrooms not accom-modate wheelchairs or provide rails – ask when you book.

The **tourist office** (www.parisinfo.com) has excellent information for travellers with dis-abilities and impairments. **Access-Able Travel Source** (www.access-able. com) also has some good links for organisations that can provide advice about reduced mobility access in Paris.

For information on wheelchair accessibility for all forms of public transport, the *Guide Practique à l'Usage des Personnes à Mobilité Ré-duite* from the **Syndicat**

des Transports d'Île de France (☎01 47 53 28 00; www.stif-idf.fr, in French) is indispensable.

Visas

There are no entry re-quirements for nationals of EU countries. Citizens of Australia, the USA, Canada and New Zealand do not need visas to visit France for up to 90 days.

Except for citizens of a handful of other Euro-pean countries (including Switzerland), everyone, including citizens of South Africa, needs a Schengen Visa, named for the Schengen Agree-ment that has abolished passport controls among 22 EU countries and has also been ratified by the non-EU governments of Iceland, Norway and Switzerland.

Check www.france. diplomatie.fr for the latest visa regulations and your closest French embassy.

Language

The sounds used in spoken French can almost all be found in English. There are a couple of exceptions: nasal vowels (represented in our pronunciation guides by 'o' or 'u' followed by an almost inaudible nasal consonant sound 'm', 'n' or 'ng'), the 'funny' *u* sound ('ew' in our guides) and the deep-in-the-throat *r*. Bearing these few points in mind and reading our pronunciation guides below as if they were English, you'll be understood just fine. The markers (m) and (f) indicate the forms for male and female speakers respectively.

To enhance your trip with a phrasebook, visit **lonelyplanet.com**. Lonely Planet iPhone phrasebooks are available through the Apple App store.

Basics

Hello.
Bonjour. — bon·zhoor

Goodbye.
Au revoir. — o·rer·vwa

How are you?
Comment allez-vous? — ko·mon ta·lay·voo

I'm fine, thanks.
Bien, merci. — byun mair·see

Please.
S'il vous plaît. — seel voo play

Thank you.
Merci. — mair·see

Excuse me.
Excusez-moi. — ek·skew·zay·mwa

Sorry.
Pardon. — par·don

Yes./No.
Oui./Non. — wee/non

I don't understand.
Je ne comprends pas. — zher ner kom·pron pa

Do you speak English?
Parlez-vous anglais? — par·lay·voo ong·glay

Eating & Drinking

..., please.
..., s'il vous plaît. — ... seel voo play

A coffee	*un café*	ewn ka·fay
A table for two	*une table pour deux*	ewn ta·bler poor der
Two beers	*deux bières*	der bee·yair

I'm a vegetarian.
Je suis végétarien/végétarienne. (m/f) — zher swee vay·zhay·ta·ryun/vay·zhay·ta·ryen

Cheers!
Santé! — son·tay

That was delicious!
C'était délicieux! — say·tay day·lee·syer

The bill, please.
L'addition, s'il vous plaît. — la·dee·syon seel voo play

Shopping

I'd like to buy ...
Je voudrais acheter ... — zher voo·dray ash·tay ...

I'm just looking.
Je regarde. — zher rer·gard

How much is it?
C'est combien? — say kom·byun

It's too expensive.
C'est trop cher. — say tro shair

an you lower the price?

ous pouvez
isser le prix? — voo poo·vay bay·say ler pree

mergencies

elp!
u secours! — o skoor

all the police!
ppelez la police! — a·play la po·lees

all a doctor!
ppelez un
édecin! — a·play un mayd·sun

m sick.
e suis malade. — zher swee ma·lad

m lost.
e suis perdu/
erdue. (m/f) — zhe swee pair·dew

here are the toilets?
ù sont les
ilettes? — oo son lay twa·let

ime & Numbers

hat time is it?
uelle heure
st-il? — kel er ay til

's (eight) o'clock.
est (huit)
eures. — il ay (weet) er

's half past (10).
est (dix) heures
demie. — il ay (deez) er ay day·mee

orning	matin	ma·tun
fternoon	après-midi	a·pray·mee·dee
vening	soir	swar
esterday	hier	yair
oday	aujourd'hui	o·zhoor·dwee
omorrow	demain	der·mun

Monday	lundi	lun·dee
Tuesday	mardi	mar·dee
Wednesday	mercredi	mair·krer·dee
Thursday	jeudi	zher·dee
Friday	vendredi	von·drer·dee
Saturday	samedi	sam·dee
Sunday	dimanche	dee·monsh

1	un	un
2	deux	der
3	trois	trwa
4	quatre	ka·trer
5	cinq	sungk
6	six	sees
7	sept	set
8	huit	weet
9	neuf	nerf
10	dix	dees
100	cent	son
1000	mille	meel

Transport & Directions

Where's ...?
Où est ...? — oo ay ...

What's the address?
Quelle est l'adresse? — kel ay la·dres

Can you show me (on the map)?
Pouvez-vous
m'indiquer
(sur la carte)? — poo·vay·voo mun·dee·kay (sewr la kart)

I want to go to ...
Je voudrais
aller à ... — zher voo·dray a·lay a ...

Does it stop at (Amboise)?
Est-ce qu'il
s'arrête à
(Amboise)? — es·kil sa·ret a (om·bwaz)

I want to get off here.
Je veux
descendre ici. — zher ver day·son·drer ee·see

Behave the Scenes

Send Us Your Feedback

We love to hear from travellers – your comments help make our books better. We read every word, and we guarantee that your feedback goes straight to the authors. Visit **lonelyplanet.com/contact** to submit your updates and suggestions.

Note: We may edit, reproduce and incorporate your comments in Lonely Planet products such as guidebooks, websites and digital products, so let us know if you don't want your comments reproduced or your name acknowledged. For a copy of our privacy policy visit lonelyplanet.com/privacy.

Our Readers

Many thanks to the travellers who wrote to us with hints, advice and anecdotes: Katrin Flatscher & Christian Oberdanner, Roger Hart, Lizet Hoenderdos, Jay Lee, Sophie Masson, Ashley Perkins, Ingrid Sandahl.

Catherine's Thanks

Un grand merci first and foremost to Julian, and to all the Parisians who offered insights and inspiration. And *merci encore* to my parents, brother and *belle-sœur* for my lifelong love of Paris.

Acknowledgments

Cover photograph: Notre Dame Cathedral/Vittorio Sciosia. Many of the images in this guide are available for licensing from Lonely Planet Images: www.lonelyplanetimages.com.

This Book

This 3rd edition of Lonely Planet's Pocket Paris guidebook was researched and written by Catherine Le Nevez. The previous two editions were also written by Catherine Le Nevez. This guidebook was commissioned in Lonely Planet's London office, and produced by the following:

Commissioning Editors Joanna Cooke, Imogen Hall **Coordinating Editor** Sophie Splatt **Coordinating Cartographer** Hunor Csutoros **Coordinating Layout Designer** Joseph Spanti **Managing Editors** Bruce Evans, Annelies Mertens, Angela Tinson **Managing Cartographers** Anthony Phelan, Amanda Sierp **Managing Layout Designer** Chris Girdler **Assisting Editor** Cathryn Game **Assisting Cartographers** Peter Shields, Brendan Streager **Cover Research** Naomi Parker **Internal Image Research** Aude Vauconsant **Language Content** Annelies Mertens **Thanks to** Laura Crawford, Janine Eberle, Ryan Evans, Liz Heynes, Laura Jane, David Kemp, Trent Paton, Piers Pickard, Lachlan Ross, Michael Ruff, Julie Sheridan, Laura Stansfeld, John Taufa, Gerard Walker, Clifton Wilkinson

Index

See also separate subindexes for:

🌐 **Eating p215**

🍷 **Drinking p216**

🎭 **Entertainment p216**

🛍 **Shopping p216**

A

À Bout de Souffle 158
accommodation 200-2
ambulance 206
Amélie 78
Arc de Triomphe 36-7
Arc de Triomphe &
  Champs-Élysées
  area 34-45, **38-9**
  drinking 44
  entertainment 44
  food 43
  itineraries 35
  shopping 45
  sights 36-7, 40-2
  transport 35
**Arc de Triomphe du
  Carrousel 59**
architecture 174-5
area codes 208
Arènes de Lutèce 135
art nouveau 102, 174
**Av des Champs-
  Élysées 40**
axe historique 37, 58

B

baguettes 83
bathrooms 208
Baudelaire, Charles 68
belle époque 102, 180

Sights p000
Map Pages **p000**

Bercy Village 87
**Bibliothèque Nation-
  ale de France 87**
**Bibliothèque Publique
  d'Information 92**
bicycle travel 40, 203-4
boat travel 204
booking agencies 64
bouquinistes 125
bread 83
bus travel 204
business hours 205-6

C

cabaret 186-7
Canal St-Martin area
  84-5, **84**
Catacombes 150
**Cathédrale de Notre
  Dame 112-117**
cell phones 16, 208
Centre Pompidou 90-3
**Champs-Élysées, av
  des 40**
Champs-Élysées area,
  see Arc de Triomphe
  & Champs-Élysées
  area
chansons 186
children, travel with 198
Chirac, Jacques 102
churches 192
  Église de la
    Madeleine 58
  Église du Dôme 30

Église St-Étienne du
  Mont 136
Église St-Eustache 58
Église St-Germain
  des Prés 151
Église St-Sulpice 150
**Cimetière de
  Montmartre 78**
**Cimetière du
  Montparnasse 151**
Cimetière St-Vincent 79
Cinéaqua 41
cinema 158, 186
**Cinémathèque
  Française 87**
**Cité de l'Architecture
  et du Patrimoine
  40, 42**
Claudel, Camille 27
climate 200
Clos Montmartre 78
**Comédie Française
  Salle Richelieu 65**
**Comédie Française
  Studio Théâtre 65**
Conciergerie 120
cooking courses 176
costs 16, 206, 207
Cour Carrée 170
courses 176
credit cards 207
**Crypte Archéologique
  du Parvis Notre
  Dame 116**
currency 16
cycling 40, 203-4

D

Da Vinci, Leonardo
  49, 50
Da Vinci Code, The
  53, 150
Dalí, Salvador 78
**Dalí Espace
  Montmartre 78**
dangers 207-8
de Gaulle, Charles 32
Delacroix, Eugène
  50-1, 150
Delanoë, Bernard 102
disabilities, travellers
  with 209
Docks en Seine 87
dogs 80
**Domaine de Marie-
  Antoinette 164**
*Down and Out in Paris
  and London* 158, 16[
drinking 184, 186-7,
  see also individual
  neighbourhoods,
  Drinking subindex

E

**Église de la Madelein[
  58**
Église du Dôme 30
**Église St-Étienne du
  Mont 136**
Église St-Eustache 5[
**Église St-Germain d[
  Prés 151**
Église St-Sulpice 15[

el, Gustave 24, 25
el Tower 24-5
el Tower & Les Invalides area 22-33, 28-9
drinking 33
entertainment 33
ood 31-3
itineraries 23
sights 24-5, 26-7, 30
ransport 23
ctricity 16, 206
ergencies 206
ertainment 186-7
quette 192, 208

hion 190-1
n 158, 186, *see also individual films*
206
heurie 68
a markets 177
ndation Cartier Pour l'Art Contemporain 150
d 182-3, 197, *see also individual neighbourhoods, Eating subindex*
rum des Halles 60
rum des Images 65
rum du Centre Pompidou 91
anco-Prussian War 73
e activities 195
ench language 137, 210-11
ench Revolution 121, 180

lerie Colbert 172
lerie Musée Baccarat 41

Galerie Véro Dodat 172
Galerie Vivienne 172
Galerie Yvon Lambert 100
Galeries du Panthéon Bouddhique du Japon et de la Chine 40
gardens & parks 189
  Jardin d'Acclimation 198
  Jardin des Plantes 134
  Jardin des Tuileries 58, 170
  Jardin du Luxembourg 144-5
  Jardin du Palais Royal 58, 170
  Jardins du Trocadéro 42
Gay Pride March 188
gay travellers 188
Ginsberg, Allen 168
Grand Palais 42
Grande Arche 175
grands projets 102, 174
Guimard synagogue 100

H
Haussmann, Baron 174
haut Marais 94-5, **94**
haute couture 44, 188
Hemingway, Ernest 63, 168, 169
highlights 8-13
history 32, 102, 121, 164, 180-1
  belle époque 102, 180
  Franco-Prussian War 73
  French Revolution 121, 180

WWI 37, 102
WWII 32, 63, 102
holidays 207
Hôtel de Cluny 128-9
Hôtel de Ville 99
Hôtel des Invalides 30
Hunchback of Notre Dame, The 116

I
ice cream 122
Île de la Cité & Île St-Louis 110-125, **118-119**
  drinking 123
  food 122-3
  itineraries 111
  shopping 124
  sights 112-117, 120
  transport 111
Île St-Louis, *see* Île de la Cité & Île St-Louis
inline skating 101, 153
Institut du Monde Arabe 134
itineraries 14-15, 170-1, 172-3, *see also individual neighbourhoods*

J
Jardin d'Acclimation 198
Jardin des Plantes 134
Jardin des Tuileries 58, 170
Jardin du Luxembourg 144-5
Jardin du Palais Royal 58, 170
Jardins du Trocadéro 42
Jeu de Paume 59
Joyce, James 168, 169

K
Kandinsky, Vassily 92
Kerouac, Jack 168
Klein, Yves 92

L
La Dame de Canton 87
La Défense 175
La Môme 158
language 137, 210-11
Latin Quarter 126-139 **130, 132-3**
  drinking 138
  entertainment 138-9
  food 136-8
  itineraries 127, 130-1
  shopping 139
  sights 128-9, 134-6
  transport 127
Le Ballon Air de Paris 194
Le Batofar 87
Les Invalides area, *see* Eiffel Tower & Les Invalides area
Les Misérables 158
lesbian travellers 188
Letters to Emil 169
Life: A User's Manual 158
literature 158, 168-9, 185, *see also individual titles*
local life 12-13
Louis XIV 58, 162, 163, 164, 170, 180
Louvre 48-53
Louvre, Tuileries & Opéra area 46-69, **56-7**
  drinking 63-4
  entertainment 64
  food 60-3
  itineraries 47, 54-5
  shopping 66-9

Louvre, Tuileries & Opéra area *continued*
sights 48-51, 58-60
transport 47

M

Maison de Balzac 185
Maison de Victor Hugo 98
Maison Européenne de la Photographie 98
Marais 88-109, **94**, **96-97**
drinking 105-7
entertainment 107-8
food 101, 103-5
itineraries 89, 94
shopping 98-9
sights 90-3, 98-101
transport 89
Marché aux Puces de St-Ouen 177
Marie-Antoinette 121, 162-4
markets 177
mass skates 101, 153
Matisse, Henri 92
Mémorial de la Shoah 100
Mémorial des Martyrs de la Déportation 120
Ménagerie du Jardin des Plantes 134
metro travel 204-5
Michelangelo 52
Midnight in Paris 158
Miller, Henry 169
mobile phones 16, 208

Mona Lisa 49-50
Monet 58
money 16, 206-7
Montmartre 70-83, **74**, **76**
drinking 81
entertainment 82
food 79, 81
itineraries 71, 74-5
shopping 83
sights 72-3, 78-9
transport 71
Morrison, Jim 161
Mosquée de Paris 134-5
Moulin de la Galette, Le 75
Moveable Feast, A 158
multiculturalism 193
Musée Carnavalet 98
Musée Cognacq-Jay 99
Musée d'Art et d'Histoire du Judaïsme 98
Musée d'Art Moderne de la Ville de Paris 40
Musée de Cluny 128-9
Musée de la Marine 42
Musée de la Mode et du Textile 53
Musée de la Monnaie de Paris 152
Musée de la Poste 152
Musée de la Poupée 100
Musée de la Publicité 53
Musée de la vie Romantique 78
Musée de l'Armée 30
Musée de l'Érotisme 78-9

Musée de l'Homme 41-2
Musée de l'Orangerie 58
Musée de Montmartre 75
Musée des Arts Décoratifs 53
Musée des Égouts de Paris 30
Musée d'Orsay 142-3
Musée d'Orsay area, *see* St-Germain des Prés
Musée du Luxembourg 145
Musée du Parfum 60
Musée du Quai Branly 30
Musée Galliera de la Mode de la Ville de Paris 42
Musée Guimet des Arts Asiatiques 40-1
Musée Jacquemart-André 40
Musée Marmottan 179
Musée National d'Art Moderne 91-2
Musée National d'Histoire Naturelle 135
Musée National du Moyen Âge 128-9
Musée National Eugène Delacroix 150
Musée Picasso 100-1
Musée Quai Branly 40
Musée Rodin 26-7
museums 178-9

N

Napoleon I 30, 36, 59-60, 121
Napoleon III 164, 180

nightclubs 186-7
NoMa, *see* haut Mara
Notre Dame 112-117
Notre Dame area, *see* Île de la Cité & Île St-Louis

O

opening hours 205-6
Opéra area, *see* Louv Tuileries & Opéra area
Orwell, George 168

P

Palais de Chaillot 41
Palais de Tokyo 40,
panoramas 194
Panthéon 134
Parc de la Villette 18
Parc des Buttes Chaumont 85
Parc du Champ de Mars 30
Pari-Roller 153
parks *see* gardens & parks
Passage Choiseul 17
Passage des Panoramas 173
Passage Jouffroy 17
Passage Verdeau 173
Passerelle Simone d Beauvoir 87
Pavillon de l'Arsenal 99-100
Père Lachaise 160-1
Périphérique 80
Petit Palais 42
philocafés 106
Piaf, Édith 161
Piscine Joséphine Baker 87
Place de la Bastille 101

Sights p000
Map Pages **p000**

ce de la Concorde
60
ce des Vosges 98
ce du Tertre 75
ce Vendôme 59-60
tzl 100
ice 206
tics 102
mpidou, Georges 32
nt de l'Archevêché
171
nt Neuf 120
nt St-Louis 120
oulation 80
und, Ezra 169
menade Plantée
100
oust, Marcel 161
olic holidays 207

noir, Auguste 27
R travel 204-5
er cruises 196
din, Auguste 26-7
llers & Coquillages
101, 153

cré-Cœur 72-3
cré-Cœur area,
  see Montmartre
fety 207-8
nd, George 78
rkozy, Nicolas 102
urat, Georges 161
opping 197
ating 101, 153
rbonne 136
utheastern Paris
  86-7, 86
uare du Vert Galant
  120, 170
e-Chapelle 120
ein, Gertrude 169

St-Germain des Prés
  140-159, 157, 148-9
drinking 155-7
entertainment 157
food 152-4
itineraries 141,
  146-7
shopping 159
sights 142-3, 144-5,
  150-2
transport 141
swimming 87

T
taxis 205
telephone services
  16, 208
**Théâtre du
  Luxembourg 145**
**Théâtre du Vieux
  Colombier 65**
theatre tickets 64, 156
**Théâtre-Musée des
  Capucines 60**
Thinker, The 27
time 16
tipping 16
toilets 208
top sights 8-11
Tour de France 40
Tour Montparnasse 152
Tour St-Jacques 101
tourist information
  208-9
tours 196
train travel 204-5
transport 17, 202-5
Tuileries area, *see*
  Louvre, Tuileries &
  Opéra area

U
Ulysses 168, 169
universities 136

V
vacations 207
Van Gogh, Vincent
  27, 75
Van Gogh's House 75
Venus de Milo 50
Verlaine, Paul 168
Versailles 162-5, 164
views 194
visas 16, 209

W
walks 168-9, 170-1,
  172-3
Water Lilies 58
weather 198
websites 16, 201-2
Wilde, Oscar 161, 169
windmills 75
wine-tasting courses
  176
WWI 37, 102
WWII 32, 63, 102

⊗ **Eating**

58 Tour Eiffel 32

A
À la Cloche d'Or 79
Alain Ducasse au
  Plaza Athénée 43
Angelina 163
Apparemment Café
  104
Arnaud Delmontel 81
Au Pied de Cochon 54
Au Rocher de
  Cancale 55
Aux Lyonnais 62

B
Besnier 27
Bouillon Racine 152

Brasserie Bofinger
  105
Brasserie de l'Île
  St-Louis 123
Brasserie Lipp 152

C
Café Campana 143
Café de la Butte 81
Café de l'Alma 32
Café La Fusée 105
Café le Flore en
  l'Île 123
Café Marly 61
Charbon Rouge 43
Charlot, Roi des
  Coquillages 79
Chez Marianne 101,
  103
Chez Marie 79
Chez Nicos 131
Chez Prune 85
Chez Toinette 81
Christ Inn's
  Bistrot 55
Crêperie Bretonne 104

E
El Mansour 43

F
Frenchie 61

G
Georges 91
Grom 154

H
Hôtel du Nord 85

L
La Boutique Jaune
  104-5
La Coupole 154

La Maison Rose 75
La Tour d'Argent 136
L'Arpège 31
L'As du Felafel 104
L'Atelier de Joël Robuchon 153
L'Atmosphère 85
L'Avant-Goût 87
Le Bistrot du Sommelier 43
Le Buisson Ardent 136-7
Le Clown Bar 104
Le Comptoir du Panthéon 137
Le Coupe-Chou 136
Le Dôme 33
Le Grand Véfour 62
Le Hide 43
Le J'Go 61
Le Jules Verne 31
Le Loir dans la Théière 101
Le Miroir 81
Le Petit Bofinger 105
Le Petit Château d'Eau 85
Le Potager du Marais 104
Le Procope 146
Le Relais Gascon 79
Le Roi du Pot au Feu 61
Le Salon d'Hélène 153
Le Soufflé 61
Le Tambour 55
Le Train Bleu 86-7
Les Deux Abeilles 32-3
Les Deux Moulins 78

Les Ombres 31-2
L'Escargot 63
L'Estaminet 85
L'Ilot Vache 122
L'Ourcine 136

M

Ma Salle à Manger 122
Maison Berthillon 122, 171
Maison Prunier 43
Marché aux Enfants Rouges 95
Marché Bastille 103
Marché Beauvau 105
Marché Brancusi 155
Marché des Batignolles 81
Marché Maubert 137
Marché Monge 137
Marché Raspail 154
Michel Rostang 183
Mon Vieil Ami 122

P

Passage 53 61
Passage Brady 193
Pères et Filles 154
Pho 67 137-8
Polidor 145
Pozzetto 103

R

Restaurant Musée d'Orsay 143
Roger La Grenouille 154
Rose Bakery 94

S

Stohrer 62-3

T

Tante Marguerite 27

Y

Yam'Tcha 60

🍷 **Drinking**

3W Kafé 107
Andy Wahloo 106
Angelina 63
Bar à Champagne 25
Bar Hemingway 63
Bistro des Augustins 155
Buddha Bar 44
Café Baroc 107
Café Branly 33
Café Charbon 85
Café de Flore 155
Café de la Nouvelle Mairie 139
Café des Phares 107
Café Le Refuge 81
Café Panis 138
Duplex Bar 106-7
Harry's New York Bar 63
Kong 64
La Charlotte de l'Île 123
La Closerie des Lilas 155-6
La Fée Verte 106
La Fourmi 81
La Palette 156
La Ruche 156
Le Baron Rouge 106
Le Cox 107
Le Pantalon 138
Le Pré 156
Le Progrès 95
Le Pub St-Hilaire 138
Le Pure Café 105

Le Quetzal 107
Le Select 156
Le Vieux Chêne 131
Le Wagg 156-7
Les Deux Magots 1[
Les Etages St-Germain 156
Mariage Frères 106
Open Café 107
Panic Room 95
Sir Winston 44
Taverne Henri IV 12
Verjus 63

🎭 **Entertainme**

Au Lapin Agile 75
Au Limonaire 64
Cinéma des Cinéastes 82-3
Comédie Française 65
Folies-Bergère 82
La Chapelle des Lombards 108
La Cigale 82
La Flèche d'Or 187
La Pagode 33
La Scène Bastille 1[
Le Baiser Salé 65
Le Balajo 108
Le Baron 44
Le Caveau de la Huchette 138
Le Champo 139
Le Divan du Monde 82
Le Duc des Lombards 65
Le Grand Rex 65
Le Lido 44
Le Nouveau Casino 85
Le Queen 44

Le Showcase 44
Le Tango 188
L'Olympia 65-6
Moulin Rouge 82
Opéra Bastille 107-8
Palais Garnier 64
Point Éphémère 85
Rex Club 66
Social Club 64
Sunset & Sunside 65
Théâtre des Bouffes
    Parisiens 173

Shopping

A La Recherche De
    Jane 157
Abbey Bookshop 139
agnès b 69
Album 139
Alexandra Sojfer 147
Androuet 131
Antoine 68
Au Plat d'Étain 147

Bazar de l'Hôtel de
    Ville (BHV) 108
bouquinistes 125
Boutique Maille 68

Cacharel 191
Carré Rive Gauche
    150
Carrousel du Louvre
    69
Chloé 45
Chocolaterie
    Joséphine Vannier
    108-9

Chocolats Mococha
    131
Cine Reflet 159
Clair de Rêve 124
Colette 69
Comptoir de la
    Gastronomie 55
Cour du Commerce
    St-André 146

D

Delizius 131
Deyrolle 147

E

E Dehillerin 55
Eres 66
Ets Lion 83

F

Fauchon 66
Frivoli 85
Fromagerie Alléosse
    197

G

Galeries Lafayette 66
Galignani 69
Gérard Durand 159
Guerlain 45

H

Hédiard 66

I

Il Campiello 125

L

La Boutique
    Extraordinaire 95
La Grande Épicerie
    de Paris 147

La Maison de la
    Truffe 67
La Maison de Poupée
    147
La Maison du Miel 67
La Petite Scierie 124
Lancel 45
Le Bain Rose 147
Le Bon Marché 147
Le Mots à La Bouche
    109
Le Printemps 66-7
Legrand Filles & Fils
    67-8
L'Habilleur 95
Librairie Gourmande
    55
Librairie Ulysse 125

M

MadeinUsed 95
Marché aux Fleurs
    124, 171
Marché aux Fleurs
    Madeleine 68
Marché aux Puces
    d'Aligre 109
Marché aux Puces de
    St-Ouen 177
Marché Mouffetard
    130
Maroquinerie Saint-
    Honoré 69
Max Maroquinerie
    Bagagerie et
    Accessoires 157
Merci 95
Mouffetard Folie's 131

N

Nomades 101

O

Oliviers & Co 125

P

Passage Molière 105
Pauline Pin 95
Plastiques 157
Poilâne 147
Pring 95
Publicis Drugstore 45

R

Red Wheelbarrow
    Bookstore 109
Rue Cler 33
Rue d'Alésia 191

S

Shakespeare &
    Company 139,
    169, 171
Shine 95
Sonia Rykiel 159

T

Tati 83
Temps Libre 74
Tombées du Camion
    83
Transmondia 83
Triangle d'Or 44

U

Un Chien dans le
    Marais 109

V

Viaduc des Arts 109
Village St-Paul 108
Village Voice 157

Z

Zut! 83

Our Writer

CATHERINE LE NEVEZ

Catherine first lived in Paris aged four and she's been returning here at every opportunity since, completing her Doctorate of Creative Arts in Writing, Masters in Professional Writing, and postgraduate qualifications in Editing and Publishing along the way. In between revisiting her favourite Parisian haunts and uncovering new ones, she wrote this book in a tiny (but charming) garret in the city's heart. Catherine's writing on the city includes numerous Lonely Planet guides, as well as newspaper and radio reportage covering Paris' literary scene – in addition to authoring, co-authoring and contributing to dozens of Lonely Planet guide books covering all corners of France, Europe and beyond. Wanderlust aside, Paris remains her favourite city on earth.

Published by Lonely Planet Publications Pty Ltd
ABN 36 005 607 983
3rd edition – May 2012
ISBN 978 1 74179 691 9
© Lonely Planet 2012   Photographs © as indicated 2012
10 9 8 7 6 5 4 3 2 1
Printed in China